BRECHT

Brecht in Lidingö, 1939. "Once again I have ended up on a little island where the people are friendly."

BRECHT

Jan Needle
AND
Peter Thomson

The University of Chicago Press

The University of Chicago Press, Chicago 60637
Basil Blackwell, Oxford

87 86 85 84 83 82 81   12345

Library of Congress Cataloging in Publication Data

Needle, Jan.
  Brecht
  Bibliography : p.
  Includes index
  1. Brecht, Bertolt, 1898 – 1956—Criticism and
  interpretation. I. Thomson Peter W., joint author.
  PT2603.R397Z7858   1981   832'.912   80–29387
  ISBN 0–226–57022–3

Printed in Great Britain

This book is dedicated to Rita

Contents

Illustrations

Acknowledgements

The authors would like to thank Frau Barbara Schall-Brecht for a generous letter, some permissions and some corrections; Nick Hern of Eyre Methuen, for sending us advance copies of new Brecht translations; Jane Collins and Nick Jones for the loan of a house in Belper when we needed a bolt-hole; and Sarah Batchelor for typing and consistent good humour.

The publishers also thank the Bertolt-Brecht-Archiv for their assistance with photographs and acknowledge the following:

Ruth Berlau and Johannes Hoffman (pages 54, below and 169)
Bertolt-Brecht-Erben (pages 52 and 126)
George Grosz Estate, Princeton, N.J. (page 36)
Museum of the City of New York, Theatre and Music Collection (page 197)
Phaidon Press (pages 134 and 212)
Vera Teuschert, Berliner Ensemble (page 42)
Hans Tombrock (frontispiece)
Zander and Labisch (page 54, left)

A Note on Texts and Titles

This book is intended primarily for those who have to read their Brecht in English. There is no point in denying that the difficulties are legion, and many of them unresolvable. But progress is being made.

When, in 1970, the first volume of the Willett and Manheim *Collected Plays* was published by Methuen, the prospect brightened considerably. Alas, the subsequent history of that crucial series has been bedevilled by inconsistencies. Volumes 1 and 7 alone have been published in Britain. America has been luckier. Volumes 2, 5, 6 and 9 (the last is not, evidently, intended for British publication) have also appeared there. Meanwhile the British policy has changed, and the translated plays are being published singly. The unwary reader may find that he has bought, from the same publisher (now Eyre Methuen) an earlier unannotated translation, and *not* the annotated text that forms part of the *Collected Plays*. Then again, the American versions are sometimes by different translators (this is true of each of the three plays in Volume 7). What all this confusion means, of course, is that the Willett and Manheim *Collected Plays* cannot confidently be called the standard translation it had so brightly promised to become.

Even so, it is the most consistent, the most extensive, and the most reliable translation on the market. We have used it wherever it has been possible, though not exclusively. For example, Eric Bentley's version of *The Private Life of the Master Race*, and the Grove Press editions of *Man Is Man*, and *Roundheads and Peakheads* have proved useful for particular purposes, and we have had, infrequently, to provide our own translations.

It would greatly help if a standard translation of Brecht's titles could be agreed upon: but once again there are problems. We had intended to settle for the Willett and Manheim titles throughout, accepting with regret *Man Equals Man* (rather than *Man Is Man*) and *Round Heads and Pointed Heads* (rather than *Roundheads and Peakheads*), but we stuck over *The Measures Taken*. Willett and Manheim have chosen to retitle their translation *The Decision* (which could equally well be the title of any of the *Lehrstücke*) despite the existence of a previous Methuen volume in which *The Measures Taken* is the title play. This is the outstanding example, but there are two others, listed below, where we have felt bound to differ:

> *The Didactic Play of Baden-Baden on Consent* (Willett and Manheim, *The Baden-Baden Cantata*)
>
> *The Good Person of Setzuan* (Willett and Manheim spell the town *Szechwan*)

Rather than reiterating the full titles of plays under discussion, we have employed standard abbreviations (e.g. *Mother Courage*, *Galileo*, *Puntila*) after the initial reference.

We have attempted to keep the text as clean as possible, by restricting the number of footnotes, and by referring readers to notes at the back of the book for the location of sources and references.

Sources of Quotations

Unless otherwise stated in the text or footnotes, quotations from Brecht's poems are always from *Poems 1913–1956*, ed. John Willett and Ralph Manheim, London, 1976. For the translations of the plays we have used the following editions:

Collected Plays Volume 1, ed. John Willett and Ralph Manheim, London, 1970, for:

 Baal (trans. Peter Tegel)
 Drums in the Night (trans. John Willett)
 In the Jungle of Cities (trans. Gerhard Nellhaus)
 The Life of Edward II of England (trans. Jean Benedetti)

Collected Plays Volume 2, ed. Manheim and Willett, New York, 1977, for:

 A Man's a Man (trans. Gerhard Nellhaus). This translation is also available as Volume Two Part One of the English edition, London, 1979, under the title *Man equals Man*.
 The Threepenny Opera (trans. Ralph Manheim and John Willett). This translation is also available as Volume Two Part Two of the English edition, London, 1979.

Collected Plays Volume 5, ed. Manheim and Willett, New York, 1972, for:

 Life of Galileo (trans. Wolfgang Sauerlander and Ralph Manheim)
 Mother Courage and Her Children (trans. Ralph Manheim)

Collected Plays Volume 6, ed. Manheim and Willett, New York, 1976, for:

 The Good Person of Szechwan (trans. Ralph Manheim)
 Puntila and Matti, His Hired Man (trans. Ralph Manheim).
 The Resistible Rise of Arutro Ui (trans. Ralph Manheim). This translation was also published in London by Eyre Methuen in 1976,

confusingly separate from the *Collected Plays*.

Collected Plays Volume 7, ed. Willett and Manheim, London, 1976, for:
    Schweyk in the Second World War (trans. William Rowlinson)
    The Caucasian Chalk Circle (trans. James and Tania Stern with W. H.
    Auden).This translation was first published in *Plays. Volume 1*,
    London, 1960, when Methuen was Eyre-less. In the American
    Collected Plays Volume 7, the same plays appear in translations by
    Max Knight and Joseph Fabry (*Schweyk*) and Ralph Manheim
    (*Caucasian Chalk Circle*). If there is a clearer case of confusion, then
    this case is that case!

The English edition of the *Collected Plays* is published by Eyre
Methuen. The American edition, with the same editors in reverse
order, is published by Vintage Books. For plays not yet available in
either edition, we have used the following translations:

The Didactic Play of Baden-Baden on Consent (trans. Lee Baxandall)
    appears in the *Tulane Drama Review*, Volume 4, May 1960.

He Who Says Yes | He Who Says No (trans. Wolfgang Sauerlander), *The
    Measures Taken* (trans. Carl R. Mueller) and *The Exception and the
    Rule* (trans. Ralph Manheim) from *The Measures Taken and other
    Lehrstücke*, Eyre Methuen, London, 1977.

Saint Joan of the Stockyards (trans. Frank Jones) was published as a
    separate volume by Eyre Methuen, London, 1976, having first
    appeared in *Plays, Volume II*, Methuen, London, 1962.

Round Heads and Pointed Heads (trans. N. Goold-Verschoyle) was first
    published in *International Literature* 5, May, 1937, and later in *Jungle
    of Cities and other plays*, Grove Press, New York, 1966.

The Private Life of the Master Race, Eric Bentley's version of *Fear and
    Misery of the Third Reich*, was published by New Directions, New
    York, 1944 and by Victor Gollancz, London, 1948.

The Rise and Fall of the City of Mahagonny presents a particularly
    difficult problem. Neither Michael Feingold, in his translation from
    Volume Two of the American *Collected Plays*, nor W. H. Auden and
    Chester Kallman, in theirs as Volume Two Part Three of the English
    Collected Plays, has succeeded in establishing a text. We have pre-
    ferred the translation by Arnold Weinstein and Lys Symonette in the
    revised Universal Edition (Theodore Presser Co., Bryn Mawr,
    Pennsylvania, 1969) and the literal translation that accompanies the
    splendid U.S. Columbia KL 5271–3 (Philips L 09418–20) recording.

Preface

This book is the result of a collaboration that began, unwittingly, in 1970, when Peter Thomson was a lecturer in the Drama Department at Manchester University, and Jan Needle was a student. It was sparked off, more than likely, by a disagreement, and it would be disingenuous to claim that all the disagreements have been ironed out. On the contrary, they have continued to stimulate us during the months of writing, and they have not been scrupulously excised from the text. There may be more inconsistencies, more disparities in emphasis than we realize — though we recognize some. Our view is that it would be a disservice to a magnificent and controversial dramatist to modify the controversy and make cautious common cause on the magnificence.

The controversial aspects of Brecht, then, very definitely remain. For one thing we are firmly agreed on is that any attempt at a single approach to so complex a writer is bound to fail: we offer no "overview", psychological or political, that is meant to provide a key to all his secrets. Our examinations of plays that are rarely considered, and our resistance to the idea that Brecht, as a classic, is more likely to have succeeded than failed in every work, spring from this. The dangers of lionization now seem at least as real as those of denigration.

We have also tried, whilst providing a broadly chronological survey of Brecht's plays, to pay particular attention to the staging theories and practice and to the political and dramaturgical principles of a writer whose influence on the contemporary theatre seems, if anything, to be on the increase. We make the assumption — it seems common sense to us but is against the bias of much earlier criticism — that an appreciation of Brecht's practice will be enhanced by an evaluation of Brecht's theories.

In all this, we have been helped beyond measure by the advice and experience of Vivien Gardner of the University of Manchester Drama Department — not least for occasionally suggesting that we might *both* be right.

1

The Phenomenon of Brecht

When Bertolt Brecht died in Berlin in 1956, aged fifty-eight, he had already achieved an international stature unequalled by any other theatrical writer, director or producer this century. Now, almost three decades later, the phenomenon shows no sign of diminishing: Brecht has become a classic, a model and a rallying point for people all over the world who believe at once that theatre suffers from a crippling, potentially terminal, malaise and also that it can not merely survive, but *live*. The other side of the Brecht phenomenon also remains, however. Always a controversial figure, he attracted and continues to attract antipathy which borders on the hysterical and frequently spills into the realms of pure hatred. He has been the most influential man of the theatre and the most vilified; the most followed and the most misunderstood. In Germany today there is an awareness of what they call "Brecht fatigue"; as early as February 1976 Kenneth Tynan — Brecht's earliest and most voluble post-war champion in Britain — wrote a long article in *Plays and Players* describing the "crisis" in the Berliner Ensemble. He dated this as having begun in the mid sixties when Helene Weigel, Brecht's widow, allowed it to decline into a stagnation which worsened after her death in 1971. Both the fatigue and the crisis are real, and both were probably inevitable; it is very much part of the phenomenon that one can confidently predict that the tensions they have created will keep the debate — and Brecht — alive.

Although the dual attitude to Brecht is not peculiar to Britain or America, it remains absolutely vital to take account of it in reviewing approaches to him in those countries. Perhaps the most remarkable single fact in the American experience is how early the polarization that has become a characteristic of reactions to him manifested itself. When he arrived in New York from Denmark in October 1935, to participate in the socialist Theatre Union's production of *The Mother*, he was hopeful — if not exactly confident — that he would be widening his tragically limited opportunities for performance as a dramatist in exile from his native land. But both politically and artistically, the Theatre Union and Brecht were worlds apart. As we will see in a later chapter, he had no sympathy for the "People's Front" policy of world communism then current, and the Theatre Union's ideas of what a play should be were more or less exactly what Brecht had spent most of his writing life trying to alter radically. The director, an inexperienced 23-year-old called Victor Wolfson, was apparently unimpressed by Brecht both as a dramatist and a theoretician; and the distance of translator/adaptor Paul Peters' concept of a play from Brecht's can most simply be illustrated by the fact of his entitling it *Mother* rather than *The Mother*. He was after warmth, tenderness and sentimentality — everything, in fact, that Brecht's version of Gorky's novel had specifically excluded. After a rehearsal period which involved frequent and violent clashes, culminating in the director barring Brecht and his musical collaborator Hanns Eisler from the theatre and Brecht threatening to get a court injunction preventing the performance, it played to only thirty-six houses, most of the tickets for which were in any case sold in advance.

Among the people involved in the production, an antagonistic attitude to Brecht was forged which was to be lifelong. The level of criticism, characteristically, ranged from ill-informed views of his theories as pretentious nonsense to complaints that he smelled because he never changed his shirt. Almost alone, Mordecai Gorelik, the designer, allowed himself to listen, became convinced and became a friend and an advocate of Brechtian theory. But other people were influenced too. Joseph Losey, who had seen Brecht performed in Europe, was turned down as a director for the play by the Theatre Union but retained an interest and admiration that never diminished. Press responses — none of which took into account the fact that nobody really knew by this time just whose play it *was* — are also significant. The non-left-wing newspapers were scathing, and their response was remarkably similar in tone and detail to that of the German commercial Press after the original production (of which details are given in Chapter 3); the *Brooklyn Daily Eagle*, for example, described it as "a simple kindergarten for communist tots". The leftist papers tried their best to be kind, but were palpably completely in the dark about what Brecht was up to. The weekly *New Masses* went some way towards rectifying this in an article by Eva Goldbeck, which remained the most accurate assessment of areas of Brecht's theories in America until Eric Bentley took up the cudgels in the early 1940s.

Although Brecht was not widely known in America, even to left-wing theatre practitioners, before the production of *Mother*, he was, significantly, invited there (and paid) to participate in a production of one of his plays. What is more, in 1931 the Philadelphia Orchestra had performed *The Flight of the Lindberghs, The Threepenny Opera* had played briefly and unsuccessfully in New York in 1933, and the film he had worked on with a German collective, *Kuhle Wampe,* had been shown in New York in the same year. Although misinterpretation and critical enmity were rife, at least they were related to performances, however inadequate, and at least the picture was not entirely one-sided. In Britain, however, to a certain and important extent Brecht was a product, almost a creature, solely of the critics. Although he became, by practice, a concern of the theatre, and by awareness of his importance a concern of more serious academic critics, he entered the consciousness of the British theatre- and drama-oriented public through the pages of their newspapers. What is more, most of their responses and attitudes to him even today are fed and moulded through the same channels. The pity of this lies in the fact that much of the newspaper criticism is ill-informed to the point of straightforward ignorance, much of it is grotesquely hostile, and little of it tries to relate the production under review to the intentions and methods of the author, either as playwright or theatrical theorist. Its danger lies in the fact that despite the anti-intellectualism, the arrogance and the ignorance of most newspaper drama critics, they are the point of contact with Brecht for the vast majority of the play-going public. Not only are views of specific plays thus disseminated and digested, but truly half-baked views of the theoretical writings are put about; and many people in the theatre, amateur and professional, accept such glosses as an alternative to finding out for themselves. Although British newspaper and magazine critics are, fortunately, less powerful than their counterparts in America, there are some fields in which their potential for destruction is tragically great.

Although Brecht did not become a notable force in Britain until 1956, even before World War II the general public could scarcely have learnt anything of him except through newspapers. Two widely spaced reviews uncannily foreshadow the sort of response he has suffered under to a greater or lesser extent ever since. The first, of the original Berlin production of *The Threepenny Opera*, in *The Times* of 25 September

1928, is not unsympathetic, although with traditional journalistic accuracy the whole is attributed to one "Herr Kurt Brecht"! It is mainly remarkable, however, for the blandness with which it explains away the elements of newness, the rough edges, of this "interesting example of the more earnest efforts now being made to break new ground on the German stage". The review concludes:

There are regrettable omissions, such as the appearance at the execution of Macheath's former loves with their babies, and some doubt may be expressed as to whether such *revue*-like additions as the brothel-scene, in which Macheath is arrested, are really in the spirit of John Gay. The ballads after Villon and — so it is said, though one failed to identify them — Mr. Kipling, sung by Peachum and Macheath, almost give the piece at times the air, deliberately fostered by music and effects, of a morality play. But *Die Dreigroschenoper* is not, of course, a morality play, it is not a *revue*, it is not a conventional burlesque, and it is not *The Beggar's Opera*; but it is an interesting combination of them illustrating the progress of a movement towards freeing music, acting, and the cinematograph from the ruts of the Italian opera, Wagnerian music-drama, drawing-room comedy, and Hollywood, and creating something new in them.

By February 1935, however, the more instantly recognizable "critical" attitude had emerged, fully-fledged, in a small *Sunday Times* item about the radio version (*The Tuppeny-ha'penny Opera*) broadcast by the BBC. Under the crosshead "A Beggarly Opera", Ernest Newman wrote:

"The Beggar's Opera" we all know, to our delight. On Friday night the BBC, in one of its concerts of what it calls contemporary music, treated us to an opera that can only be described as beggarly. The "Dreigroschenoper" of Bert Brecht (text) and Kurt Weill (music), which was all the rage in Germany a little while go, is described by its authors as "after 'The Beggar's Opera' of John Gay". It may be after that masterpiece, but it will certainly never catch up with it: these two dull dogs achieve the almost incredible feat of making even crime boring. It is difficult to say which is the feebler, the libretto or the music — perhaps the latter, which has the worst faults of more than one bad style and the qualities of not a single good one, even at second hand.

Although this sort of "quasi-criticism" is still the rule rather than the exception, it is to another drama critic that the honour of forcing Brecht on the public and the theatre is generally given. Despite the early championship of Eric Bentley, despite the support of the intelligent and influential journal *Encore*, despite the fact that a small body of people in the theatre had heard of Brecht and were interested in trying to stage him, it was Kenneth Tynan's eloquent advocacy in the *Observer* from 1954 to 1963 that made Brecht required reading and a household word (in those households interested in theatre, let one hastily add). It is a sad fact that this advocacy caused as much enmity as friendship for Brecht, in the first instance by the equal and opposite reaction it inspired in other critics.

On the Continent, of course, the picture had been completely different. As early as November 1952 the Théâtre Nationale Populaire in Paris performed *Mother Courage and Her Children* (directed by Jean Vilar), while Roger Planchon, founder/director of the theatre at Villeurbanne, near Lyons, not only produced him earlier but began to apply his methods to the classics, including Shakespeare. The Italian Giorgio Strehler, still one of the world's most noted producers of Brecht, also seized upon him within a very short time of his re-establishment in the German theatre in 1949.

Tynan's reviews of the *Mother Courage* performance in Paris in January 1955 by the TNP, and the Berliner Ensemble's Paris performance of *The Caucasian Chalk Circle* in June of the same year, contained the sort of enthusiasm which can only have made lovers of live theatre in Britain (where dead theatre was certainly the norm in those days) wistfully determined to come to grips with the mysterious German. "Never before have I seen a thousand people rise cheering and weeping from their seats,"[1] he said of *Mother Courage*. In his review of *Chalk Circle* he stated: "Once in a generation the world discovers a new way of telling a story; this generation's pathfinder is Brecht, both as playwright and director of the Berliner Ensemble."[2] Brecht's method he described as being "as shocking and revolutionary as a cold shower" and the whole production as "superb". That he also in this review attempted an extremely simplified gloss of "Brecht's theory of acting, the famous *Verfremdungseffekt*, or 'alienation effect' ", is interesting in that it foreshadowed a major area of controversy that is still nowhere near resolved by critics, ephemeral or academic. It is an area where Tynan, in trying to get Brecht accepted, set the tone for those who followed: a tendency to get round the theories, not by serious attempts to learn by them or even to understand them, but to cut them down to a manageable size. It is this lack of seriousness that is the single greatest difference between Brecht himself and his critics (both pro and anti).

In the summer of 1955, the energetic and ebullient Joan Littlewood directed *Mother Courage* for the Devon Arts Festival. It had its premiere in Barnstaple, with Littlewood herself in the title role. Tynan thought it "a production in which discourtesy to a masterpiece borders on insult",[3] but Miss Littlewood's discourtesy (real or imagined – we did not see the production) was as nothing compared with the insults heaped upon Brecht's own production of the play in London in the summer of 1956.

On 5 August, in East Berlin, Brecht — who was to die on 14 August — had posted a notice of warning to the company about their forthcoming presentations, at London's Palace Theatre, of *Mother Courage, Chalk Circle* and *Trumpets and Drums*, his version of Farquhar's *Recruiting Officer*:

For our London season we need to bear two things in mind. First: we shall be offering most of the audience a pure pantomime, a kind of silent film on the stage, for they know no German. (In Paris we had a festival audience, an international audience — and we ran for a few days only.) Second: there is in England a long-standing fear that German art (literature, painting, music) must be terribly heavy, slow, laborious and pedestrian.

So our playing needs to be quick, light, strong. This is not a question of hurry, but of speed, not simply of quick playing, but of quick thinking. We must keep the tempo of a runthrough and infect it with quiet strength, with our own fun. In the dialogue the exchanges must not be offered reluctantly, as when offering somebody one's last pair of boots, but must be tossed like so many balls. The audience has to see that here are a number of artists working together as a collective (ensemble) in order to convey stories, ideas, virtuoso feats to the spectator by a common effort.

It would be foolish to deny the accuracy of Brecht's view of the British attitude towards German art, however unpalatable it may seem. Only three weeks before he pinned up his notice, T. C. Worsley had reviewed a production of *Chalk Circle* by students of the Royal Academy of Dramatic Art and had stated (in the *New Statesman* of 14 July) "But, oh dear, what a terrible old Germanic bore this Brecht can be and what aeons of fatigue we shall have to suffer in the future owing to the Communist deification of this stuck-in-the-Twenties playwright!" As well as the specific assumption that to be Germanic is to be boring, Worsley quite blatantly, in other parts of his review, displays several of the prejudices that have constantly dogged Brecht, as well as the smug device of pretending not to prejudge, then going ahead and doing so. Thus:

We must wait before pronouncing on [Brecht's formal approach] until we have seen his own productions and his own company, which are expected at the Palace Theatre in the late summer. By all accounts – and not all of them Communist accounts – this company is a remarkable ensemble and he is a remarkable producer. He has been given the most lavishly equipped theatre in the world and – so they say – he makes the most of it, though I can't help feeling from the accounts that I have read and heard that his methods are too close to an out-dated expressionism. We shall see. Meanwhile, and without having seen his productions – indeed all the more clearly for not being dazzled by them – I find his approach to play-writing old-fashioned, dull and arty. . .

One thing I am sure of is that *The Caucasian Circle of Chalk* would bore the pants off any average English audience. . .

In the event, Worsley seems to have been proved right by the visit of the Berliner Ensemble. Even Tynan's long and enthusiastic review in the *Observer* of 2 September smacks of defeat. Harold Hobson's, in the *Sunday Times* of the same date, is a masterpiece of (deliberate?) mis-understanding. What is not taken into account by either man is that very few members of the audience were doing much more than watching "a pure pantomime". The British are not noted for their excellence at foreign languages, and in any case bilingualism is extremely rare. Even rarer is an admission by a critic that he is not bilingual; one wonders how many members of the audience for the three plays had more than a very shadowy idea of what was going on on stage. Both reviews are worth quoting at length, however, as once again they reveal several things that were to become almost the hallmarks of attitudes to Brecht, and unfor-tunately not only among ephemeral critics.

First Tynan:

When the houselights went up at the end of *The Caucasian Chalk Circle* (Palace), the audience looked to me like a serried congress of tailor's dummies. I probably looked the same to them. By contrast with the blinding sincerity of the Berliner Ensemble, we all seemed unreal and stagey. Many of us must have felt cheated. Brecht's actors do not behave like Western actors; they neither bludgeon us with personality nor woo us with charm; they look shockingly like people, real potato-faced people such as one might meet in a bus-queue. Humanity itself, not the exceptional eccentric, is what their theatre exists to explore. In their lighting, an impartial snow-white glow, and their grouping, which is as panoramic as Breughel's, life is spread out before you. It does not leap at your throat and yell secrets in your ear.

Let me instance the peasant wedding in *The Chalk Circle*, a scene more brilliantly directed than any other in London: a tiny cell of a room, ten by ten, is cumulatively jammed with about two dozen neighbours and a sottish monk. The chances for broad farce are obvious, but they are all rejected. Reality is preferred, reality of a memorable and sculptural ruggedness. I defy anyone to forget Brecht's stage pictures. No steps or rostra encumber the platform; the dominant colours are browns and greys; and against a high, encircling, off-white backcloth we see nothing but solid, selected objects – the twin gates in *The Chalk Circle* or Mother Courage's covered wagon. The beauty of Brechtian settings is not of the dazzling kind that begs for applause. It is the more durable beauty of *use*.

The same applies to the actors. They look capable and practical, accustomed to living in the open air. Angelika Hurwicz is a lumpy girl with a face as round as an apple; our theatre would cast her, if at all, as a fat comic maid. Brecht makes her his heroine, the servant who saves the governor's child when its mother flees from a palace rebellion. London would have cast a gallant little waif, pinched and pathetic; Miss Hurwicz, too busy for pathos, expresses petulance where we expect her to "register" terror and shrugs where other actresses would likely weep. She strengthens the situation by ignoring its implications: it is by what it omits that we recognize hers as a great performance.

As Eric Bentley said, "Brecht does not believe in an inner reality, a higher reality or a deeper reality, but simply in reality." It is something for which we have lost the taste: raised on a diet of gin and goulash, we call Brecht naive when he gives us bread and wine. He wrote morality plays and directed them as such: and if we of the West End and Broadway find them as tiresome as religion, we are in a shrinking minority. There is a world elsewhere. "I was bored to death," said a bright Chelsea girl after *Mother Courage*. "Bored to life" would have been apter.

Through intelligence and a preparedness to do his homework, Tynan illuminates some important aspects of Brecht's theatre, but the difficulties that the theories had caused, were causing and sadly still cause are hilariously captured in the contrast between his account of the Berliner Ensemble's treatment of the British national anthem and Hobson's.

Here is Tynan's:

. . .the clearest illustration of the "A-effect" comes in the national anthem, which the Berliner-Ensemble have so arranged that it provokes, instead of patriotic ardour, laughter. The melody is backed by a trumpet *obbligato* so feeble and pompous that it suggests a boy bugler on a rapidly-sinking ship. The orchestration is a criticism of the lyrics, and a double flavour results, the ironic flavour which is "A-effect". . .

And here is Hobson's:

I fear that Miss Helen Hayes would describe the work of the Berliner Ensemble as slipshod. The much-heralded presentations we saw last week are characterized by an apparent carelessness. A small but typical example of this is provided by the orchestra. There seems to be no rule what its members shall wear. Some are in lounge suits, others in dinner jackets.

One guesses, however, that this carelessness is deliberate. Uncertain though they may appear to be about their clothes, they know exactly what their instruments are capable of. Their playing of "God Save the Queen", hauntingly arranged by Elisabeth Lutyens, on Monday evening came as a revelation, with its high, tense, silver trumpet note. When this company ignores a convention to which we are accustomed, it is evident that it does so because it considers that convention either irrelevant or positively injurious to its purposes.

Hobson is evidently doing his best to seem responsive to the intentions of the Berliner Ensemble, but his hankering after a theatre of illusion cannot be long resisted. He concludes his review like this:

The Berliner Ensemble's conception of the theatre is. . .an austere one; but now and again beauty breaks through, as in the charming episode of the swan and the young lovers on the banks of the Severn in *Trumpets and Drums*, or in the servant girl's love for a child in *The Caucasian Chalk Circle*. The company's acting is of a very high standard, the scenery often enchanting. There are performances of deep originality and lofty ambition.

I am bound in honesty to add that, except for parts of *The Caucasion Chalk Circle*, they bored and annoyed me. I believe the thesis on which I take them to be founded is false. To claim that the theatre, where hundreds of people are crowded together in conditions of more or less discomfort, is a suitable place for clear thinking seems to me childish. I do not believe that, fundamentally, there is any more rational illumination in *Mother Courage* or the other plays of Brecht than there is in *Uncle Tom's Cabin*, or that Brecht was any more willing than Harriet Beecher Stowe to follow the question wherever it led him. The audience which thinks that it is thinking at these performances flatters and deceives itself.

As an example of English parochialism at its worst, this would be hard to beat. One pines for a reference to the fact that the plays were performed in German. But Tynan's review shows up some perhaps less tractable problems. Both he and Hobson clearly wish to give the impression that they have a certain knowledge of Brecht's theories, although

Hobson's reference to the Ensemble being "deliberately careless" is a chilling pointer to just how infinitesimal his knowledge of the spirit and the letter of the theory was. Both make statements of Brecht's intentions that few people were in a position to refute, given the almost total lack of available material in English (or German) at this time. Where Tynan's response is possibly more dangerous, however, is over the knotty matter of boredom. Hobson at least admits to it, although his reasons border on the philistine. Tynan tries to explain it away with his highly unconvincing "Chelsea girl" who should have been "bored to life". The implication that although Brecht is boring he is good for you is not one that any sane theatre-goer should allow any credit at all. It is certainly not a view that Brecht would have admitted. Even the most austere of his works, the *Lehrstücke* or "teaching plays", he expected to entertain. In an essay published in London by the *Left Review* in 1936, he wrote:

With the teaching plays, then, the stage begins to be didactic. (A word of which I, as a man of many years of experience in the theatre, am not afraid.) The theatre becomes a place for philosophers, and for such philosophers as not only wish to explain the world but wish to change it. . .

For theatre remains theatre even while it is didactic, and as long as it is good theatre it is also entertaining.

The three plays presented at the Palace were by no stretch of the imagination didactic, and by no stretch of the imagination could they be described as boring plays (which Brecht was as capable of writing as the next playwright, incidentally). Tynan's castigation of an English-speaking audience for being bored and therefore having subtly failed as people is the sort of double-think which has provided much ammunition for the anti-Brechtian camp. One can sympathize with them for having taken it up so gratefully.

In the years since 1956, a considerable amount of material by and about Brecht has become available in translation, although in a sadly piecemeal and haphazard fashion. John Willett's *Brecht on Theatre* remains a vital if slightly eccentric guide, but misunderstanding of the theatrical theories would be far less widespread if a collected translation *in chronological order* of the *Schriften zum Theater* were available.

Inadequate as the translated material may be, however, there is very little excuse nowadays for professional critics to display the lack of knowledge their earlier counterparts suffered from (even if they refused to admit it). But sadly the situation has generally deteriorated even further. The one single, simple thing that shines out from the most cursory study of Brecht, as theoretician, playwright or practitioner, is his seriousness: his whole relationship with the theatre could be summed up in that word. Most critics have proved themselves incapable of taking Brecht seriously — let alone the theatre they are presumed to be fascinated by and practitioners of (if only to the extent of being aware that they are part of a process which is, among other things, intellectual). The critics remain arrogant and the ignorance if anything seems more wilful.

Harold Hobson (later Sir Harold Hobson) was succeeded as drama critic of the *Sunday Times* by Bernard Levin. The tone of the reviews remained in many cases uncannily similar. Thus Levin on 6 November 1977:

The full horror of Brecht's *The Days of the Commune* (RSC, Aldwych) cannot be conveyed; I do but hint at its unendurable tedium and leaden stupidity by saying that it has the depth of a cracker-motto, the drama of a dial-a-recipe service and the eloquence of a conversation between a speak-your-weight machine and a whoopee-cushion. The brave, doomed rebellion of the Paris Communards in 1871 involved them in great suffering, from eating rats to being shot when they finally lost. But at least they were spared this.

The month before, Levin had been more general, if no less vitriolic, in his attack.

The Brecht boom is, God save the mark, almost over, and another look at *The Good Woman of Setzuan* (Royal Court) only reinforces my astonishment that it ever began. It was always an artificial creation (the Court on Monday was full of Courtiers, poleaxed with boredom, trying to convince themselves that they were having a transforming ideological experience), but the works, many of which (particularly this one) combine the mawkishness of A. A. Milne with the intellectual profundity of a Pekin wall-newspaper and the character-drawing of a telephone directory, insist on giving the game away. (It is interesting that his best plays – *Mother Courage* and *Galileo* – are the ones which most completely contradict the theories with which he larded his work, and which for twenty years have lighted fools the way to dusty death.)

He went on to praise the performance of Janet Suzman in a title role which he can hardly have believed Brecht wrote, so good did he find it. The downright contradiction of the penultimate sentence is fascinating: "Such things as the rapture of Shen Te's declaration of love, the chill of Shui Ta's callous refusal of help to the indigent, convey an emotional truth that bypasses everything except the nerves, along which her performance sizzles throughout."

What seems to have been Levin's bid to become the most confused, contorted and anti-intellectual critic in London would probably have succeeded (on these two efforts alone, perhaps) had it not been for the determination of another man, Sheridan Morley, in a piece which appeared in the *Sunday Times Magazine* on 28 August 1977. From a mass of insults, half-truths and idiocies, it is worth quoting only a few.

Yet of the major Brechtian works only *Mother Courage* can truly be considered his alone: *The Threepenny Opera* owed a good deal to John Gay (on whose *Beggar's Opera* it was loosely based), and even more to Kurt Weill (for whose remarkable and haunting score Brecht memorably paid not the 50 per cent that is usual in composer-lyricist relationships but instead a mere 25 per cent), while *The Caucasian Chalk circle* had already been adapted by the poet Klabund from a Chinese original and was being used as Socialist propaganda long before Brecht happened upon it.

And later:

Better, then, to think of Brecht as a showman: the Phineas T. Barnum of the eastern European world, able to unite composers and actors in one memorable evening for which the plot had often been better treated elsewhere (usually by Shakespeare) and the action depended on a decent director. Like James Bridie, J. M. Barrie and many other perennial seven-year olds, Brecht believed that a basic moral point about good or evil, wealth or poverty, imprisonment or freedom, could be restated several times in the same play and that an audience (far from screaming to be released at the interval from the sheer simple-mindedness of the whole affair) would in fact emerge from the theatre better able to cope with the complexities of their present-day lives. As a moral and political philosopher, Bertolt Brecht had much in common with Rod Hull's Emu.

On the theories:

For his supposedly revolutionary staging techniques Piscator had been more than somewhat responsible several years earlier.

Among his concluding remarks he claims that most of Brecht's work "now inhabits that worst of all limbos, the one composed of critical adoration and public indifference" – which presumably means Morley is neither a critic nor a member of the public.

Silly as the piece was, it cannot, unfortunately, be dismissed as unimportant. The *Sunday Times* is one of the most influential moulders of middle-class opinion, and Morley is a professional drama critic who demands, therefore, to be taken seriously. It is little wonder the "average theatre-goer" so deeply doubts and mistrusts Brecht.

Since the mid-fifties, also, there have been the counterparts in the Press to Kenneth Tynan, and here again little has changed significantly, although David Zane Mairowitz has done a useful service by his refusal to allow bad direction and lack of understanding of Brecht to be sufficient reasons for condemning the plays or the writer. His review (*Plays and Players*, January 1978) of *The Days of the Commune* which Bernard Levin chose to be so flippant about, is interesting, although too long to quote in full. At one point he wrote:

Precious little of [Brecht's] clarity survives the current production. The confusion is overbearing. Davies [Howard Davies, the director] imposes two narrators on the play, presumably to facilitate the historical line for the uninitiated, and cleverly places them on opposite sides of the political fence. But they speak in such bland fashion, showing no real interest in the subject of their narration, that no one listens to them; they are just another of many stage obstacles thrown up between the argument and the spectator. Then comes the predictably xenophobic attempt to reduce the play's foreign-ness with a discord of local accents. There is the usual equation of working-class English Northern, and Mme Cabet (for some inexplicable reason) has an Irish brogue.

But the overriding fault is the production's almost complete lack of stress and dramatic tension. There seems no recognition that the play depicts a life-and-death situation from the outset, with the Parisians starving and dying between the war with Prussia and the imminent Civil War (during Davies' staging of the banquet scene a loaf of bread breaks over someone's head and is allowed to roll to the side of the stage without being retrieved).

A new note which recurs in Mairowitz, and which he is clearly committed to, is the idea that Brecht's texts are not to be treated as sacred and unchangeable. In reviewing the Oxford Playhouse production of *Happy End*, he wrote in *Plays and Players* (November 1975): "It is almost sacrilege *not* to tamper with Brecht when he warrants it (witness G. W. Pabst's successful film of *Threepenny Opera*, more Brecht than Brecht), yet this cannot be done without a prior commitment to his content." Apart from his peculiar choice of example, it is clear that Mairowitz presupposes seriousness when he postulates the possibility of changing the text and the manner of production. In fact he ends his review:

[This production] wants clarity, mood, intent, above that a *reason* for being performed in the first place by *these particular players*. It wants an *attitude* that will approximate, if not accommodate, Brecht's own.

Without going into the question, at the moment, as to how Brecht should be played and how reasonably he can be "tampered with", it must be noted that Mairowitz has here put his finger on a major point. However serious *he* may be about the attitude with which practitioners should approach a Brecht production, it is a sad fact that time after time he has himself observed that Brecht is nowadays being almost butchered. In a review (*Plays and Players*, December 1976) of *The Seven Deadly Sins* at the Citizens Theatre, Glasgow, he reports that director Geoffrey Cauley "has expanded the 35-minute ballet into a full evening's theatrical venture." Mairowitz goes on:

In itself the idea of turning *The Seven Deadly Sins* into a play with music is not unthinkable. More and more as Brecht is performed in this country (i.e. out of context) it is first of all necessary to learn how to *use* him (or rather, re-use him), even "re-interpret" him (as long as this has the implication of "re-*think*" and keeps the basic Brecht of him) for audiences with no grounding in (and little taste for) historical critique. Brecht never held any other playwright beyond adaptation, freely borrowing right up to his last works, always however with an eye on change and the needs of the specific historical moment.

Yet there seems little point in expanding the boundaries of a work unless you can enhance its central experience. The Citizens *Seven Deadly Sins* adds only stage excess.

He concludes that the version dismantles Brecht's *case*, as well as his text, to the extent that it "in fact supports the lie Brecht chooses to uncover."

One may turn to a review by Martin Esslin (*Plays and Players*, December 1977) to complete the point. After praising Janet Suzman's performance as The Good Woman of Setzuan at the Royal Court, he continues:

All the more distressing are the excesses of the production. Why should it, for example, be necessary in every production of a play by Brecht to drag in songs from *The Threepenny Opera*? This is provincialism carried to absurd lengths: why not put the Hamlet-monologue into productions of *Romeo and Juliet* just on the grounds that that is even better Shakespeare? Altogether, Keith Hack, the director, seems to have *The Threepenny Opera* on his brain: there the whole play rests on the assumption that it is an attempt by beggars to stage a play as sentimental and as false as a bourgeois opera. The poverty of the sets and costumes therefore, the whole pretence that we are witnessing a pathetic attempt to stage *kitsch* with the financial resources of beggars, is part and parcel of a *parodistic intention*. But then, in *The Good Woman of Setzuan*, there is no such parodistic intention. The author wants the play to be taken at its face value as a serious statement. To dress it in rags, therefore, and to build a whole set from old oil cans and rags is nonsense.

The continuing correspondence between the more serious of the "ephemeral" critics and British theatre practitioners can be seen at work here. Mairowitz (and others) while pleading for commitment and care, makes the idea of "tampering with Brecht" respectable, and the people who perform his plays go blindly ahead and tamper. What neither side realizes, in assuming that Brecht may be treated in so cavalier a fashion because he was a great alterer and borrower himself, is that he did not do it easily or glibly to "improve" an existing text, but to make a new text or a new statement altogether. One can see no justification at all (as Esslin saw no justification in putting *Threepenny Opera* songs in *The Good Person*) in tinkering with a good play unless for a specific and overwhelming reason. A vague feeling that "it doesn't work" is the sort of sloppiness that Brecht spent his whole life in the theatre fighting, and is an endemic disease in the British theatre. Until somebody has *fought* to make Brecht's plays work, then the idea of "improving" them by "tampering" is intellectually indefensible.

The American experience is in some ways depressingly similar to the British. But because America is so vast a country, with no interested audience sufficiently mobile to be called "national", an accurate evaluation is extremely difficult. When he returned to the United States, some six years after the *Mother* debacle, Brecht chose to live on the West Coast. It is almost certainly an over-simplification to attribute this to a desire to avoid the main base of the American left-wing theatre, but it is undeniable that Brecht had learned from it the bitter lesson that "tampering" was not only considered reasonable but could almost be seen to be its "method". And while he continued to hope for — even strive for – American performances, it seems equally an over-simplification to maintain as Willett and Manheim have done[5] that his theatre writing while in America was undertaken with Broadway in mind. *The Life of Galileo, Schweyk in the Second World War* and *The Caucasian Chalk Circle* may be many things to many minds: serious possibilities for the American commercial stage they are not, nor were ever meant to be, except as manifests that Brecht was prepared to continue the artistic struggle against gargantuan odds. After years of close and fruitful collaboration with Charles Laughton, a version of *Galileo* was completed that was performed in 1947 in Los Angeles and New York. This time the commercial Press and the left-wing Press were in agreement. The "script" [sic] was a bore.

While he lived on the West Coast, however, Brecht met a small group of people who were prepared to listen, learn and ultimately fight on his behalf. In terms of later influence, Eric Bentley was by far the most important, and it is his own seriousness, and his insistence that Brecht must be taken seriously, to which the great, and growing, influence of Brecht in America is largely due. To be sure, Eric Bentley is a university man, and to be sure it is in the universities that the deeply-rooted American attachment to Stanislavsky, to "the method", to theatre of illusion, to raw emotion and empathy, is being most surely broken down. But Bentley, unlike most academics in the "Old World", has been prepared to take the fight far beyond the lecture room and tutorial. He has translated Brecht, adapted Brecht, directed Brecht. As general editor of the Grove Press editions he also gathered round him a team of translators and men of the theatre of the calibre of Lee Baxandall, Martin Esslin, H. R. Hays and Desmond Vesey (to name only four of many) to make Brecht available in far greater quantity and quality than many European countries enjoyed until much more recently.

Availability of good texts, and the existence of serious and extremely capable academic critic/practitioners did not, unfortunately, mean that everything in the American garden became lovely overnight, nor does it mean that the situation is entirely healthy now. It is true that Brecht – as in Britain – is quite frequently performed in the commercial theatres, but as in Britain the general standards leave a great deal to be desired. In 1968 Bentley expressed the view that there was no "American way" of doing Brecht, because "I have seen Brecht done the American way, and this is how I know there is no American way."[6] He added scathingly: "When Brecht is a big deal on Broadway, he becomes theatre of the absurd in a sense Martin Esslin didn't intend." Bentley did say, however, that many of the "rough and (un)ready" productions across the States were much better, and that "even an amateur production can show, first, sympathy with the point of view and, second, an intelligent grasp of Brecht's art. Broadway has nothing to offer that can match these two assets. . . " From the late sixties to the mid seventies, during the powerful upsurge of "non-legitimate" professional theatre that became known as off-Broadway and off-off-Broadway, Brecht was, in name at least, a potent influence indeed. But again as with the British experience, "fringe" Brecht must be treated with extreme circumspection. Very many productions "based" on Brecht or "inspired" by Brecht had, and have, far more affinity with the ideas and teachings of Stanislavsky (usually filtered through those of Antonin Artaud and/or Jerzy Grotowski) than with those of Brecht. It was, and is, the politics that were the attraction and the apparent link. The Living Theatre's *Antigone* of 1967, the Performance Group's four-hour *Mother Courage and Her Children*, which opened early in 1975, the Shaliko Company's *The Measures Taken*, which was performed in 1974 and early 1975, the San Francisco Mime Troupe's *The Exception and the Rule* (1965), *The Congress of the Whitewashers* (1970) and *The Mother* (1974) – all these and many others were chosen, adapted and presented with immeasurably more respect for Brecht as a political writer than as a playwright or theatre practitioner.

Just how apparent this was to the people concerned is a matter for debate. Richard Schechner of the Performance Group, for example, defended himself against charges of directorial infidelity to Brecht's *Mother Courage* by pointing out that very few textual changes had been made – which falls rather short of explaining why there was no wagon in the production, why the audience were invited to eat a meal (including Swiss cheese) during the course of a half-hour interlude early in the action, and why some later scenes were performed *outside* the Performing Garage in Wooster Street, New York City, with the audience dressed in their winter coats against the February chill, passers-by blundering across the "set", and the occasional taxi-driver stopping to ask what was going on! To relate this last point to Brecht's famous theoretical street scene essay – as Schechner did – makes the seriousness he claimed for his approach difficult indeed to accept. The Mime Troupe's *The Mother*, while it received a critical response extraordinarily and amusingly similar to both the original Berlin production and the 1935 Theatre Union production (words like "childish", "condescending" and "offensive" were much in evidence) was totally dissimilar to both. The text was extensively altered (in a scarcely comprehensible attempt to make things less difficult for an American audience even some names were changed: Pelagea to Anya and Masha to Katya, for example), some songs were rewritten, and the play opened with a choral rendering of a song from another Brecht play – although *not*, mercifully, *The Threepenny Opera*! The affinities with Artaud and Grotowski can best be illustrated by the fact that the eight-strong company did their warming up in front of the audience; a process which involved acrobatics to a small jazz group and much singing of revolutionary songs. Leonard Shapiro, who directed *The Measures Taken* with the Shaliko Company, went so far as to ban references to Brecht's theories during rehearsals, and to create individual characterizations to replace faceless, impersonal members of the chorus in the text. His stated purpose was to make the play "more dramatic". The fight for Brecht is still going on, for which we must be grateful; and indeed, some lively and fascinating productions have resulted from it. But defining the battle-lines still seems to be demanding a major part of the available energy.

As we saw earlier, Brecht became a powerful force throughout Europe very quickly after his return to Berlin in 1949. Not only was the process much slower for Britain, but there was an essential difference in approach. European directors, after a certain tendency to try and slavishly follow Brecht's productions, either through his notebooks or "model-books", began to apply an enormous amount of thought, and to give an enormous amount of weight, to what Brecht had written as text, his methods of staging and his political impulse. Anyone who has studied Brecht's theories ought to know that he demands a certain serious and unified approach. The Europeans evolved productions of his plays which were not as he would have presented them; but they were evolved. The use of the word "tampering" to describe their approach would be an insult.

The process was not, of course, without its dangers and disasters. The Berliner Ensemble after the death of Weigel certainly went through a period of near-ossification, and throughout Europe there was a feeling in the late sixties and early seventies that the slavishness the best producers had always striven to avoid had at last become a real cause for concern. The best-known expression of the problem is probably the address the Swiss playwright Max Frisch gave in Frankfurt in 1964 when he described Brecht as having achieved the "sweeping ineffectiveness of a classic".[7] Frisch was, in fact, talking in more or less political terms (he doubted whether any of the millions of people who had seen Brecht and would see him again had changed their political views as a result, or even examined them seriously) but the importance of the statement in terms of Brecht as a theatrical phenomenon must not be underrated. By the late seventies, however, the position in Europe appears to have altered yet again, led perhaps by the much healthier situation at the Berliner Ensemble. By 1977/8, after the return of

Manfred Wekwerth to the company, which Tynan had pleaded for as early as February 1976, they began to regain critical approval. As Michael Billington ecstatically put it (*Guardian*, 20 February 1978): "The moral of the Berlin celebrations [of the playwright's eightieth anniversary] was unequivocally that Brecht Lives." Once more, though, one must strike a cautionary note. The play Billington was most enthusiastic about, *Galileo*, with Ekkehard Schall in the title role, certainly did not appear to us, in a performance seen in East Berlin in 1979, to indicate that the Berliner Ensemble was by any means out of the woods of stultification. Not only was the production unelectrifying to a degree, but it was received with a general indifference bordering on the impolite. A fair number of people in the audience talked sporadically throughout, as they did during a later performance of *Schweyk in the Second World War*. In conversation with East Berliners afterwards, it was hard, as foreigners, to establish exactly how normal a practice this is for theatre audiences there: some said one thing, others the opposite. But it was perhaps significant that during a performance of Dario Fo's *Bezahlt wird nichts*, which the Ensemble did brilliantly, the only noises from a totally absorbed audience were laughter and applause. In conversations with directors and performers of other East German theatres, too, a feeling emerged that the dangers of reverence for, and overexposure of, a limited repertoire are still felt to be very real – if not insoluble – where Brecht and the Ensemble are concerned.

That Brecht is a classic, with all the problems implicit in that state, can no longer be doubted. Frisch described him in 1964 as a genius, and a mere five days after his death the *Observer* published an extremely intelligent obituary by Sebastian Haffner (19 August 1956) which not only described him as being the nearest equivalent to Shakespeare ever, but added, "indeed, if one believed in the transmigration of souls, one could be tempted to think that he was Shakespeare reborn." Less fancifully, he described Brecht's work as being probably the central event in twentieth century drama, and said he had created "a new style and school of the theatre which today looks like saving the theatre from threatening sterility for the next generation or two."

In Britain, sadly, Brecht has achieved classical status without having gone through the fiery process of working and reworking by men like Vilar, Planchon, Strehler, Palitzsch, Wekwerth and so on. The first Brecht "interpreters" in this country, both pro and anti, set up a body of theory and prognostication, which although dubbed "Brechtian" had very little to do with anything he said, wrote or thought. "English

Seneca read by candlelight" was Thomas Nashe's apt description of the
theatrical excesses of an earlier era: it is hardly less apt if applied to most
of what has happened to Brecht in Britain. The great danger in many of
the received ideas of what Brecht advocated and practised is that, wrong
as they may be, they have been absorbed; and people who have absorbed
ideas and worked by them, naturally resist any attempt to prove they
have got them wrong from the start. Thus, not only is he a classic, but he
is a classic who has not been given anything like his deserts in performance terms. Instead of taking Brecht's theories seriously, British
practitioners (and to a certain extent this applies in America too) have
chosen deliberately to undervalue them, to distort them, to ignore them
or to resent them. The academic critics have been as guilty as the
ephemeral ones on this point, as will be seen later, but the real damage
has been done in the theatres. The one element one might have expected
to have been absent *there* – hostility – strangely exists. Brecht must bear
some of the "blame" in that he insisted on commenting on his own style
and method throughout his working life, thus requiring of his interpreters a great deal more intellectual effort and serious thought than
most "men of the theatre" have ever been prepared to expend on a
"mere writer". Whatever the reason, however, the result has been for
directors to adopt the view that Brecht may have been able to write
plays, but he should have kept his mouth shut about performing them.
Perverse as Ronald Bryden's prognostication (in a 1965 review of *Mr
Puntila and his Man Matti* that he was prepared to have reprinted in
1969[8]) that "some day when the fever's subsided we'll be able to play
Brecht properly, against his own instructions" certainly is, it equally
certainly encapsulates the attitude of most British and many American
directors today. This resentment is more likely to grow than dimish the
longer everyone goes on refusing to understand that Brecht was not the
boring, pompous, tendentious old wizard he is usually seen as.

The comparison of Brecht with Shakespeare, made by Haffner, is an
interesting one, if only because Shakespeare sums up the problems of
the classic better than any other writer. Brecht himself was aware of the
problems, and used Shakespeare many times as a focus for his doubts.
Shakespeare's theatre *in its time*, he reckoned, could "automatically
assume that the audience would not think about the play but about life"
(that is, Shakespeare was neither ineffective, nor a classic, when he was
first performed), but out of his time the dangers were manifold.
Shakespeare, along with the German classics, was in a state which
Brecht found terrifying as a young critic and playwright, and the

"unduly respectful attitude" was the root cause. "The worst," he wrote, "is the laziness in thinking and feeling amongst people who live in a rut. There is a tradition of performance which people regard unthinkingly as part of the cultural inheritance although it only damages the work, the real inheritance."[9] True as this is for Shakespeare in our time, it does not go far enough in a consideration of Brecht. Even on the Continent a "tradition of performance" is unlikely ever to become established because his theories are (deliberately?) too difficult, too complex and too suggestive to allow it; while in Britain and America he is all too frequently treated with a contemptuous lack of seriousness which has fostered something remarkably like sloppiness of approach as an apology for a tradition. The fact remains, however, that Brecht, being a classic, is *performed*; and that in itself is a problem.

Brecht, like Shakespeare, wrote great plays, good plays, mediocre plays, bad plays. Being, like Shakespeare, a classic, he now suffers from the problem that no one agrees where the lines which divide those categories should be drawn. It is inevitable that scholars and students, academics and critics, should argue about this; it will keep thousands of people happily occupied for centuries. But Brecht is performed, and the effect is a complex one that may be likened to throwing a stone in a pond – the ripples hit the bank, then rebound to meet more ripples. In short, Brecht's plays are now performed for reasons which have nothing to do with their merits as plays. A bad play is shown, bad critics or less well-informed people react by blaming Brecht (although the piece is one he would not have dreamed of giving a performance of at this late date, let us say) and other people respond by leaping to his defence, usually distorting the actual value of the play in question as an inevitable part of the process.

The problem goes further. Not only do bad or mediocre plays get performances, but the great and good plays get performed *badly*. Shakespeare illustrates the point best: he is given more disgustingly inadequate performances than any other writer, for the worst possible reasons. It usually reaches its nadir in Britain in the O-level text season, when the lack of intelligence of the people who stage *Measure for Measure* or *King Lear* seems only to be exceeded by that of the people who set it, but time and again his plays are staged, butchered, insulted (and praised) for no other reason than the idea that Shakespeare is Britain's national poet. So, equally unfortunately, with Brecht. The critic R. W. Shakespeare put his finger on it in *New Manchester Review* (March 1978) when he described a performance of *the Good Person of Setzuan* by

Contact Theatre Company as its "annual homage to Brecht". Homage could hardly have been a less apt word in view of the scantness of the respect shown to Brecht as playwright or theoretician, but the attitude is accurately revealed nevertheless. It is a fact that Brecht is one of the most widely performed writers in British theatre today; apart from Shakespeare it is difficult to imagine one who is consistently more inadequately performed. (Whether it is because of the theories or because he is a classic, Brecht, like Shakespeare, tends to "get away with" these bad performances, too. As with the directors, so with the audiences: people leave the theatre arguing not so much whether the *play* is successful, but whether the *performance* was "Brechtian" – and there are usually as many opinions as there are people! Genuine criticism can be easily deflected by accusing the critic of failing to have understood what Brecht wanted.)

Brecht, then, understood very clearly the problems that face the classic. It is at least possible that one of the reasons he erected the spiky (and for some, impenetrable) barrier of theory around his plays was to prevent the process ever occurring to him (he never suffered from false modesty about his creative ability). But if this is so, he failed. One fears that it is as vain to plead that this "classicization" be reversed, or even halted, as it would be to plead for an end to the hysterical antipathy of many of his detractors, but one may still hope. Although his status as a classic has been the result of many factors – his politics, his theories, his practice as exemplified by the early Berliner Ensemble, and latterly his poetry – it is as a playwright that he must, in the name of sanity, be judged first and foremost. Whether or not he would have written the plays in the way they exist had he not always formulated and tabulated his thoughts as he went along, those plays do exist: concrete, complete and available to read, perform, ponder over, analyse. Some are great, some are *pièces d'occasion,* some are partially or totally unsuccessful. Some deserve performance, some do not even call for it. It is vital to test them on their own merits, and that, surely, is the acid test.

During his lifetime and since his death, Brecht has suffered from what he said, what people think he said, and the seemingly limitless desire of critics to distort and damage as well as criticize, which is much harder. One must look at the areas of controversy which have most consistently obscured the clear and important questions, as well as trying to establish what Brecht actually said and meant. He is a phenomenon and he is a classic. Neither of which is sufficient reason either to misrepresent him or to become lost in reverence.

2

The Early Plays

Brecht started writing presentable poetry at an unusually early age, and his first full-length play was written (in one draft) by the time he was twenty. When he was twenty-one he wrote another full-length drama, and his third was started before he was twenty-four. Because of his lifelong habit of revising and rethinking, there is little point, in a book more concerned with Brecht as a dramatist and theatrical phenomenon than as a source of academic and psychological speculation, in agonizing over the minutiae of textual variation: the texts as they are generally available to readers (and directors) give more than sufficient insight into the processes by which Brecht achieved maturity as a writer.

Max Spalter, in his intelligent book of 1967, has made a case for placing Brecht solidly in a tradition of German writers stretching from Lenz to Karl Kraus who "suggest at the same time that the world is such a cesspool that it *must* be changed and that the world is such a cesspool that it *cannot* be changed. Like Brecht, they are all incongruous mixtures of moral outrage and cynical perception."[1] The writers (Lenz, Grabbe, Büchner, Wedekind, Kraus) share "his pitiless debunking attitude, his corrosive anti-romanticism, his hardheaded refusal to idealize or glorify, his suspicion of all sentimentalities".[2] While the general position embodied in these two quotations from Spalter is a convincing one, the details of the case are not so simple to come to terms with. It is, with a writer as great as Brecht turned out to be, a dangerous and possibly irrelevant exercise to try and place him in a tradition, although his early plays, even on a cursory examination, do reveal some interesting influences, as one might expect. There is no doubt that he knew, and admired, the work of the writers mentioned, and there are formal and thematic elements in the early plays which owe something to all of them. One may list the structural similarities with Büchner and

Wedekind embodied in *Baal* and *In the Jungle of Cities*; the overall sense
of cynicism that reflects all these writers in *Baal*, *Drums in the Night*,
Man Equals Man and *The Threepenny Opera*; and the use of language
which makes an especial link between Wedekind and *Baal* or *Drums in
the Night*. Undoubtedly the single most important influence, and not
only in the early plays, is that of *Woyzeck*; it will be looked at in more
detail in Chapter 9. The last main reason for accepting Spalter's tradition theory is a nebulous one, but none the less real for that: it is a
question of "feel". Brecht, who suffered from charges of plagiarism
almost from the start, was never afraid of borrowing, but invariably
creatively transformed the material he used. From the writers of
Spalter's "tradition", he borrowed and "transformed" something more
than an attitude, and more than habits of language. He used them and
others to establish his own peculiar stance towards the intricate relationship between a story and the manner in which that story is told. The
cynicism and anti-romanticism of the early plays is mixed with a
decidedly romantic and youthful view of the world, exhibiting through
its confusion a conscious debt, but the mature work retains little more
than a "feel" for the best of his creditors.

To a considerable extent, then, particularly concerning the early
plays, Spalter is reliable; but it must not be overlooked that there was
another dynamic which gave impetus to Brecht's work from the very
first: the urge to write answers, or present oppositional viewpoints, to
other dramatists. (*Baal*, his first full-length work, was, in fact, a
counter-play (*Gegenstück*) to Johst's *Der Einsame*, based on the life of
that oddball of Spalter's Brecht tradition, Grabbe.) He also wished to
oppose the hidebound bourgeois German theatre, which he saw much
of in Augsburg, and the Expressionists with their emotionalism and
sometimes hysterical idealism. *Drums in the Night* was written at the
time of a positive rash of plays about homecoming soldiers, and its
delightfully cynical treatment of both its love theme and its revolution
theme is a neat example of his oppositional quirkiness and technique.
This dynamic led fairly rapidly to Brecht's becoming an opponent of
everybody else; he wanted to rewrite the lot, to convert the world to epic
and Brecht.

Had it not been for his oppositional temperament, one might reasonably, in view of his youth, have expected *Baal* to be not merely "in a
tradition", but even a straightforward copy of the writers Brecht
admired. It is not, although the debts owed to *Woyzeck* in particular and
Wedekind in general are enormous. The story is a slight one, told in

self-contained episodes, interspersed with songs, that takes as its starting point the fact that the amoralist Baal cannot be contained within the drab, false world of the bourgeoisie, and takes as its finishing point his death, alone under the stars, rejected and misunderstood even by the woodcutters of the forest, one of whom comments: "He had a way of lying himself down in the dirt, and then he never got up again, and he knew it. It was like a readymade bed to him. . .Did anyone know him?" Brecht's picture of the bourgeois world, and the low drinking haunts he saw as the other side of the coin, owes much to his own background and apparently free and easy days and nights as a fairly well-heeled youth; the confusion of the story probably springs from this confusion too: Brecht wished to excoriate the bourgeoisie and hymn the lower depths; but he was of the one and a dabbler in the other. It is hardly surprising that *Baal* is so full of the intentionally shocking amorality that everybody noticed and which some still try to base a picture of Brecht's psyche on. But in fact it is an adolescent fantasy which kicks around some of life's profundities like so many footballs – drink, women/whores, homosexuality, murder – and wraps them in oodles of exotic poetry with the accent on excrement and decay.

There is, though, always danger in thus dismissing a play by Brecht. For however excessively romantic it may seem, however unsuccessful it can certainly be on stage, *Baal* has many possibilities that can be revealed by a director with sufficient imagination and grasp of the text. It also contains some examples of writing technique that can be identified by reference to later work as being characteristic. Very near the end of the play, two policemen are seen hunting down Baal after he has murdered Ekart, his friend and lover. The dialogue is sparse, but it reveals an enormous amount about not only the quarry, but the hunters too. The First Policeman asks: What is he?

Second: Above all, a murderer. Before that, revue actor and poet. Then roundabout proprietor, woodsman, lover of a millionairess, convict and pimp. When he did the murder they caught him, but he's got the strength of an elephant. It was because of a waitress, a registered whore. He knifed his best and oldest friend because of her.

First: A man like that has no soul. He belongs to the beasts.

Second: And he's childish too. He carries wood for old women, and nearly gets caught. He never had anything. Except for the waitress. That must have been why he killed his friend, another dubious character.

First: If only we could get some gin somewhere or a woman. Let's go. It's eerie.

Here, almost in sketch form, is the archetypal Brechtian soldier/ policeman – corrupt, brutal, by implication worse than the enemy/ criminal: the Ironshirts of *The Caucasian Chalk Circle* in embryo.

The writing of *Baal* helped Brecht to identify his enemies, but not his friends. He associated himself with its "hero", of that there can be no doubt. He wrote in his diary on 18 June 1920, when he was trying to shake off the play in order to get on with new projects:

How this Germany bores me! It's a good middling country, with lovely pale colours and wide landscapes: but what inhabitants! A degraded peasantry whose crudeness however doesn't give birth to any fabulous monsters, just a quiet decline into the animal kingdom; a middle class run to fat; and drab intellectuals. The answer: America. . .[3]

Confined to Germany, the Baal-like response to boredom is monstrous self-assertion, an iconoclasm as thrilling as Christ's overturning of the moneylenders' tables. Baal embodies a dark energy and a fearlessness that make him a potent symbol of revolt. In detail, of course, his revolt is petty and disgusting, but the ecstatic language, the defiance of small-minded decency, and above all the association of the outcast with the natural world that engulfs him, gives Baal a figurative force that actuality denies him. He becomes, for the young Brecht, an image of the artist, triumphant over neglect – like Van Gogh, whose letters to his brother inspired this diary entry on 8 July 1920:

The overriding thing must be the greatness of the conception, the dark piled-up mass, the trembling light over everything and the fearlessness of the human heart which shows things as they are and likes them that way.[4]

It is cause for celebration that Brecht overcame the impulse to seek his glory in magnificent mischief-making. He came to associate *Baal* with *In the Jungle of Cities*. One hymned the wildness, darkness and mystery of the countryside, the other of the city. But *Baal* succeeds where the later play fails. In its degenerate way, it is a monument.

Drums in the Night, the second play, is as interesting from the point of view of Brecht's personal politics and his subsequent development as it is from a dramatic standpoint. In later years he considered suppressing it altogether, but decided in the name of history to let it stand, with minor alterations (no Russian communist he). It tells the story of Andreas Kragler, a soldier returning from the war, who finds that his fiancée has agreed to marry another man and is pregnant to boot.

Wooed by Red revolutionists, he decides rather to take back his shop-soiled lady, and turns his back on the bright tomorrow with the famous words, "I am a swine, and the swine's going home."

Brecht's subsequent dilemma over *Drums in the Night* is obvious. Several times after his study of Marxism had started seriously he tried to explain away his apparent attitude in the play to the revolutionary activity in Germany after World War I. He described Kragler variously as a "disastrous type of Social Democrat", a "fake proletarian" and a "petit-bourgeois who defends his own interests". Kragler, he wrote in 1954, saw the revolutionary activity as "something romantic", and Brecht failed to make his audience see it differently because "the technique of alienation was not yet open to me." The problem for most people is that his retrospective awareness that he was politically "wrong" in his portrayal of Kragler seems a pity; for it is hard to suppress a feeling that he was actually "right". Even among people who still believe communism to be a way forward, it is the element of naive Utopianism (especially concerning revolution itself as part of the process) that sticks in the gills. In *Drums in the Night* Brecht's view of the revolutionary process was a cynical and clear-sighted one. It (the "revolution") was caused, the play suggests, more by chaos than political awareness, and was a romantic notion that he (however romantic himself at the time) recognized as such. Even ten years later he was unable to deny that the world then had been full of Kraglers, and in 1954 he was not prepared to deny that the play contained "comparative approval" of Kragler's conduct. Brecht probably did not know it, but Hitler himself was in one of the Red Army units for a short time after the war, and was arrested for it by right-wingers!

Brecht's first play about revolution, then, was profoundly anti-revolutionary. But although it may be tempting to say that as a young man he expressed a clearer vision of the implications of revolution than he allowed himself ever again, one cannot in reality make too much of the point. The simple fact is that *Drums in the Night* is a pretty feeble play and also a squib against, among other things, Brecht's own class and background. The story is extremely thin, and to spread it over five acts was ridiculously hopeful. Brecht described it later as "an ordinary romantic love story with no particular depth to it" which was helped along by the use of off-stage drums. It would be difficult to better that summing up.

Like *Baal*, *Drums in the Night* was solidly in the tradition outlined by Max Spalter. It was also an oppositional play to some of the worst excesses of Expressionism (although its first production, in September 1922, clearly made use of some of the trappings of Expressionist presentation). But it was very different in tone and intent to the first work, which is a not-unimportant point in any consideration of Brecht. To a certain degree, and despite his insistence on using "labels" to describe his methods, his whole writing life consisted in confounding and confusing by never following any given work with the sort of play one might have expected next. At this stage in his development the difference between *Baal* and *Drums in the Night* can best be explained by the fact that he was trying things out, testing the water, perhaps even looking for a form. He was also living in a specific time and place, and *Drums in the Night* was a specific response. It is worth noting that it is his only play (except for three "propaganda" pieces) that deals directly with a contemporary matter, without any hint of the exotic or "distancing" setting that he later came to consider almost vital for his examination of any subject. In a tradition then – and also quite close to the norm of some of his contemporaries. He probably saw it as being much closer to everybody else than he ever wanted to be, and he clearly decided that whatever he wanted to say, that way of saying it was wrong.*

To claim that the next play, *In the Jungle of Cities*, is either in a tradition or an oppositional work is probably stretching things too far. One does not have to seek hard to identify some of the writers and preoccupations that triggered it – Brecht himself mentions J. V. Jensen and Arthur Rimbaud, and the attempt to make concrete man's isolation owes a great deal to Büchner's *Danton's Death* – but the play is such a morass that it stands unmajestically alone. As an exercise in alienating an audience in the sense which Brecht did *not* mean, it can hardly be matched!

In the Jungle of Cities is mysterious from the word go, and from its first Berlin performance in October 1924, Brecht both acknowledged and enhanced this mysteriousness by appending a prologue exhorting his audience not to seek motives for the "inexplicable wrestling match" they were about to see, but to concentrate on the stakes, judge the contenders' techniques impartially, and "keep your eyes fixed on the

---

* It had the lantern moon, of course, and the waterless river, and later on the distancing sets, nebulous music, and slogans that Brecht recommended. The delightful "Don't stare so romantically", addressed to Kragler's audience, is in some ways the daddy of them all; he probably never wrote anything that so neatly encapsulated his theories. But in the case of this play, the need to be so anti-romantic is, unfortunately, absolutely in proportion with the romanticism of the piece itself.

finish." Even given that Brecht was fascinated by sport at this time (he saw it as, in some ways, a theatrical experience more valid than one could get in the theatres) and may have *believed* sports audiences were not wildly partisan, this prologue smacks of disingenuousness. Later he was to explain, in a fine example of his *penchant* for rather unconvincing hindsight, that the play had changed in the writing from being about "the pure enjoyment of fighting" to something very close to an idealization of the class struggle. A diary entry for 30 September 1921, when he had just begun work on it, supports the relationship of people and systems on the portentous mumbo-jumbo of "curves":

If I want to portray a struggle, it will probably be one between two people, not between two systems. This conditions all the characters' outer curves; the struggle has to be portrayed by them. The fate of the characters remains a matter of taste. The extent to which the individuals become aware of their curves, then resist them, is what produces the personal climate, in other words the poetic element. Acts of resistance create the cosmic aspect. Each of the protagonists in the struggle has to be given every possible opportunity, but one mustn't set out to prove anything.

Both early and late, one feels, he was unwilling to recognize the piece as a mere blind alley. Indeed, it has the kind of generalized hostility to things as they are that particularly appealed to certain British theatre groups in the seventies, and it is disturbingly easy to envisage a revival of interest that will further encourage the shriller anti-Brechtians.

The apparently motiveless "fight" which makes up the action is between a weird easterner called Shlink and a poverty-stricken young man called George Garga, who has emigrated to Chicago "from the prairie" with his family, whom he supports by his work as a librarian. The fight starts when Shlink arrives at the library and tries to buy Garga's opinion of a book. Garga immediately recognizes this as an attack on his integrity as a human being (he is a great deal more perceptive than the audience!) and refuses. The first problem has been set up: how are we to understand this totally disproportionate reaction to an apparently harmless proposition? Shlink makes it clear that a fight is on in an exchange that is a nicely theatrical evocation of the boxing ring:

Garga: Ninety four degrees in the shade. Noise from the Milwaukee Bridge. Traffic. A morning like every other morning.

Shlink: But this morning is different; I'm starting my fight with you. I'm going
to start by rocking the ground you stand on. (The [shop] bell rings. . .)

In the second scene Garga accepts the challenge "without obligation. . .and no question why".

From this point on, the play catalogues the moves in the fight, in
which the only concretely observable element is the slide to degrad-
ation, both mental and physical, of the two protagonists and everyone
around them. Shlink gives his lumber business to Garga (a gift tor-
tuously designed to *harm* him!), works for a pittance hauling coal, then
uses the money to support Garga's family, meanwhile engineering a
three-year term in jail for him, while Garga turns his fiancée into an
alcoholic, his sister into a whore, leads his mother to "disappear" into
the city, and finally brings about a situation in which Shlink is hunted
by a lynch mob. Shlink refuses to leave him and die alone, so the pair of
them end up in a deserted railway workers' "tent" near Lake Michigan.
Here Shlink declares his love for Garga, they agree that "man's infinite
isolation" makes even enmity "an unattainable goal", Garga declares
"the important thing is not to be stronger, but to come off alive. I can't
defeat you, I can only stamp you into the ground" and he leaves. Shlink
poisons himself.

One danger in giving a digest of the story is that, confusing as it may
be, it is clearer than the action of the play as it emerges from a reading or
a performance. It also conceals the play's most unattractive element –
the feeling that Brecht was trying to manufacture ambiguity. For all the
faults of *Baal* and *Drums in the Night* they were honest attempts to
convey by poetic and dramatic means ideas which were, by their nature,
to some degree ambiguous. With *Jungle,* it is extremely difficult not to
see the ambiguity as inorganic – tacked on (ladled on would perhaps be
closer) to give the impression of a depth of meaning that just is not there.
It is the more unfortunate because there are scenes and speeches which
are not only powerful and effective, but *truly* suggestive and ambiguous. The first scene, for example, contains a great deal that is brilliant
although it is overwritten, as is so much of the play. The mysterious
situation set up by Shlink's assumption of a fight is engaging, however;
it has a kinetic energy which is deliberately dissipated in the following
scenes by Brecht's refusal to give us something tangible to key it to.
Towards the end of the play Shlink and Mary Garga appear on the
shores of Lake Michigan in a scene of great beauty and bitterness,
broken by an extraordinary monologue by Garga's friend Manky, who

is searching for her although he imagines her now as "lying around like a fishbone" in a greasy saloon. Shlink and Mary emerge from the woods with this exchange:

Shlink: You ran into the bushes like a rabid bitch and now you're running out again like a rabid bitch.
Mary: Am I what you say? I'm always what you say. I love you. Never forget that, I love you. I love you like a bitch in heat. That's what you said. But now pay me. Yes, I'm in the mood to get paid. Give me your money, I'll live on it. I'm a whore.
Shlink: Something wet is running down your face. What kind of a whore is that?
Mary: Don't make fun of me, just give me the money.

The final scenes similarly make one regret that Brecht for the most part chose to fudge the story with a narrative "ambiguity" at once unsuccessful and uncharacteristic.

There is a chance, of course, that his failure in *Jungle* was not one of intent, but execution, that he merely failed to forge a dramatic shape which was capable of serving his vision. On reading Brecht's early poems, it is easy to see how *Baal* emerged from them. Although there is no such ease of correspondence between *Jungle* and the poems, it is very like many of them in impulse. Had he chosen to write it as a long poem, some of its major areas of failure would probably have been successfully transformed. In the play, the suspicion of pretentiousness is hard to avoid.

It is possible to *find* meaning in *Jungle*, and many people have tried. We have already mentioned human isolation, and a more general point about Brecht's nihilistic view of the world is often made. However convincing this world-view may be in his poetry of the same era, though, in this play the vision is flawed. Everything is overdone. One can sympathize (but not for the right reasons) when Garga responds to the much quoted speech by Shlink which contains the line "If you cram a ship full to bursting with human bodies, they'll all freeze with loneliness" by saying "Shlink, I've been listening to you now for three weeks. . . I realize that your drivel irritates me"! The oft-made point about homosexuality (oft-made about all the early plays), with its implicit speculation about the young Brecht's sexual make-up, seems merely a waste of time; even the most ardent Freudian in unlikely to convince anyone on that score.

It is heartening that when Brecht became a performed playwright in the early 1920s there was at least one critic who had the perception to see beyond the faults of the first plays. Herbert Ihering, of the *Berliner Börsen-Courier*, was not only perceptive but powerful, and he secured for Brecht the important Kleist Prize for his first three plays. Ihering thought them indicative of a major talent that had "changed Germany's literary complexion overnight", and what he recognized was the emergence of that hard-to-pin-down creature, a *writer*. This is a nebulous concept, perhaps, and almost impossible to define. The element Ihering chose to isolate was Brecht's language – "a language you can feel on your tongue, in your gums, your ear, your spinal column", and later, "Brecht is a dramatist because his language is felt physically and in the round." He realized that however flawed the plays, Brecht had something to say and said it in a way that was a joy and fire compared with most of his contemporaries.[7]

As an illustration that Brecht sprang fully-armed into the arena as a *writer*, his next work (written during winter 1922-1923) is of great significance. In 1954, writing of his early works, Brecht said it was hard for him to come to terms with *The Life of Edward II of England*, which is a pity. It was a tremendous achievement to have taken one of the finest history plays ever written and to have made a version that is almost certainly even better. Apart from the remarkably Elizabethan flavour of the verse – more moving in many places than Marlowe's amazingly moving original – he strengthened the play immensely by simplifying the story and giving far more depth to many of the characterizations.

The most important step forward, though, was that taken away from romanticism, overt or buried. The death scene, for instance, is far less rich and horrible than Marlowe's (although tremendously powerful still). The manner of Edward's death is not dwelt on (the stage direction says specifically "Lightborn smothers him") and even the sewer is evoked with less involvement than one might have expected from a young poet who had tended to wallow in the excremental. The play is permeated with a bitter cynicism that owes much to the original but is yet a clear, unflawed, poetic expression of a world view that is bleak indeed. When Edward, a prisoner in Shrewsbury castle after a four-year civil war made inevitable by his devotion to his "male whore", is invited to confess to the Lord Abbot, the exchange goes thus:

Edward: The starving fishermen of Yarmouth
              I pressed for rent.
Abbot: What else weighs on thy heart?

Edward:	I kept my wife Anne in the city in fifteen.
	In the August heat. A whim.
Abbot:	What else weighs on thy heart?
Edward:	I spared Roger Mortimer for malicious pleasure.
Abbot:	What else weighs upon thy heart?
Edward:	I whipped my dog Truly till he bled. Vanity.
Abbot:	And what else weighs upon thy heart?
Edward	Nothing.
Abbot:	No bloodshed, no offences against nature?
Edward	Nothing.

Later, when the King is being shipped from pillar to post, always under guard, there is a scene – the best in a play almost bursting with good scenes – in which Mortimer, now Queen Anne's lover, instructs the murderous brothers Gurney to keep Edward on the move. While the wolfish and bitterly humorous conversation goes on ("Where is your prisoner?" "North east south west from Berkeley, my lord") Anne talks to herself in dislocated, dreadful images like: "Here among the tapestries of Westminster it reeks / Of strangled chickens." At the end of the scene, having finally given up all resistance to Mortimer, in whatever awful deed, she laughs twice.

Mortimer:	Why do you laugh a second time?
Anne:	I laugh for the world's emptiness.

Perhaps what Brecht later found hard to "come to terms with" was the clear expression in this work that the world is unalterable, and its frightfulness an irrevocable concomitant of the human condition.

By early 1924, when *Edward II* was first performed, many of the trappings of "epic" theatre were clearly there, to be used specifically in performance. Even earlier, on his twenty-fourth birthday, Brecht had noted that in *Baal* and *Jungle* he had avoided the "common artistic error" of "trying to carry people away". He did not want his audiences to empathize because a "higher type of interest [can] be got from making comparisons, from whatever is different, amazing, impossible to take in as a whole."[8] What can be seen from a study of these four plays is that Brecht was moving in a certain direction from the start. This is not greatly surprising, and fits in with Spalter's "tradition" very well; for although Brecht may have been the most vociferous proponent of non-involvement, he was by no means the first to believe it was the way to present drama. More interestingly, one may speculate that at least part of the reason he built up a body of theory was not to provide an aesthetic for anyone else, nor even a series of formal guidelines for himself, but to explain and *encadre* the way he naturally wrote. In the end, one feels, his decision was that form – a more nebulous concept than is often allowed – was merely content plus a little help from his friends the acting and staging theories.

One of the major strengths of *Edward II*, already noted, is Brecht's treatment of the story. Whether the exercise of simplifying, clarifying and strengthening the original was one which he consciously found valuable we can never know. But coming after *In the Jungle of Cities*, in which he told a story of such confusion and mystification that some critics have made a virtue of failing to understand it, it may well have been crucial to his further development. What is more his next play, *Man Equals Man*, like *Edward II*, tells a story of great simplicity which seems to offer, but refuses to yield, a simple *meaning*.* This is fascinating, for while *Jungle* deliberately (it appears) sets out to conceal something which almost certainly is not there in any worthwhile quantity, *Man Equals Man* sets out an apparently naive tale which seems to reveal everything about itself and yet is capable of many interpretations. This mixture of simple story and complicated intent became a central strand in Brecht's technique as a writer, and one which we will examine in more detail later. *Man Equals Man* was also the high point, so far, in the use of the trappings of performance which became part of the theories; it indicates a growing conviction on Brecht's part that he had to tell his stories in a certain way for certain reasons. This development did not, of course, proceed in a straight line; there were to be failures and blind alleys along the route.

The problem with *Man Equals Man* that has proved a major stumbling block with commentators is that it is a comedy. It was his first full-length comedy (although he later described *Drums in the Night* as one), and it is very funny; but critics, determined to find deep significance (often to do with Brecht's personal psychology) in all his works, have overlooked this point with depressing regularity. It has been seen as a pacifist play; a super-prescient anticipation of brainwashing; yet another proof that Brecht had unconquerable identity problems; yet another example of his repressed homosexuality; and inevitably, an

---

* Brecht had had the idea in his mind for years before the play gelled, and it was revised and re-pointed several times over the years; clarity of story and ambivalence of meaning, however, are constant.

illustration (before Brecht became a Marxist!) that communism was the way forward but that, to become a communist, and therefore to survive in the new world, one had to be prepared to submerge one's individuality in the mass. Clearly, the play does have a serious intent, was not written merely to provide a few laughs; but the po-facedness of some of the opinions listed above is really quite extraordinary. What cannot be overlooked, in the light of contemporary art movements in Germany, is Brecht's ability to review with lightness and good heart the mechanization of twentieth century man. George Grosz and even John Heartfield could not do that. Theirs is the satiric mode. Brecht's is the ironic.

In a delightfully Kiplingesque India, a porter called Galy Gay from the seaport of old Kilkoa goes out to buy a fish, telling his wife that he will be back in ten minutes. Meanwhile four drunken British colonial soldiers (the lucky owners of four of Brecht's witty and surprising "English" names – Uriah Shelley, Jesse Mahoney, Polly Baker and Jeraiah Jip) are robbing a pagoda. Jip is caught in a cunning "pantomime" trap, and loses a large tuft of hair. The others put him in a palanquin and decide to come back that evening and shave his head, so that the bald patch will not betray him. But Sergeant Bloody Five, a weird and wonderful killer who got his name by shooting five Hindus to test that his pistol was not jammed, is looking for the bald pagoda thief, and arranges a roll call. The three soldiers, learning through an overheard conversation between Gay and the canteen owner Widow Begbick that Gay is a man who cannot say no, decide to recruit him to stand in for Jip. This ruse works well enough, although Bloody Five smells a rat, but back at the pagoda the chief monk, Mr Wang, has "metamorphosed" Jip into a god by the simple process of putting him in a prayer box. When the god knocks (Jip is wondering where he is) the faithful pay. The other three soldiers try to recover him, but by liberal applications of steak and whisky, Wang keeps him too befuddled and comfortable to move. The three decide that "we won't let this porter out of our hands so long as Jip is still out on the tiles."

Polly: How do we manage it, Uriah? All we have is Jip's paybook.
Uriah: That's enough. That'll give us a new Jip. People are taken much too seriously. One equals no one. Anything less than two hundred at a time is not worth mentioning. . .
Jesse: They can stuff their 'personalities'.
Polly: But what's he going to say if we turn him into Private Jeraiah Jip?

George Grosz, "Daum marries her pedantic automaton George in May, 1920. John Heartfield is very glad of it."

Uriah: His kind change of their own accord, you know. Throw him into a
pond, and two days later he'll have webs growing between his fingers.

The point is adequately proved when they wake him up.

Uriah: Are you of Irish extraction?
Gay: I think so.

At first, though, even the super-amenable Galy Gay is unprepared to
lose his identity. So the soldiers play on his greed by offering him a
"deal". This, the comic centre of the play (which some critics mis-
understand to the point of perversely calling it unconvincing!), involves
giving him a make-believe army elephant called Billy Humph, which
consists of Jesse and Polly under a map holding an elephant's head and a
whisky bottle full of water so that it can urinate to prove its reality. Gay
agrees to sign as the owner of the elephant (as long as his name is kept
out of it!), which he then sells to Widow Begbick. He is immediately
arrested, to be tried on the double charge of selling an elephant that was
not his, and selling an elephant that was not an elephant, which is fraud
(and is also a variant of the old Service story that one pays twice for lost
or broken equipment – once for the item in question and again for its
replacement). He is condemned to death, and in fear agrees to be Jip.
But in the course of the next few minutes, totally confused, he vacil-
lates. The scene of his execution, which is at once funny, affecting and
extremely nasty, brings out his key speech about lost identity:

If you shoot now you're bound to hit me. Whoah! No, not yet. Listen to me. I
confess! I confess I don't know what has been happening to me. Believe me,
and don't laugh: I'm a man who doesn't know who he is. But I am not Galy
Gay, that much I do know. I'm not the man who is supposed to be shot. Who
am I, though? Because I've forgotten. . . if you come across a man who has
forgotten who he is, that'll be me. And it's him I am beseeching you to let go.

He is shot, with blank cartridges, and faints.
   While this part of the story has been unfolding, the second strand has
also emerged. Bloody Five, the epitome of military discipline and
savagery, has a fatal flaw. When it rains he becomes mad with lust. It
has rained, he has succumbed (the Widow Begbick has three daughters
who follow camps for the traditional reasons, although they disappear
from later versions) and in the process he too has lost his identity. As
Galy Gay lies in his faint, Bloody Five enters in civilian clothes to find

out what the shooting is about. Uriah bangs his hat down over his eyes and tells him, "Stop your gob, civvy!" Later, Bloody Five, in the grip of his normal disgusted reaction to his "weakness", blows off his testicles with his revolver and the amazing line, "Mutineers will be shot." He adds: "I accept full responsibility. I have to do it if I am to go on being Bloody Five. Fire!" Galy Gay, who has watched (and who remains the only person ever to know) comments:

On account of his name this gentleman has done something extremely bloody to himself. He has shot off his manhood. Witnessing that was a great stroke of luck for me. Now I realize where such stubbornness gets you and what a bloody thing it is when a man is never satisfied with himself and makes so much fuss about his name.

Up until this moment, Galy Gay has continued to vacillate. He has even presented a tragi-comic funeral oration, in the persona of Jip, over the coffin of the supposed Gay, but given away his disbelief in the proceedings by referring to the "shot" man as "I". But now he turns to Widow Begbick, admits that he knows who she is (that is, who *he* is – Galy Gay – because they met earlier), obtains some information essential for a soldier, and assumes the persona of Jeraiah Jip, using his papers to prove it. In the final scene he becomes the complete soldier, the "Human Fighting Machine" and destroys a fortress, singlehanded, with (significantly) five shots. Jeraiah Jip turns up, without papers, and his three former comrades refuse to recognize him. Galy Gay gives him "the papers of the bloke you used to tease me about: Galy Gay." Jip accepts them and leaves. Bloody Five enters and demands who the "Human Fighting Machine" is. Gay replies that he is Jip. Bloody Five is speechless: it has been proved to him that, had he been prepared to lose his name, he could also have lost his sexual "weakness". Alternatively, he could, with a new name, have ceased to care about his sexual "weakness". *Or* he could have asserted his continuing right to his name despite his "weakness". For it is the name, and the name only, that makes a man what he is: he has castrated himself unnecessarily.

This play absolutely crackles with fine scenes, cynical and vulgar lines ("It's as full of vomit as a spittoon on the third day of Christmas") and satirical commentary on the life and times of colonial soldiery. For example, Wang, on finding Jip in the palanquin, remarks: "I knew it must be a white man as soon as I saw what a disgusting state the palanquin was in. . . A soldier of his Queen, coated with sicked-up drinks, more helpless than an infant hen, too drunk to recognize his own mother. . . Our best answer is to make a god of him." It also contains some interesting sketches, which Brecht returned to more than once: the Widow Begbick, for example, full-blooded, bawdy, tough – and the owner of an army canteen. In feel *Man Equals Man* could hardly be more different from *Mother Courage*, but some of its details prefigure that play and several others. (Begbick reappears in name, of course, in *The Rise and Fall of the City of Mahagonny*.) It might be argued that Galy Gay and Bloody Five, representing the opposite faces of man, introduce a theme that Brecht returned to several times, most notably in *The Good Person of Setzuan*. Trying to find an overall, pat "meaning" for the play, however, is a pointless exercise. Those set up are easily shot down. If Brecht was making a tentative plea for communist acceptance of group identity, for instance, why should Galy Gay end up a monster of colonialistic savagery? One could quite convincingly counter the inter-pretation with an oppositional one – that it was a warning that normal, easy-going, harmless German citizens could be transformed into murderous lunatics by Nazism. As to the question of the problems of identity, Brecht has so many balls in the air at once that his intent is clearly comic: civilian turns to soldier, soldier to civilian, man into god, canteen into empty space! And if, as those who believe they can see into Brecht's mind so frequently reiterate, he believed the loss of identity was ultimately necessary for progress and happiness, why is the "brain-washing" scene and Gay's mock execution so heartrending an example of man's inhumanity to man? The play is a savage, cynical, bitter comedy, in which, Widow Begbick tells the audience, Mr Brecht is showing us that you can take a human being to pieces like a car and rebuild him like one, thus demonstrating (with scant regard for logic) that "the world is a dangerous place." It is also an absurd (one might almost say absurdist) tale, with the constant and incomprehensible references to elephants running through it like a streak of uneasy and unresolved madness. (The "interval piece" removed from the first versions and published as an appendix in 1927, *The Elephant Calf*, takes Brecht's mild obsession with elephants to its nth degree. It also, interestingly, uses a version of the chalk circle story which later became one of his masterpieces.) The references to elephants in *Baal* (and likewise red moons in *Drums in the Night*) were juvenile and a little tedious. In *Man Equals Man* the effect is disturbingly successful. What-ever Brecht meant this play to be "about", it was not something so glibly concrete as is usually suggested. More convincingly, it is another expression of his bleak, if at this time confused, view of mankind.

If the long-faced reactions to *Man Equals Man* have made it difficult to respond to in the spirit in which it was written, a similar problem is magnified enormously with *The Threepenny Opera*. Many thousands of words have been expended on it, most of which at best damn it with faint praise. The most frequent judgement is that while it was, and remains, a great theatrical success, it is basically deeply unserious, and should therefore not be made too much of. That it fails as a play by a Marxist writer has become axiomatic, usually because Brecht is judged to have failed to excoriate the bourgeoisie in that they actually enjoyed it. Neither of these views stands up to a close examination.

Brecht and his musical collaborator Kurt Weill wrote the play in the time-honoured chaos and confusion that people who have never worked in the theatre find incomprehensible. It was written in haste, parts of it were apparently "merely" cobbled together, and the song which remains the most famous thing either man ever wrote, Macheath's "Moritat", is said to have been written virtually overnight and stuck at the beginning because an actor demanded a better entrance. The whole process of creation and production was a melting pot of fun, fights, expected failure and bombshell success, which is just not commensurate with the naive but clearly widespread view that visible effort, a grim creative sweat, is the price which must invariably be paid for achieved literary weight. Brecht and Weill, fortunately, were not so self-important. Their youthful and exuberant genius bubbled away to produce some of their very best songs, and a theatrical whole which remains totally alive and more stimulating politically than it was even when first performed.

The idea of *fun (Spass)* is one which is all too easily lost when someone like Brecht (who used the word all the time) becomes the subject of "serious" study. It is at the core of much of his writing, especially in the early plays, and it was also an important part of his personality. The problems in this instance are somewhat compounded by his perfect understanding that seriousness of intent is not somehow embodied in seriousness of the *process* of writing (for example, he wrote *The Threepenny Opera* in an almost haphazard way, yet was deadly earnest in his *message*) and by his lifelong habit of writing notes about his plays after performances or publication which are at best tongue-in-cheek replies to the reactions of others and at worst downright lies. Thus, in his notes to *The Threepenny Opera*, Brecht is clearly mocking when he insists that Tiger Brown's "affection for Macheath is entirely genuine", since it has been very firmly shown to be a ludicrous and hilarious theatrical joke (with the sentimental brutality of Brown possibly being a sketch for Pierpont Mauler in *Saint Joan of the Stockyards*); while his insistence that Macheath is an embodiment of the bourgeoisie, like his attempts to make the filmed version politically more in line with Marxism and his writing of the rather drab *Threepenny Novel*, are examples of Brecht being almost as miserably po-faced as some of his detractors.

However surprised Brecht may have been, or claimed to have been, about the success of this play, it was certainly no accident, and it is certainly not the pot-boiler it has so often been called. The plot is superbly integrated, and unfolds in an organic way which is very far from his normal technique. Not only is it in three acts, but the rythmic placing of scene and counter-scene and the sharing out of the dramatic steps between the most important characters in an almost schematized way make it by far the nearest he ever got to writing a "well-made play", despite the aggressive use of placards and lighting and despite his insistence (again in the notes) that the plot did *not* proceed in a straight line. His use of characterization too is remarkable and is one of the great strengths. Macheath is the "hero", but the events do not happen to him alone. Peachum, Polly, Lucy and Brown all interact on each other and Macheath, and his downfall is the end-product of a process of cross and double-cross, betrayal and counter-betrayal, which involves all of them almost equally. Even the gang, taken as an entity, is a part of this process: Macheath is prepared, even planning, to have them hanged when it suits him; and when it suits them they have exactly the same idea.

Another aspect of the play's excellence and power which is consistently overlooked is the actual characterization of Macheath. If Brecht genuinely wanted to make a point about gangsters being bourgeois and the bourgeois being gangsters (and we have only his word for it!) he probably failed. From the start, it is hard to believe in Macheath's villainy, impossible to be worried by the tales of his murders and misdeeds. What Macheath actually is, though, is not a portrait of a murderer or an unpleasant and greedy burgher but a picture of a man ruled by sex, by an enormous lust for life and women. Mrs Peachum's song about his downfall, as well as her complete (and correct) conviction as to his inability to miss his Thursday visit to the whorehouse, are central, while the barefaced gaiety with which the themes of sexual jealousy are handled both in song and scene is little short of amazing in view of Brecht's enormously complicated relationships with women at this time

". . . a man ruled by sex, by an enormous lust for life and women." *The Threepenny Opera* as performed by the Berliner Ensemble in 1960

(and indeed with his original cast and collaborators). It is hard to escape the thought that some of the words Polly and Lucy have to say to each other must have been very close to home for the women originally involved. Brecht may have been politically serious, but he refused to write a politically simple or drab play; his love-life may have been difficult at this time, but he wrote about such matters, through Macheath and his women, in a brazen, even callous, way. Brecht liked Macheath too much to make him a convincing gangster. But he is a thoroughly convincing characterization of a human being who suffers and inflicts suffering because of sex. The characterization in the novel, incidentally, is entirely different, and pretty unsuccessful: *that* Macheath Brecht definitely did *not* admire (or know).

He later described the text as "little more than the prompt-book of a play already given over completely to the theatre", and it is vital that this should not be overlooked, especially when the political aspects are being considered. High quality recordings of the songs and music are readily available, and the absurdity of many of the arguments levelled against the play becomes apparent when the glory of Weill's score and the tremendous verve and fun of the piece as a whole are realized. Many of the apparent political confusions which arise from a reading just do not come into the question in performance – the ending being a good case in point. Peachum says the play has shown the difficult life of the downtrodden, which it has not, and he goes on to reveal the impenetrable paradox that Mounted Messengers come far too infrequently, if you kick a man he'll kick you back, and *therefore* one must not be too eager to combat injustice! A *non sequitur*, a bitter joke, a nonsense? It matters not at all in the context of the amazing finale. (And in many versions available today two last verses of the "Moritat" – from Brecht's film treatment – which are far less ambiguous, linger after the finale: rich men can buy happiness, and the poor live in darkness.)

What does matter, politically, is that the play is successful, funny and forces an audience to think, then as now. (To expect more from it, up to and including the provoking of revolution, is merely ridiculous; but is implied, even stated, quite frequently by those determined to prove it a failure.) Although it is full of clever but largely superficial digs at the bourgeoisie and the capitalist ethic ("What is the robbing of a bank to the founding of a bank? What is murdering a man compared to employing a man?") and everyone in it is said to be middle-class and dishonest (even the whores), much more serious is the feeling that permeates it that the world is intensely evil and its denizens intensely greedy – a feeling that almost all the songs state specifically and with brutal clarity. The crux may be that Brecht feels this evil and greed to be not only intense, but possibly irredeemable. A gangster is *of course* not necessarily a bourgeois, nor *vice versa*; but a gangster is always a human being, and this may be the source of the darkness that underlies *The Threepenny Opera*. Brecht makes a very feeble case for convincing us Macheath is a bourgeois (he tries much harder in the novel), but he presents us with a very complete human being. The only way it could succeed as a specifically left-wing or Marxist attack would be if it made us believe that it is a genuine and complete picture of a specifically bourgeois world, and that to survive in such a world it is necessary to be evil. But if it can be seen more as a picture of the world as a whole, as it exists, through all classes and strata, and that it is necessary to be evil to survive, it must fail as a narrowly political attack.

It is very doubtful that a narrow political attack is what Brecht was trying to make. He wanted the effect of the piece "hardened up" in the film and the novel, but he stated in later life that the reaction of the bourgeoisie did not surprise him, and what is more, he went on to write *Happy End* and *Mahagonny* – both extremely jolly and exuberant "attacks" in similar form. Despite any weakness in narrow political terms, *The Threepenny Opera* is a bleak, compelling and convincing portrait of us all, not just the petit-bourgeois, which is all the rarer (and all the harder for critics to take seriously) for being in the form of a genuinely funny comedy. The idea that Brecht somehow failed (with this, his greatest theatrical success) is a widespread and long-lived one which is in reality a sham: for the play still shows us misery as a result of greed even if it hides the misery in a series of bitter jokes, and few people would be cynical enough to believe that mankind is so far lost as to be incapable of being jolted by, and learning from, such a reminder. What is more, that was just as true for the audiences who first saw the play. It is a political play, a successful one, and it is also about deeper problems of existence. It continues to *defy* a reverential or over-solemn approach, and it continues to make people think. Far from being a minor play, or a failure, it is one of Brecht's most suggestive and fascinating works.

3

Brecht and Politics

Beware of willing judges
For Truth is a black cat
In a windowless room at midnight
And Justice a blind bat. [1]

As we have seen, it is absolutely vital to examine the role of the critic in any area of study concerning Brecht. Nowhere is this more true than over the vexed question of politics. Few writers have suffered more than Brecht at the hands of biased and hostile commentators, and one may safely say that much of the bad "scholarship" is at least in part attributable to the fact that Brecht was a Marxist; certainly the political field is the area of the worst critical excesses. As in so many other areas, however, Brecht had the unique distinction of attracting hysterical or near-hysterical reactions from the camp which one might reasonably have expected to have applauded him; for the communists, as well as the non-communists, for many years found much in his writing to fear and hate, and little to applaud.

The facts of Brecht's political life are unexceptionable enough on the face of it. After a perfectly normal adolescent patriotism, not to say jingoism, at the start of World War 1 (in 1914 he exhorted the schoolchildren of Augsburg, his home town, to "render a small service to the common cause of your beloved Fatherland"[2] and in January 1915 composed a panegyric for Emperor Wilhelm II's birthday), Brecht had already before he was eighteen begun to develop the pacifism which was to be his most powerfully felt belief for the rest of his life. In June 1916 he was almost expelled from school for an essay on Horace's line "Dulce et decorum est pro patria mori" which concluded, among other things, that the idea was merely propaganda, and in November 1918 he wrote his notorious "Legend of the Dead Soldier" in which a medical commission dig up and declare fit for battle the corpse of a soldier who has already given his life for the Kaiser.

On 21 October 1919 Brecht began to review theatre and films in Augsburg for the Independent Socialist newspaper *Der Volkswille*, which became communist in 1920.* Although by now clearly broadly aligned with the left, however, the young poet seems to have been remarkably uncommitted. Writing, women, liquor and cigars appear to have been his greatest passions; which is perhaps not too surprising considering his age, his talents and his boundless attractiveness to the opposite sex.

It was not until mid 1926, while collecting material for a (never-completed) play called *Joe P. Fleischhacker*, that Brecht started studying economics, and more specifically the works of Karl Marx. In view of the widely held (and possible rightly so) opinion that Brecht never understood economics, it is worth quoting him on his research for this project. He wrote later:

I had thought that by a few inquiries among specialists and practitioners I could quickly acquire the necessary knowledge. It turned out quite differently. Nobody . . . was able to give me an adequate explanation of what goes on in the Corn Exchange. . . The ways in which grain is distributed around the world are flatly incomprehensible. From any point of view except that of a handful of speculators, the grain market is one large morass. The projected drama did not get written, instead I started to read Marx, and then, not until then, was reading Marx.

A few months later Brecht wrote to his collaborator Elisabeth Hauptmann: "I'm eight feet deep in *Das Kapital*. Now I must know the whole thing." It was not for another three years, however, that Brecht's purely didactic, political pieces *The Flight of the Lindberghs* and *The Didactic Play of Baden-Baden on Consent* were premiered at the Baden-Baden Festival. By 1930 the didactic phase was apparently fully established. Brecht was suing the Nero Film Company because he did not like the way they were proposing to film *The Threepenny Opera* (he finally settled before an appeal court hearing was due to start); he was

*In a 1920 review, he incidentally mentioned just having read Upton Sinclair's *The Jungle*, "the story of a worker starving to death in the Chicago stockyards". Sinclair's Chicago, fused with other more or less mythical elements of early twentieth century America, became one of the founts of Brecht's more specifically socialist writing.

engaged in making another, definitely left-wing film (*Kuhle Wampe*, later banned, then released in a cut version); and his plays were all specifically communist and many of them straightforward propaganda.

Where Brecht may have gone as a communist writer had he stayed in Germany, we shall never know, of course. As late as February 1933 he was attending lectures on Marxism at the Karl-Marx-School in Neukoelln, followed by workshop sessions in his own home. But on 28 February 1933, the day after the Reichstag fire, Brecht, his second wife Helene Weigel and one of their two children fled the country. At the time, he was reputed to be Number Five on Hitler's death list. On 8 June 1935 he was deprived of his German citizenship.

The psychological problems of enforced exile are unfathomable, and the writer, divorced from his language, the people and society he uses as source material, and in Brecht's case the theatre, probably suffers more than most. Many German artists did not survive the disaster: the suicide rate among them was hideously high. Brecht, who at the very least may be described as among the toughest-minded of men, never allowed himself to complain (at least in public or in his writings). But it was fourteen years before he was to return. During those years he suffered personal tragedies, he watched helpless while his homeland led the world into the most terrible war in history and Russia, the great communist hope, revealed herself for all to see as a country suffering under the heel of a dictator with enough affinities to Hitler to drive the most ardent believer to the borders of despair.

In the early part of his exile, Brecht saw the fight still in terms of communism versus fascism. In June 1933 he was proposing to Johannes R. Becher, Secretary of the Alliance of Proletarian-Revolutionary Writers, a conference to discuss the problems of continuing the struggle from outside Germany and talking about the possibility of winning over "bourgeois writers of the left" for real political schooling. (It is perhaps illuminating to note here that Brecht did not consider himself to be of the bourgeois.) In 1934 he wrote *The Threepenny Novel*, as well as the didactic play *The Horatii and the Curiatii*, and in 1935, at the end of a visit to Russia, said in a newspaper interview: "On May 1, I saw the triumph over the difficulties which the transformation of a new world brings with it: the triumph that here those difficulties are unknown which affect all the rest of the world and which it cannot overcome."[1] But as the decade grew older, and bleaker, so the overt political element in Brecht became subordinated to the more pressing need to oppose Hitler as a "pure" force rather than as a counterforce to communism, a

shift which can perhaps best be illustrated by the series of playlets
written between 1935 and 1938 which became the sequence *Fear and
Misery of the Third Reich*. By 5 August 1940 Brecht no longer considered
himself a member of the proletariat, but rather as a bourgeois writer
who had espoused their cause – "on a par with the bourgeois politicians" who had done the same. In his *Arbeitsjournal* for l6 September
he wrote perhaps the most moving expression of his state that exists:

It would be unbelievably difficult to express the frame of mind in which I
follow the Battle of Britain on the radio and in the bad Finnish-Swedish
papers, and then write *Puntila*. This psychic phenomenon explains both that
such wars can be and that literary works can still be produced. *Puntila*
concerns me hardly at all, the war concerns me utterly; about *Puntila* I can
write almost anything, about the war nothing. And I don't just mean 'may', I
really mean 'can'. It is interesting how far literature, as a practical activity, is
removed from the centres of the all-decisive events.[5]

It is indeed. Brecht wrote all his great masterpieces in these bitter years
of exile.

From 1941 until 1947 Brecht lived in America, where, to quote his
own words, "As a guest . . I refrained from political activities concerning this country, even in literary form."[6] This did not save him
from being subpoenaed to appear before the House Un-American
Activities Committee, which he did on 30 October 1947. Although the
event itself was a prolonged exercise in triviality, it had wider implications than its surface idiocy might suggest. To quote Eric Bentley: "this
tragi-comedy goes far beyond the question of the HUAC. It transcends
the spectacle of a communist-sympathizer cannily evading questions
and winning a compliment from his arch-enemies. We have here,
among other things, the intellectual confronting the philistine, the man
of Mind confronting the man of Power . . . There is a drama here of
human types who have never seen eye to eye and never will."[7] It might
be noted that a similar irony underlay Brecht's life after he had finally
settled in the Eastern bloc some two years after his return to Europe.
One can never know how his creativity was affected by the quiet
confrontation with the powers of philistinism that was such a large, and
constant, part of his life as an artist in East Berlin, but he adopted an
approach to the descendants of Zhdanov and Stalin who dominated the
arts "establishment" there not dissimilar to the one he used before the
American committee. He had noted wryly of the Americans that they

were not as bad as the Nazis because they let him smoke. The East Germans let him do far more than that; but Mind and Power retained their (eternal?) polarity.

Brecht's faith in Marxism, however, apparently stayed with him until the day he died, and it was occasionally illuminated by flashes of revolutionary optimism. On 18 January 1949 he wrote: "Through all these weeks I keep in the back of my head the victory of the Chinese Communists that totally changes the face of the world. It is in my mind constantly, and engages me every few hours."[8] This was in opposition to his awareness, expressed early the previous December, that the German proletariat, even with the Russians there to provide the "driving force", did not want "rule by the people in the form of dictatorship."[9] (The distance between the bourgeois intellectual and the masses, as well as one of the problems of long-term exile in time of war, may perhaps be illustrated here very clearly indeed: Brecht obviously believed the German masses should or could welcome the Russians. Considering the practically unbelievable savagery of the war they had just fought, with losses and atrocities on both sides which beggar imagination, his belief seems at best hard to comprehend.) Such oppositional forces were the very stuff of life to Brecht, and a main source of the tensions from which some of his greatest art sprang. He died before the Cold War had really begun its long thaw; one may wonder how he would have viewed the warlike stance which so firmly characterizes the relationship between Russia and the Chinese communists now.

The complexities, the ambiguities, not least the impossibility of entering the mind and psyche of another human being, have, unfortunately, left many Western critics unamazed, undaunted and unembarrassed. Responses to Brecht the Marxist range from the merely snide to much more serious attacks. Willy Haas, for example, "reveals" that Brecht was something of a poseur in the matter of dress. "He was always fully masqueraded: his costume consisted of an old, dark, close-fitting, well-worn jacket of soft leather like a motorcyclist's or a truck driver's, yet underneath he wore an expensive silk shirt which only men of substantial income could afford." At the other end of the scale one observes the phenomenon of a far more seriously considered academic like Ronald Gray apparently almost finding the rise of communism in Germany, or at least Brecht's espousal of it, more disturbing than the rise of Nazism. At one stage, in his book *Brecht the Dramatist*, after giving a brief sketch of the chaos and misery into which Germany was slipping in the late 1920s, he concludes of the Nazis and the communists:

Both were intolerant of opposition, and street-fighting between rival factions became increasingly widespread. Together, they made the moderate parties seem helpless, and there was some excuse, in politics, for a man who decided to plump for one or other of the dictatorial parties.

   For a dramatist, a wrong choice was less excusable, though a defence of Brecht can be offered. One of an artist's main concerns is with truth, and to sacrifice this for a temporary advantage can only be justified in terms of a conviction that some synthetic, comprehensive theory of universal development is over-ruling. Up to the time of *Mahagonny*, Brecht was still uncertain about where his allegiance ought to lie. By 1929, he had made up his mind: only Marxism could provide a solution, and the propagandist works of the early 1930's were the result.[11]

Quite apart from the extraordinary assumption that Brecht sacrificed a concern for the truth as he saw it in the plays of this period, one can perhaps be forgiven for thinking — in view of what happened to Germany in 1933 and to the world in 1939 — that he deserves a medal rather than a defence. But it emerges clearly enough that Gray disapproves of revolutionaries *per se*, whoever they might be fighting against. He speaks sympathetically of Ernst Toller because although "his convinced belief in Communism could hardly be doubted" his work was "deeply despairing". Toller, Gray notes, "was crushed by the inhumanity which revolutionaries seemed to take in their stride, and by his exile after 1933."[12] No such sympathy is extended to Brecht (who did not, as Toller did, commit suicide). In his next paragraph Gray writes:

Brecht was also confronted with these issues of humanity and revolution; he found them easier to solve, in fact even in his earliest plays brutality is portrayed without a qualm, and by his thirties he was allowing characters in his plays to advocate it without contradiction. Even in the milder period of his forties and fifties he could still unleash a spurt of violent hatred without obvious political necessity. He was, in fact, the only one of the German and Austrian 'literary' dramatists of his day to do so.

   It will be necessary, when we come to discuss individual plays, to return to Gray and his apparent inability to see beyond the merest surface of the problem of the political writer. His refusal to accept the possibility of deeper human motives and confusions is almost the exact antithesis of the approach made by Martin Esslin in his famous book

Brecht: A Choice of Evils, first published in 1959. This is a huge, almost baroque, edifice, constructed in Freudian terms, presumably to explain away the unswallowable fact (for Esslin) that a writer he so greatly admires could have been an adherent of a political philosophy he so deeply abhors. In his introduction he wrote: "The most intriguing question, however, posed – and largely answered – by Brecht's experience is: how far is it possible for a great writer to adhere to a creed so rigidly dogmatic, so far divorced from the reality of human experience as our latter-day brand of Communism without doing violence to his talent?"[13] As late as 1969, the question for Esslin was simple enough and easily answered. He wrote:

The main contention of my exposition of Brecht's life and political career was that, while he was a fervent believer in the Marxist creed, he had been highly critical of the party's theory and practice and bitterly opposed to the official doctrine of socialist realism; that he had hesitated a good deal before finally deciding to settle in East Berlin and in accepting the East German invitation had been largely motivated by his desire to get his own theatre; that, once settled in East Berlin, he had been subjected to a good deal of harrassment in the final phase of Stalinism and had consistently, albeit very prudently and diplomatically, opposed the more oppressive manifestations of totalitarianism and state interference in the arts; that the workers' revolt of 17 June 1953 had deeply shaken him; and that his disillusionment with the realities of life in a Communist-ruled country might have been a contributory factor in his early death.[14]

On the face of it there is not too much to argue about in that summary, but it hides more than it reveals. The fact is, Esslin had decided that Brecht had *become* a Marxist for complex psychological reasons that sprang from a "deep feeling of inability to establish genuine human contact" and a "longing for meaningless authority". In 1959 he had admitted that his picture of Brecht's character and the main events of his life was "fairly circumstantial", but as more and more facts emerged over the years, Esslin displayed no willingness to accept that his view was being proved to be hopelessly inaccurate, if not ridiculous. Brecht, we now know, consistently and from his earliest years, formed relationships which were not only deep, but extremely long-lasting. In the months before his death he was working with Caspar Neher, with whom he had gone to school (the friendship survived despite the fact that Neher did not flee Germany in 1933 and in fact was conscripted into Hitler's forces in 1944), he visited his publisher and lifelong friend Peter

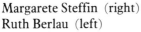

Margarete Steffin (right)
Ruth Berlau (left)

Suhrkamp in hospital in West Berlin, and he went to Milan with
Elisabeth Hauptmann, a collaborator since the 1920s and a friend since
her attempted suicide (she was presumably his mistress) on the day he
married Helene Weigel. Neither did Brecht lose contact with the far-
from-easy Ruth Berlau, who had borne him a child in America in 1944.
(The child lived a few days only.) In fact, when he left Finland for
America in 1941, Brecht's "household" had consisted of his wife and his
two mistresses, Margarete Steffin and Ruth Berlau. It may well be that
such a circumstance draws attention to Helene Weigel rather than to
Brecht, but the point is that a man who retains the love of and a concern
for his mistresses and his wife for as long as Brecht did is clearly more
capable than most of us are of "genuine human contact". And yet, in
1969, Esslin was still able to find his early analysis of Brecht's motivation confirmed by the new material that had come to light.

    In the same breath, one may comment on Esslin's almost casual
contention that Brecht's life might have been shortened by his "disillusionment with the realities of life in a Communist-ruled country".
Esslin bolsters his claim by quoting the lines:

> I was sad when I was young
> And am sad now I am old
> So when can I be gay for once?
> It had better be soon. [15]

The dangers of the biographical approach to literature hardly need reiterating. Let it suffice to quote an earlier poem, "Little Song":

> One time there was a man
> Whose drinking bouts began
> When he was eighteen. . . So
> That was what laid him low.
> He died in his eightieth year:
> What of, is crystal clear.
>
> One time there was a child
> Which died when one year old
> Quite prematurely. . . So
> That was what laid it low.
> It never drank, that's clear
> And died aged just one year.
>
> Which helps you to assess
> Alcohol's harmlessness.

It is at least as reasonable as Esslin's contention to suggest that Brecht's lifelong addiction to cheap cigars and alcohol, his phenomenal expenditure of mental and physical energy, and the fact that he produced enough words in his lifetime to fill twenty volumes, may have had something to do with his death at fifty-eight! More serious, however, is Esslin's failure to note that the first line of the quotation hardly helps his case; for Brecht was "sad when I was young" as well. To share the naive distrust and hatred of Brecht's Marxism displayed by so many Western critics, much of the history of Europe from the day of his birth to the day of his death has to be ignored: the times of confusion, militarism and rampant capitalism in Germany before and after World War I; the terrible war itself and the appalling effect on the morale of the whole German people caused by defeat and the almost insane "reparations" visited on the vanquished nation by the victors, and the concomitant rise of fascism coupled with the feeling that only the Soviet Union could keep renewed militarism in check and only a proletariat fired by communism could beat the Nazis' push for power. After the holocaust of World War II one still has much to ignore if one is to condemn Brecht's position: the Cold War and the arms build-up of the West; the fact of his pacifism and his belief that the Eastern bloc was genuinely the "peace camp" that it claimed to be; and most of all his fear that Western Germany was inevitably still fascist at heart (and it may be remembered

Brecht in Berlin, 1927 (left)
Brecht in Santa Monica, 1947
(below)
"In the earthquakes to come,
I very much hope
I shall keep my cigar alight."
(*Poems 1913–1956*, p. 108)

that by some estimates there were still ten thousand high-ranking Nazis working in high office in West Germany in 1978). One would have to ignore, too, that Brecht, Marxist or no, was deeply aware of the misery of human life, despite his optimism for a future which he did not believe was just around the corner: he would, in short, have been sad anywhere. What, for instance, may one make of the fact that Brecht's first son, Frank, born to Paula Banholzer on 30 July 1919, was killed on Russian soil on 13 November 1943 while fighting for Hitler against the communists? Life, and human motive, is not so simple as many commentators would have us believe.

It was Brecht's decision to live and work in the German Democratic Republic that stuck most firmly in the gills of the West (and evidence suggesting he may have wanted to settle in the other sector and been refused permission by the Allies is not going to alter anybody's opinion at this late stage). Even today many cannot accept the simple notion that Brecht was a Marxist, a communist sympathizer who hoped and believed that given time the creed he embraced would lead to better things — and that such an advancement was *necessary*. Perhaps the problem is that in the "Free World's" smug belief in the rightness of what is seen as a generally fair and liberal system, of what Ernst Wendt described in 1966 (talking of West Germany) as "an affluent society, a society of an at least reformed, humanized capitalism", [16] there is not a sufficient feeling that anything is actually *wrong*. Most people cannot really believe that anyone could be stupid enough to be taken in by a system seen as so direly inhuman, and they assume that the millions who live in communist countries, wherever they are on the globe, are secretly anti-communist and deeply unhappy. It is an attitude which contains as many possibilities as the assumption of old that all Germans were either actually anti-Hitler or suffering from a collective lunacy.

The Russia of the 1930s, and specifically under the mass-murderer Stalin, was the catalyst which (retrospectively) separated Western intellectuals, left-wing or not, from a belief in the Utopian possibilities of communism, and Brecht's commentators have worried the question interminably as to why he either did not know about what was happening to the "mother of revolution" or why it did not drive him, too, away from Marxism for good and all. That Brecht did know of the horrors under Stalin is in no doubt. Many of his friends (and his former mistress Carola Neher) "disappeared" after fleeing to Russia when Hitler came to power in Germany, and Brecht was also well aware of the violence being done to the cause and freedom of literature in Stalin's cultural climate. On 20 July 1938 Walter Benjamin wrote to Gretel Adorno: "As for Brecht, he explains to himself, as best he can, the reasons for Russia's cultural politics by speculating on the necessities imposed by Russia's many nationalities. But that obviously does not prevent him from recognizing the theoretical line as destroying everything we have stood for, for twenty years."[17] On 29 July Brecht told Benjamin he had no friends in Russia, and added: "And the people in Moscow themselves have no friends — like the dead."[18] When he heard in January 1939 that Mikhail Kolzov, the writer and Spanish Civil War fighter, had been arrested, Brecht noted in his *Arbeitsjournal:* "Literature and art seem shitty, political theory gone to the dogs. . .The Marxists outside are now in a position about like that of Marx relative to the German Social Democrats. Positively critical."[19] So Brecht knew; and he chose, when finally forced to flee Europe in 1941, to settle in America, not Stalin's Russia. But Brecht's belief was in Marxism; one should hardly be surprised if his faith was not destroyed by the experiences of Russia under what amounted to a one-man dictatorship. Shaken, yes, but not destroyed; for Brecht had never believed the revolution would be simple, or anything other than a long and bitter process, with innumerable, and bitterly tragic, mistakes along the way. He spent, moreover, the next six years in the United States of America. It is worth noting that he left the day after he had appeared before the House Un-American Activities Committee, where he was asked the now notorious question: "Are you now or have you ever been a member of the Communist Party of any country?"

Brecht's answer was that he had not, and despite Ruth Fischer's claim in her book *Stalin and German Communism* that he did join, in 1930,[20] there appears to be no evidence that he was lying. Erwin Leiser's statement that Brecht "declined to submit himself to party-discipline because, like the man who says no in the 'school-opera' of that name, he claimed the right 'to think again in every new situation' for himself"[21] sounds much too characteristic to be lightly dismissed; and indeed, Brecht reiterated throughout his life, not least in post-war East Germany, that he had never been a party member. It was, however, then as now, an irrelevant question. The ironies of his arraignment before the committee are legion, and the implications tragic. First and foremost may be mentioned the fact that Brecht had already obtained airline tickets to leave America the next day. It cannot, surely, be coincidental for a conscious ironist like Brecht that he fled from Germany the very day after another symbolic disaster for freedom?

It is hard, at this distance, and with the intervening hysteria about his politics, to imagine what it can have meant for a man who had spent long years of exile fighting Hitler to be required to defend himself, in the country which had played such an enormous part in Hitler's eventual downfall, against an element that must have reminded him so strongly of all he had feared and hated in the Germany which had finally embraced Nazism. Within two or three years of his appearance, indeed, the full-scale "witch-hunts" of Senator Joseph McCarthy brought an element of near-fascist irrationality to the "free" society of America that still leaves a sickening aftertaste; and it is perhaps not irrelevant to note that the committee's chairman, J. Parnell Thomas, was later jailed for corruption, and one of its members, Richard M. Nixon, brought the presidency of the United States itself into international disrepute. Accepting the history of the immediate post-war years and the emergence of the Cold War, coupled with the very existence of the House Committee, it would not have needed any very exotic or vivid imagination to foresee the possibility of a final war of the worlds in a very short time. At the very least, his arraignment can hardly have reassured Brecht that the forces of evil in Germany had disappeared merely because Hitler had lost the war; some paradox it would have been if fascism in Germany had evaporated into thin air while "the land of the free" was palpably swinging its face towards a fascist attitude.

Brecht's fears for the future of the world, and for the future of the liberal ideal in America, were in fact summarized in detail in the statement which he asked permission to read to the committee. That permission was refused, on the remarkable grounds that it was "a very interesting story of German life but it is not at all pertinent to this inquiry." It is worth quoting at length.[22]

After a brief resumé of his early years, Brecht talked of becoming a playwright: "For a time," the statement went on,

Germany seemed to be on the path of democracy. There was freedom of speech and of artistic expression. In the second half of the 1920s, however, the old reactionary militaristic forces began to regain strength. I was then at the height of my career as a playwright, my plays being produced all over Europe. But in Germany voices could already be heard demanding that free artistic expression and free speech should be silenced. Humanist, socialist, even Christian ideas were called 'undeutsch' (un-German), a word which I hardly can think of without Hitler's wolfish intonation. At the same time, the cultural and political institutions of the people were attacked.

Brecht's daring, not to say cheek, in the use before a committee invest-
igating "un-American activities" of the word *undeutsch* and coupling it
with the memory of Hitler, is still startling even after more than thirty
years. He followed it up with a bleak portrait of the destruction of
culture under the Nazis, and a scarcely concealed warning:

At the very beginning, only a very few people were capable of seeing the
connection between reactionary restrictions in the field of culture and the
ultimate assaults upon the physical life of a people itself. The efforts of the
democratic anti-militarist forces, of which those in the cultural field were, of
course, only a modest part, then proved to be weak indeed. Hitler took over.

Finally Brecht, having justified it on the grounds of being called before
the committee, allowed himself a direct statement about America and
the current world picture:

Looking back at my experiences as a playwright and a poet in the Europe of the
last two decades, I wish to say that the great American people would lose much
and risk much if they allowed anybody to restrict the free competition of ideas
in cultural fields, or to interfere with art, which must be free in order to be art.
We are living in a dangerous world. Mankind is capable of becoming enormously wealthy but, as a whole, is still poverty stricken. Great wars have been
suffered, greater ones are imminent. One of them might well wipe out mankind. We might be the last generation of the specimen man. Ideas of how to
make use of the new capabilities of production have not been much developed
since the days when the horse had to do what man could not do. Do you not
think that, in such a predicament, every new idea should be examined carefully
and freely?

Had the committee seen fit to allow this statement, it is just possible
that some of the more violent anti-communist attacks on Brecht over the
years would have been stillborn or modified. But the right-wing faction
that appeared to be taking control of America was clearly very little
interested in anything except its own obsessions. The stink of fascistic
crassness that arose from the "investigation" of Brecht's collaborator
Hanns Eisler is scarcely believable. At one point, several of Eisler's
songs were referred to as having "no place in any sort of a civilization",
in fact "obscenity is a poor word for it." When Eisler protested to John
E. Rankin that the material was not "filth", that committee-member
replied: "I am conscious that anybody that would write that stuff would
certainly not have much respect for the Congress of the United States.

But this Committee has given you more than a fair deal, more than a fair trial, more than you would have gotten in any other country in the world."[23] The "more than a fair trial" was on the "charge" of being un-American. One almost wonders why Brecht stayed so long.

What emerges most clearly from an examination of the facts of Brecht's life over the next year or two is that he trusted neither side. Tragically, the biggest and most expensive war in the history of mankind had ended in a terrible form of stalemate. The Allies and the Axis had fought themselves to a standstill only to leave the "victors" face to face across the ruins of Europe with a potential new enemy which had already proved itself during the past few years to be, if not invincible, virtually indestructible and inexhaustible. A mere *five days* after arriving in Zurich from America, Brecht helped draft a proclamation which it was hoped would be signed by the writers of every nation. It read: "The expectation of another war paralyses the reconstruction of the world. Today, the choice we face is no longer between peace and war, but peace or destruction. To those politicians who still do not understand this fact, we state emphatically that the peoples want peace." The accompanying text noted "that the existence of two different economic systems in Europe is being exploited for a new war propaganda. Anxious about the fate not only of their own countries but of the whole world [the signatories] beg the writers of all nations to add their signatures to the attached proclamation, and to support it in practice."[24]

As a stateless person, Brecht was in the thick of the chaos. As a pacifist who feared the world was on the brink of another war, he was in an agonizing position. As a man of the theatre (and aware of his own destiny, perhaps, as the most important man of the theatre of his century) he was possibly desperate. When he did finally settle in East Berlin, it was doubtless for more complex and serious reasons than that he was merely a communist, as it has so often been represented. And as is well-known, it was only after he had applied for Austrian citizenship (a long, complicated process completed finally only in September 1950) that he moved to East Berlin. Earlier, Brecht had hoped to work with Gottfried von Einem at the festival in Salzburg, and had written to him in April 1949, asking him to help obtain "asylum" — "meaning a passport". The letter continued: "If it were at all possible, it should be done without any publicity. . .a passport is really enormously important for me. I simply cannot sit down in some one part of Germany, and be dead for all the rest of Germany."[25] Even getting to Salzburg, in the country which finally granted him citizenship, proved almost impossible except for fleeting visits. It should be noted, too, that Brecht had not been free to visit even Berlin until he obtained documents in September 1948, and then he had to go there via Prague (in October) because the American authorities would not grant him a visa to enter their zone. According to evidence given to Eric Bentley, he may even have been more or less forced to settle in the East because of the American attitude to his attempts to settle in Munich. Brecht was a very wily bird, in a very difficult situation; any idea that he did anything lightly, or that we may understand his motives and thought processes as commentators on both sides of the political fence have claimed to do, is patently absurd.

What the East did offer Brecht, and what he must desperately have wanted, was a theatre. In the event it was a subsidized theatre which had facilities and available cash that must have been beyond his wildest dreams. Willett's idea that he need not have gone there, that "many provincial and city governments [in West Germany and Switzerland] might have been proud to sponsor a Company like the Ensemble"[26] is facile in the extreme considering the events of Brecht's past and his political alignment. With hindsight the West may well regret their treatment of, and attitude to, Brecht; but there is precious little evidence so far of the gratitude we should extend to the Eastern sector for having provided him with a base, money, and a kind of security (even accepting that they did it largely for the propaganda that could be extracted from the exercise) from which sprang possibly the greatest and most important theatre company of the century.

As Brecht remained in East Berlin (albeit as an Austrian citizen insisting on exercising his right to freedom of travel), and as the Ensemble became more and more famous, the bitterness against him grew. It culminated in a positive orgy of vilification after his response to the workers' uprising on 17 June 1953, which was followed by similar trouble in other parts of East Germany and the calling in by the government of Russian troops. In the West, naturally, the rising was taken as a popular expression of revolt by a repressed people — and clearly, as Frederic Ewen puts it, "There can be no doubt that justified grievances sparked the outbreak."[27] But there were other elements to it, equally clearly, and the West, more interested in propaganda than in truth, was far from prepared to admit or consider them. On 17 June Brecht wrote a letter to the First Secretary of the Socialist Unity Party (SED), Walter Ulbricht, which said: "History will pay its respects to the revolutionary impatience of the Socialist Unity Party of Germany.

The full-scale dialogue with the masses on the tempo of socialist reconstruction will lead to a sifting through and a guarantee of socialist
achievements. I feel the need at this time to express my loyalty to the
Socialist Unity Party of Germany." On 21 June the last sentence only
was published in *Neues Deutschland* — to be greeted with howls of
hatred and rage in the West. Two days later he was allowed to elucidate:

When it became clear to me on the morning of June 17 that the demonstrations
of the workers were being misused for militaristic purposes, I expressed my
solidarity with the Socialist Unity Party of Germany. I now hope that the
provocateurs will be singled out and their communications networks destroyed
and that the workers who have demonstrated because of justified grievances
will not be placed on the same level as the *provocateurs*, in order that the full and
open discussion, so very necessary, of the mistakes made on all sides, might not
be vitiated from the start.

Brecht also explained to his friend and (West German) publisher Peter
Suhrkamp that "from Unter den Linden one could see the column of
smoke rising from the Columbus Building which is on the sector
boundary at the Potsdamer Platz, just as on a previous day of disaster we
once saw the column of smoke rising from the Reichstag building." In
the streets, he went on, were "all kinds of *déclassé* young people who had
poured in streams through the Brandenburg Gate, the Potsdamer Platz
and across the Warsaw Bridge" as well as "tough brutal figures of the
Nazi period which had not been seen together in flocks for years, but
which had always been there."[28]

Brecht's fears of a third world war had been latent throughout these
years. In January 1951 he had spoken to Paul Dessau of the "hysterical"
threats of the Americans and in September of the same year had called
upon German artists and writers, in an open letter, to oppose the threat
of a new war and to fight for the reunification of the country. He ended:
"The great city of Carthage waged three wars. After the first she was
still powerful, after the second still inhabitable. After the third she
could not be found."[29] That his feelings about the uprising and the way
it was put down were not simple can be seen in a poem called "The
Solution":

> After the rising on 17th June
> The secretary of the Writers' Association had
> Leaflets distributed in the Stalinallee
> In which it said that the People

Had forfeited the confidence of the Government
And that only redoubled effort
Could win this back. Would it not
Be easier, however, if the Government
Dissolved the People and
Elected another?

It was written in the summer of 1953 and not published until after his death. For Brecht, nothing was simple. But he was certain of one thing: Germany was Carthage.

The whole vexed question of Brecht and politics has obstructed an honest appreciation of his plays. So many critics have cryptically expressed their own frustration at the fact that the man who was certainly one of the greatest playwrights of the twentieth century was not prepared to agree with them, was not prepared to leave the communists, was not prepared, in short, to cut his losses and say, "You were right, God forgive me, I recant." One of Brecht's greatest plays depicts a man who denied what he believed, but Brecht, unlike Galileo, would not. He has not been forgiven.

An important exception to this rule is Keith Dickson's *Towards Utopia*, a study of Brecht published in 1978, and standing like Canute against the tide of British political antagonism. Dickson's thesis, argued with scholarly thoroughness and an engaging enthusiasm, is that Brecht believed the primary function of his writing to be that of ensuring the free passage to its Marxist goal of the human urge to happiness. There is a lot to be said for this view, and Dickson is a splendid spokesman. We find ourselves in the odd position of wishing wholly to agree with his immensely intelligent book, but finding those plays of Brecht's that Dickson neglects (and even some he mentions) less single-minded than he is. Dickson is making an important statement, and he is not wrong. What he has observed in Brecht was certainly there: a conscious commitment to and belief in man's ability to change the world for the better. We have not found, though, the consistency in Brecht that Dickson has found, nor the relentlessly maintained relationship between political beliefs and their dramatic expression. It may be that *Towards Utopia*, in trying to correct Martin Esslin's skid into psychological speculation, has over-compensated. What must be stressed is that Dickson's book, given the popularity it deserves, could help significantly to revitalize Brechtian scholarship in the English-speaking world.

In fact, though, and this is a point Dickson ducks and weaves his way round, when one comes to examine the *oeuvre* in relation to Brecht's position as a communist, most of the fears and miseries of the Western critics became ridiculous. For if ever he *was* a straightforward political playwright, he was certainly a failed one — especially in the eyes of the communists. There was only a short period when he consciously and deliberately attempted to harness his talent to the rise of the communists, and he succeeded with almost every effort in frightening and infuriating them. For even at his apparently most straightforward, Brecht's inability to see only one side of any question was absolute. Irony and ambiguity, which were two of the elements that combined to make him a great playwright, combined also to make his propaganda efforts many-sided weapons that could as easily discomfit the communists as their enemies. Dialectics, that all-purpose Marxist word that never has been (and probably never can be) adequately defined, was Bertolt Brecht's essence and his watchword; but for his fellow Marxists, he was too dialectical by half. Throughout this short period too (the *Lehrstücke* date from 1928/9 to 1930/2, with *The Horatii and the Curiatii* of 1934 a sort of postscript) Brecht continued to write plays which were not specifically Marxist, although they were all definitely left-wing.

The new, austere Brecht was presented to the public (at the music festival at Baden-Baden) just eleven months after the wild, anarchic, cynical Brecht had shocked and delighted Berlin with *The Threepenny Opera,* and just one month before its successor, *Happy End,* was to flop resoundingly before the same audience. Two pieces were performed under Brecht's direction at Baden-Baden in July 1929, his radio play for children *The Flight of the Lindberghs* and the oratorio *The Didactic Play of Baden-Baden on Consent.* The latter sets the tone of Brecht's failure as a propagandist more than adequately; it is dense and ambiguous to the point where one may be forgiven for deciding it is merely confused (Martin Esslin got out of the problem amusingly by dubbing it "an obscure but significant work"![30]), but if one cares to take it as a representation of a communist line, it sets out its doctrinal points in a way which invites distaste for them; if that is Marxism, one may say, then I want none of it.

In its strange mixture of religious format, poetic aspiration, and slap-stick, the Baden-Baden play harks back to *Mystery Bouffe,* though we have found no evidence that Brecht knew Mayakovsky's play of welcome to the Russian Revolution. The key "characters" of the piece are The Flier, his Three Mechanics, the Trained (or Skilled, or

Learned) Chorus, and The Mass. At the start the four airmen report on the achievement of the human race, who "Late in the second millennium. . .arose. . .showing what is possible." At this time, they point out, they had not forgotten what still needed to be achieved. However, in the second part, entitled The Fall, that necessary brake on human greed and unbridled, destructive progress-for-the-sake-of-it had been forgotten. The airmen, having forgotten not only the goal they set out for but their very names and features, have crashed. And they ask the Mass, through the Trained Chorus, for help, in the shape of some water and a pillow under the head, "for we do not want to die."

Because of the enormity of their admission (and critics who dismiss the whole piece as being unmotivated are surely deliberately overlooking the fact that Brecht is postulating a "Fall" in human society equivalent in its symbolic magnitude to the Fall of Man in *Genesis*, not only in the actual words and events, but also in choosing the form of an oratorio/cantata in the first place), the Chorus asks the Mass if the Fallen airmen are to be helped. The answer, immediate and definite, is Yes; the Mass (humanity) has not yet realized the painful implications inherent in real (that is, communist) progress, nor the enormity of what the airmen have admitted to. The Chorus asks another question: "Have they helped you?" The immediate and definite answer is No. So the Chorus sets out, by three "investigations", to discover if man customarily helps man.

The first "investigation" is directly related to the airmen's admission. The Leader of the Chorus and the Chorus tell us that despite various scientific advances, "for example, while you flew", bread was no cheaper for the masses and people crawled on the earth beneath the symbolic aircraft "not like a man". The Leader of the Chorus asks the Mass: "So. Does man help man?" The answer is No. In the second investigation (and demonstration of a doctrinal view is, of course, what all three actually are) twenty photographs "which demonstrate how, in our time, men are slaughtered by men" are shown to the Mass. Which responds (with as little political awareness as a Pavlov dog) by shouting: "Man does *not* help man!" In the third "investigation" the anarchic theatre iconoclast in Brecht surely got the better of his desire to write a highly disciplined, quasi-religious piece showing the Marxist way to the future. It is a grotesque knockabout involving three clowns, one of whom (Herr Schmitt) is a giant. Because of his size the other two wish to ingratiate themselves ("crawl up his arse") which they do in the first instance by sawing off his left foot because it hurts. In the next few minutes (with the same helpful intention) they saw off the other foot, pull off his left ear, saw off an arm and the top of his head, then tear his head off completely. When Herr Schmitt, now sufficiently weakened, complains that he is lying with a stone sticking into his back, they inform him that "one can't have everything", and roar with laughter. Whether or not this was intended to be a parable about the danger for the masses of *accepting* piecemeal alleviation for their plight or a warning against the *offering* of such alleviation in the first place is not clear, and may not matter. It was certainly a show-stopper. Hanns Eisler recalled years later: "This rough joke [the sawing off of the feet] appalled many spectators. Some fainted, although only wood was being sawed, and the performance was certainly not naturalistic. I sat next to a well-known music critic who fainted. I helped him out and got him a glass of water." Whatever the effect on the audience, however, the Mass responds by deciding yet again that "Man does *not* help man." The pillow is torn up and the water poured away.

That piecemeal alleviation is one of Brecht's targets (as it would later be in *The Measures Taken*) should become clear from the next section, in which the Mass tell the airmen that they are not to be helped. But the ambiguity, not to say downright difficulty, of the verse makes simple understanding an impossibility, especially in performance:

> No doubt you have seen
> Help in many a place
> Of many kinds, begotten by the condition
> Of not yet to be renounced
> Power.
> Nevertheless, we advise you to confront
> Grim realities more grimly
> And with the condition
> Which begot your demand. Therefore,
> Not to count upon help;
> To refuse to give help, power is needed.
> To obtain help, power is also needed.
> So long as power rules, help can be refused
> If power no longer rules, help is no longer needed.
> Therefore you are not to demand help, but do away with power.
> Help and power are two sides of a whole
> And the whole must be changed.

The Fallen Airmen have no problems of understanding, of course. They know they are to die. But when ten very large photographs of the dead are shown, they are afraid to die. The Speaker from the Chorus reads to them from a "Commentary", apparently to help them accept death, and in some way to transcend it. Again the quasi-religious note is strong, and in the next section, "The Examination", the Three Mechanics change their attitudes from arrogance to humility in the face of death. At first, when questioned, they claim to have flown tremendously high, to have not been praised enough for it, to have flown the ocean alone and unaided, and to have many people awaiting them. At the end of the interrogation, however:

Chorus: Who dies then, when you die?
Mechanics: Those who were too much praised.
Chorus: Who dies then, when you die?
Mechanics: Those who rose a little above the earth.
Chorus: Who dies then, when you die?
Mechanics: Those for whom nobody waits.
Chorus: Who dies then, when you die?
Mechanics: Nobody.

The Fallen Flier, however, cannot achieve humility, and insists he will never die. In response, the Chorus makes the Mechanics take away the wreckage of the aeroplane, praising them, who are part of the making or creating process, while they do it. When the plane has gone, it is discovered that the Flier's features have disappeared. The Chorus decide, among themselves, that he only became recognizable by the fact of being employed, and was, in reality, nobody. Together with the Mass they exhort:

> What lies there, without a task
> Is no longer any human thing.
> Die now, you human-no-longer!

But the Flier replies: "I cannot die."

Most critics have found it impossible to decide if the Flier dies or not, but the fact is that Brecht at this point switches gear, as it were. The parable has been religious in form throughout, but from this moment forward the "religion" is clearly communism, and the "death" which the Flier cannot achieve is an acceptance of, and absorption by, communism and the "march forward". The Fallen Mechanics reply to the Flier:

> O human being, you have fallen from the flow.
> O human being, you have not been in the flow.
> You are too great, you are too rich.
> You are too much of yourself alone.
> Therefore you cannot die.

The Chorus responds, ambiguously, that "He who cannot die/Also dies" and, in the section entitled "The Expulsion", presumably offers the Flier another chance by inviting him to speak again. He does not speak, and is told to go, which he does.

For the Mechanics, there are no such problems. They "consent to the flow of things" and their "death" is in fact a transformation, a "change". The Chorus tells them:

> Arise
> Dying your death
> As you have worked at your work
> Altering what is altering.
> And thus, although dying,
> Be not governed by death.

And later:

> For we ask you
> To march with us and with us
> To change not only
> One law of the earth, but
> The fundamental law.
> Consenting that all will be changed
> The world and Mankind
> Above all, the disorder
> Of human classes while there are two kinds of men,
> Exploiters and the unknowing.
> *Mechanics:*   We consent to the change.

They also agree to build a new aeroplane (that is, progress is not to be ruled out in the new society) but this time not to lose sight of the goals of humanity (which is what first led to their Fall). And in a characteristically Brechtian finale, the whole nature of revolution as a process of never-ending *change* is emphasized:

Chorus: If you have improved the world,
   Then improve the world you have improved.

	Give it up!
The Leader:	Forward march!
Chorus:	If, improving the world, you have perfected truth,
	Then perfect the truth you have perfected.
	Give it up!
Leader:	Forward march!
Chorus:	If, perfecting truth, you have changed Mankind,
	Then change the Mankind you have changed.
	Give it up!
Leader:	Forward march!
Chorus:	Changing the world, change yourselves!
	Give yourselves up!
Leader:	Forward march!

The obscurity of the piece can best be encapsulated in two responses. Willy Haas decided: "One may well say that Brecht never was closer to his better self and farther from Marxism than here."[32] Esslin sums it up as a piece about "a group of transatlantic fliers [who] are made to consent to their own deaths in the interests of technical progress."[33] As propaganda, one may repeat, a definite failure. But that is not to say that it failed in performance terms. It must not be forgotten that the piece was written as an oratorio, with the music, by Paul Hindemith, an absolutely vital and integral part of it. Hanns Eisler, who was at Baden-Baden in 1929, wrote, "It was a great production and wonderful music",[34] and we have already noted his description of the theatrical effectiveness of at least a part of it. The dangers of discussing all these pieces as straightforward plays has not been emphasized enough, and it is the musical aspect which is most easily overlooked.

Another aspect to be remembered is that Brecht intended the *Lehrstücke* to be most "educational" for those taking part. And while this intention is often looked upon with scepticism, not to say cynicism, by non-communist critics, Brecht's next "teaching play", written as an opera for schoolchildren, in fact concerned and stimulated them to a remarkable extent. Their reaction to the lesson they learnt, however, was diametrically the opposite of the one Brecht had intended, and led him to write an alternative version.

Whereas the message of the Baden oratorio, if anyone took the trouble to sort it out, actually contained little that would provoke violent objections, with *He Who Said Yes* Brecht moved into much more dangerous waters. Not only the schoolchildren he was trying to teach, but the communists themselves, shied away from the implications. At the very least, the subject matter was politically deadly dangerous. The opera opens, uncompromisingly enough, with a declaration from the Great Chorus:

> What we must learn above all is consent.
> Many say yes, and yet there is no consent.
> Many are not asked, and many
> Consent to wrong things. Therefore:
> What we must learn above all is consent.

Almost from the first, however, the Boy who is the opera's main character fails to consent. The problem is that a terrible disease has broken out and the Boy's Teacher is going on an expedition to the "city beyond the mountains where great doctors live." The Boy's Mother also has the disease, and he wants to go too, expressly to get medicine and instructions *for her*. Whether or not the reason the Teacher and the Mother give for allowing him to go is entirely convincing ("They saw no plea / Could move him", sings the Great Chorus) may be argued. But he sets out on the "difficult and dangerous journey" which the Teacher has said would be "quite impossible" for him.

The party has not gone very far when the Boy, having "strained his heart", is too weak to go on. The terrain is too difficult for him to be carried, and the Three Students (who complete the expedition) recognize, with great sadness, that he will have to be left for the sake of the city that awaits the medicine. The Teacher tells the Boy that it is right that he should be asked his decision on being left behind, but that custom ordains that he should answer that he should be left. After reflection the Boy consents – but demands to be hurled to a sudden death in the valley, because he is "afraid to die alone". The Students refuse. The Teacher then points out to them that it is easy to decide that necessity demands the Boy's death, but harder to accept the implications by actually seeing him die. They accept their obligation and hurl him down, "None guiltier than his neighbour". The fact that they take his jar to fill with medicine proves that he need never have come in the first place.

Hard as it may seem, then, in this play there is no choice, unless a whole city is to be sacrificed for the life of one disobedient boy. He is not hurled down, or even left to die, according to a custom; the custom merely decrees that he should accept his (inevitable) fate. The Students make the hardest choice, in agreeing to recognize the implications of the inevitable, and actually killing him instead of putting it more comfortably out of sight and out of mind. The clear-sighted and tough-minded Brecht saw no problems with this parable, and he was horrified by the reaction of the communists. Frank Warschauer wrote of the premiere (at the Central Institute for Education and Instruction, Berlin, 23 June 1930) that it "infuses into the souls of young people a view of life that contains. . .all the wicked ingredients of reactionary thinking based on senseless authority",[35] and an audience of children at the Karl Marx School in Neukoelln were in broad agreement. Brecht, ever ready to listen to other people's views, wrote an alternative, stipulating that the two should be played together if possible.

Strangely enough, the new version, *He Who Said No*, was far more the play one might have expected Brecht to have written in the first place, because its message is that nothing should be done automatically or merely by custom (however "great"). In this opera there is no desperate imperative. There is no terrible disease in the city, and the Mother's illness, which the Boy wants to get medicine and instruction for, is "of no consequence", she says. A scientific expedition is planned – which by definition means that speed is not vital – to see the great teachers (not doctors) over the mountains. The Boy asks to go, and agrees to consent to "everything that may happen" to him. When he falls ill the response of the Three Students is startlingly different. They are neither disturbed nor humane. They cannot carry him, they say, so:

> Ought we not to follow the Great Custom
> And hurl him into the valley?

Even if he disagrees, they decide, they will kill him. The Boy, knowing what's afoot, actually tries to pretend he is not ill. The Teacher explains that according to the Great Custom he must be hurled down, and that he must consent. But the Boy refuses. Although he agreed to consent to everything that might happen to him, he says, he was wrong to do so. But they are more wrong. There is no great urgency in the expedition, and the situation has altered. "If, as I hope, there is anything to be learned on the other side," he says, "it can only be that in a situation like ours one must turn back. As for the old Great Custom, I see no rhyme or reason in it. What I need is a new Great Custom to be introduced at once, to wit, the Custom of rethinking every new situation." The Teacher and the Students agree that the Boy is talking sense, but they know they will face shame and disgrace if they do as he says. However there is "nothing disgraceful" in his having spoken his mind (a key problem that, as Brecht had just found to his cost) so they set out for home, "side by side. . .None more cowardly ["guilty" in *He Who Said Yes*] than his neighbour."

What Brecht did, quite clearly, was to write a play about a completely different subject rather than modify his first view. *He Who Said Yes* is about the necessity for self-sacrifice in the cause of communism (that is, by definition, in a situation of revolution). *He Who said No* is about the necessity of embracing Marxism, or becoming a communist. The trouble is that, by subtly switching the meaning of "the custom" and the "Great Custom" (the first can be taken to represent communism, the second a *pre*-communist system) he has inevitably increased the ambiguities. Although in *He Who Said No* he makes the point that the Great Custom is ancient and must be replaced, it is hard not to see it as the communist system. Further, while it may be said that anyone who advocated the death of the Boy in the second opera would be inhuman, totalitarian communism is seen by most people to be the only system under which the Students would ever have contemplated such a course. In *He Who Said Yes*, the Boy accepts communism through the expedition, in *He Who Said No*, the expedition accepts Marxism through the Boy. As propaganda both are counter-productive.

The real problem for Brecht, it appears, is that he was at this time constitutionally incapable of understanding that certain truths can never be expressed in the world of politics. Undeterred, apparently, by the row over *He Who Said Yes*, he went on to write a teaching cantata on a similar theme, *The Measures Taken*, which caused a storm of fury from the communists. Its conclusion is that the individual must be prepared to sacrifice himself up to and including death for the sake of the revolution,and the story Brecht chose to illustrate this thesis is a simple, effective, and, for him, remarkably unambiguous one. Four Agitators (who act all the parts) demonstrate to a Control Chorus why they killed a Young Comrade and threw his body into a lime pit. From the first it is made clear that the four, who are travelling from Moscow to Mukden, are politically educated, and the Young Comrade is not. When they meet him at the border he looks to them for material aid, and they explain that they are going purely to bring "instruction concerning their condition" to the ignorant, "to the oppressed, class-consciousness, and to the class-conscious, practical knowledge of the revolution". He agrees to the mission, and takes part in a quasi-religious "effacement" whereby the five Agitators "become" Chinese; for it is explained to them that the work to be done in China is illegal, and in fact that there are gunboats and armoured trains ready to attack "the moment any of us is seen there". They set out as mere tools of the revolution, nameless and faceless, prepared to die rather than risk being caught:

> He who fights for Communism
> Has of all virtues only one;
> That he fights for Communism.

The Young Comrade, however, has another "virtue", which in the context of their mission is no virtue at all; he suffers from misplaced humanity. Although he has agreed to his role, he keeps behaving from laudable motives that are likely to alleviate immediate misery at the cost of ruining the chances of a long-term change for the better. Instead of inciting some barge-hauling coolies to demand better conditions, he aids them individually by putting stones under their feet to stop them slipping. By the time he has exhausted himself and returned to his suggestion that the coolies demand better shoes, he has proved to their satisfaction that he is merely a soft-hearted "liberal" (in its modern, pejorative, sense) and they help the overseer chase him. The expediton is hindered, but it is hoped that the Young Comrade has learned from his mistake. Later, when their work has developed and cells and a printing outfit have been set up, the Young Comrade gets into a brawl with a policeman and some non-striking textile workers which leads to the striking workers being driven off. What he should have done, we are told, is persuaded the non-striking workers to side with their fellows in the face of police injustice, but the scene is rather unclear. Next he is sent to persuade a merchant to arm the coolies in a common struggle against the English rulers of the city, which will lead to the coolies gaining strength and weapons which they can turn to their own advantage. The Young Comrade finds the Merchant so despicable that he refuses to treat with him; and the coolies go unarmed. The Control Chorus asks: "It is not right to put honour above all else?" and follows it with the song "Change the World: It Needs it":

> With whom would the just man not sit
> To help justice?
> What medicine is too bitter
> For the man who's dying?
> What vileness should you not suffer to
> Annihilate vileness?

If at last you could change the world, what
Could make you too good to do so?
Who are you?
Sink in filth
Embrace the butcher, but
Change the world: It needs it!

This song (and it should be remembered that it *is* a song, first sung by the massed voices of the Greater Berlin Workers' Choir who premiered the cantata on 10 December 1930) is the core of the piece, and has many times been used (or more specifically the line "embrace the butcher" has been used) to belabour Brecht, not only in terms of *The Measures Taken* but of his whole life and philosophy. What it actually says is that if you want a revolution to succeed, it cannot be undertaken half-heartedly; and while this may be sad, tragic even, it can surely be only the bare truth. The horror it aroused in critics (both communist and non-communist) seems at best squeamish and at worst hypocritical. Brecht, we know, was a pacifist, but here he had clearly decided that in some struggles blood had inevitably to be spilled. It might be noted that not many years later the Allied forces (including Russia) sank in filth and embraced the butcher to beat Hitler. Brecht not only thought that poverty, injustice and the system that engendered them (in his view) were active evils that had to be fought, but he also saw communist revolution as the only way to destroy Hitler. Critics who are grateful to the people who sacrificed themselves by taking up arms against the Nazis might care to consider the connection.

The failure of the Young Comrade to understand the implications of the situation leads the Agitators to wonder if they should send him back across the border. But although "clearly aware of his weaknesses", they still need him for various reasons. In any case, it is too late. During hunger riots in the city the Young Comrade, overcome with pity, demands immediate action. He asks the Agitators if the "communist classics" preclude immediate aid to the suffering before all else, and when told that they do, he tears them up. The Agitators point out that his "impetuous revolution" will last a day "and be strangled tomorrow." Their revolution begins tomorrow but will "conquer and change the world." They even concede that he may be right, but beg him to realize the dangers of dividing themselves:

Do not go the right way without us
Without us it is

The wrong way.
You must stay with us.

But the Young Comrade refuses to give in "because I know I am right."
Like the Boy in *He Who Said No* (but with opposite intent on Brecht's
part) he denounces all he had agreed to and declares his course of action
"the revolution". He tears off his mask, reveals his nationality (and, to
the Agitators, his "naked face,/ Human, innocent, and without guile")
and the hunt is up for all of them.

The alternatives facing the party of Agitators, which have so often
been trivialized and distorted by critics, are extremely difficult. They
wish to get the Young Comrade over the border to safety, but the masses
are in the streets and they must be organized. If the Young Comrade is
found he will be shot, but more importantly the gun-boats and armoured trains will "attack us" (i.e. China will go to war against Russia
because of communist infiltration). Although "it is a terrible thing to
kill" they know they would be prepared to kill themselves if need be:

> For violence is the only means whereby this deadly
> World may be changed, as
> Every living being knows.

What is more the Young Comrade knows it too, and knows of no way
out. In a peculiarly tender moment, as he is unable to kill himself, they
cradle his head in their arms and shoot him, throwing his body into the
lime-pit that will obliterate his features.

Ronald Gray's reaction to this as late as 1976 is a textbook example of
why communists had to denounce *The Measures Taken*. Having decided, astonishingly, that it is the Agitators the gunboats and armoured
trains are "on the lookout for" and that "the young comrade is not even
shown to be guilty of the faults of which he is accused", he claims that
the conclusion simply does not stand up. "And for a conclusion so
repugnant to human feeling and so smugly stated in those final lines,
this is even more astonishing than the fact that the conclusion was
reached at all."[36] His next paragraph adds, with magnificent
irrelevance: "Ernst Toller would never have brought himself to write
such a work"! The fact is, far from being accepted as the clear-headed
piece of political analysis that it is, *The Measures Taken* gave the anti-
communists a club with which hypocritically to beat the communists,
and the communists a severe headache because of it. It is as obvious that

the end must justify the means in a revolution as is the oppositional point: that the power-bloc under threat will justify any means to thwart the revolution. But politics has never been about the clear, rational and unemotional analysis of truths, and Brecht's failure in this play becomes blindingly clear: it is one of naivety. He really should have realized that people who "embrace the butcher" in political or power terms can never under any circumstances acknowledge that this is what they are doing.

While the communists denounced Brecht as politically ignorant and matched the hypocrisy of non-communist critics with the straight-forward denial that anything like it could ever happen (in a public discussion a few days after the premiere one communist insisted that the Young Comrade would in fact have been expelled from the party, adding quaintly that *that* would have been a fate *worse* than his death!) perhaps the oddest view is Martin Esslin's. He describes the play as Brecht's "first real masterpiece" and "the only great tragedy on the moral dilemma of Soviet Communism".[37] What he means is that the play is great because it is, in his view, *anti*-communist; and he explains away this paradox by claiming an extraordinary extension of the poetic-subconscious: "Owing to Brecht's uncannily penetrating intuitive grasp of the realities of the problem of totalitarianism, the play transcends its author's conscious intention and becomes a classical statement of [Stalinist Communism's] basic dilemma." This is, of course, nonsense. *The Measures Taken* is neither a masterpiece, nor is it "an exact and horrifying anticipation of the great confession trials of the Stalinist era".[38] Brecht was talking about a communist revolution and the sacrifices that must be made by an individual for the good of all. The sacrifices made by Stalin's victims for the "peace of mind" of a monster among monsters have nothing to do with the better world which Brecht believed was possible, and which many people still believe might be one way towards altering a system that vast numbers in a less comfortable and privileged position than Esslin or the authors of this book find at best inadequate.

The most charming and successful (as a play) *Lehrstück* that Brecht wrote in this phase was *The Exception and the Rule*, of 1930. We will never know how the communists would have reacted to this piece (it was first performed, in Hebrew, in 1938 and in French in 1947) but it is easy to guess. For the tale is an early and brilliant example of the impish love of contradiction that characterizes Brecht's best plays and which he often explained away (and possibly aggrandized) with the beloved word *dialectic*. On the surface it seems simple. A capitalist merchant, hurrying to beat a rival caravan to the town of Urga to gain an oil concession, sacks his guide and savagely ill-treats his coolie when the pair get lost in the desert. Finally the coolie offers the merchant a drink from his water bottle, which he had kept hidden until then, but the merchant shoots him, assuming that the coolie is going to attack him. At his trial the merchant is acquitted, on the grounds that he acted in self-defence — regardless of whether he was threatened or only had reason to *feel* threatened. The coolie, it is held, was of a class that had reason to "inevitably regard it as right and just to avenge themselves on their tormentors".

The problems with a straightforward reading of the piece as an illustration that the oppressor always wins are so manifold that one needs hardly to scratch the surface before one is deep in the world of Brechtian ambiguity. For a start, the "evil merchant", although he has killed the coolie, is ruined because of it; he could not carry the baggage himself and was too late to win the concession! Furthermore he is characterized, and very strongly, as being neurotic, almost paranoid; in fact, a rather touching figure. Certainly, he is far too much a human being to be a schematic symbol of oppression. The judge, too, who acquits him, bursts any narrow political bounds the piece might pretend to. He is a sort of forerunner of Azdak, in personality at least; eccentric, grotesque, even good humoured in his total corruption. What is more, the coolie does not offer water out of kindness (as Esslin says) but because "if they find us [in the desert] and I'm still alive and he's half dead, they'll put me on trial." The water bottle he offers is shaped like a stone, and all in all one feels that a conviction against the merchant would indeed have been most unfair. Even a reading of the piece as an illustration of capitalism as a fear-system in which conflict is inevitable and in which *nobody* wins, although it could be argued, would be difficult to make wholly convincing. Any straightforward political intention Brecht might have had is very firmly obscured by the play's charm and complexity.

The only overtly political play which did meet with a certain amount of approval from the communists was *The Mother*, which Brecht adapted from the novel by Gorky. It sets out in an austere and straightforward fashion the steps by which Pelagea Vlassova of Tver moves from helpless acceptance of her lot as a member of the suffering masses to the outbreak of the 1917 Revolution, at which she proudly carries the red flag. It was first shown, privately, to workers' councils and organizations from 12 January 1932, and opened publicly at the Komoedienhaus (Theater am Schiffbauerdamm), Berlin, on 17 January, the anniversary of the murder of Rosa Luxemburg. Although Brecht classified it among the *Lehrstücke*, he stipulated that it needed professional actors; Helene Weigel played the title role and Ernst Busch that of her son.

If the communists found something, at last, to congratulate Brecht on, the "bourgeois" critics were universal in their condemnation. The *Deutsche Tageszeitung* remarked: "What took place up to the moment when the eyes of the public strayed elsewhere, is devastatingly arid and childish"; while the *Neue Preussische Kreuzzeitung* described it as "crude, inflammatory, propagandistically conceived. For the True Believers, a real festival, more powerful than speeches or newspapers. To the outsider, a madness."

There is a great deal to be said for both these views, however baldly stated. It is hard to find much merit in *The Mother* except as a sop to the converted (the importance of this aspect of agit-prop should not be overlooked, incidentally). Despite the vigour with which Vlassova is drawn (and the fact of Weigel's greatness in performance must be remembered), the play is extremely short of the characteristic Brechtian virtues. It is not so much a story, dramatically tensioned, as the unfolding of a series of scenes depicting Pelagea's advancement along the road to a communist goal. The ambiguity, which makes almost all the other *Lehrstücke* still fascinating, is totally lacking. And Brecht's great sense of fun is submerged in the rather priggish representation of a worthy and exemplary tract.

Strangely enough, Brecht was clearly infuriated by the negative response *The Mother* received, and wrote extensive notes in which he both quoted and berated the unfriendly critics. These notes are in some ways as uncharacteristic as the play itself, often hate-filled and bordering on the hysterical. Communism's opponents, he wrote, "are the opponents of mankind. . .Today, as the bare self-defence of the great masses turns into the final struggle for power, 'kindness' comes to mean the annihilation of those who make kindness impossible."[39] It seems to have been the zenith of his political fury, both as a playwright and a pamphleteer, and he was never to write another play so determinedly political or earnest. He and the party he sympathized with were quickly overtaken by history, and we may guess that he was not only shatteringly discouraged but also politically disillusioned from here on. One may also consider the odd possibility that, hateful as enforced exile may have been, it may have turned Brecht slowly but irrevocably from the arid paths of propaganda. There was no point, finally, in trying to "convert" foreigners to communism for the sake of Germany; indeed the international left had already, by the mid thirties, embraced the People's Front concept of uniting all classes to fight Hitler, although it took Brecht longer. Certainly in exile his plays matured and deepened. To write anything with no audience must have been bad; to write propaganda was impossible.

We have already noted that by 1940 Brecht had ceased to classify himself with the proletariat, although for the rest of his life he apparently retained his romantic attachment to the "masses" – that peculiarly bourgeois, middle-class attachment which is part of the phenomenon that originally gave birth to Utopian communism with Marx and Engels, and which ensures its continued existence as an ideology among intellectuals in the West today. Whether he ever admitted to himself, or recognized, the failure of his attempts to speak theatrically to the class he so admired and so completely misunderstood we will never know. Certainly by the end of the 1930s he had given up for ever the idea of stirring them, even if he had not accepted that "culinary" art is the true taste of the ignorant, just as fascism rather than communism may be their true radical movement. All his later, and great, plays were aimed once more at educating the bourgeois, and his audiences were, inevitably (and still are, even at the Berliner Ensemble's East Berlin home) predominantly middle-class. Perhaps the fact that he chose to revive *The Mother* as one of the Ensemble's earliest productions in January 1951 was a wistful indication that he still wanted to believe in theatre for the masses, although whatever agitational value it may have had would obviously have been extremely out of place in a society where the glorious revolution had already arrived! As a "classic of revolutionary art" the faults of *The Mother* reveal themselves even more completely; it is merely a sentimental piece about a good simple woman who has seen the light and fought for the good of the proletariat, whose revolution the audience knows succeeded in 1917. A heroine, in fact. (Unless Brecht had finally found a way of injecting some irony into the piece, merely by playing it; but that seems rather far-fetched.)

To say that Brecht's overtly political plays were confined to a relatively short time, and that they were in general unsuccessful, especially in the eyes of the Marxists, is not, of course, to deny that he was a political writer. All his theatre works, from the earliest to the greatest, were permeated with politics, and there are several which, if not propaganda, certainly set out to further a communist/socialist view. But almost all carry so great a weight of meaning, and are capable of so great a number of different interpretations, that it is quite impossible to look at them as tracts, propaganda, or even polemic; a narrowly political interpretation is frequently the most laboured and least likely reading of all. That Brecht could not understand this fact is one of his great fascinations. What he saw as true Marxism – a questioning, a refusal to accept anything as fixed, a coruscating disgust with smugness – translates itself in his writing into a massive and all-pervading ambiguity.

Although fascinating, it is no great surprise that Brecht could not see this; the idea that a writer is often unaware of all the elements that make up his achievement is unlikely to cause any great argument today. What is sadder is that his political stance in life (ambiguous as even *that* was) has coloured the reactions of the world to his plays. The communists see him as their property and play him to extract communist meanings, however imaginary, from his works. Westerners either do the same (if they are "left-wing") or treat him with a contempt that compounds distortion. All the great plays raise and examine moral points rather than political ones, as we will see when we study them. Practitioners and critics – indeed the whole Brecht industry – have succeeded over the years in getting the two totally confused.

4

In the Jungle of Intentions

The other day I wanted
To tell you cunningly
The story of a wheat speculator in the city of
Chicago. In the middle of what I was saying
My voice suddenly failed me.

While Brecht was a narrowly political writer for only a short period of his life, and by almost any yardstick a failed one, it is a fact that his severely political phase has had a completely disproportionate influence on the way people think about him, and indeed on the writers who have attempted to emulate him. To most people, the major connotation of the cover-all word "Brechtian" is to do with politics, and when it is applied to plays by current writers it almost always means both a "method" of writing and presentation (short scenes, straightforward exposition, etc.) and an implied left-wing stance. As a concomitant, a writer often chooses subject matter in which the dramatic possibilities are more apparent to him than he can make them to the audience, and barely digested facts and figures are often hurled about as if their very existence should convince us of the playwright's case. Most audiences, however, especially British ones, seem to have a deep dislike, even fear, of this self-important preaching stance.

Brecht's first attempt at a *large-scale* didactic play, *Saint Joan of the Stockyards*, seems to have had the greatest influence of all in this area. This is not only sad, but strange; because it is by no means characteristic of his writing, either in technique or intention, and is politically both crude and naive. As a *Gegenstück* (counter-play) to Schiller's *Die Jungfrau von Orleans*, it has some claim on an educated German audience (though none on the working classes to whom it was ostensibly addressed), and Völker has rested his admiration for it on its structure, which "follows the phases of the recurrent cycle which, according to Marx, runs through modern industry."[2] What seems clear to us is that Brecht, beguiled by the trees, lost sight of the wood. The play was not actually staged in Germany (and West Germany at that) until 1959. It is not easy to conceive of a theatrical context in which it would be genuinely appropriate now.

Written in 1929–1931, *Saint Joan* was the culmination of several attempts to write a play about the world economic crisis. *Happy End*'s failure was subsumed in restarted work on the drama of economics in *The Fall of the Egoist Johann Fatzer* and *Joe P. Fleischhacker*, only to resurface in a new project, under the proposed title of *The Breadshop*, in which the role of the Salvation Army as a supporter of big business is associated with the unemployment of 1929. Brecht had earlier written to Elisabeth Hauptmann that the operations of the world wheat markets were "incomprehensible", but he had now tried to understand them. Into *Saint Joan* he poured many of the theatrical ideas that had been in his mind before, and were to emerge again (the idea of Joan of Arc herself, the Salvation Army, the sentimental/fascist character mix of capitalists and gangsters as he saw them, some jokesy cynicism about identity that harks back to *Man Equals Man*, and so on). He also wrote it as a parody of several disparate models, perhaps in the hope that the brilliance of his poetry, coupled with the possibilities for source-hunting that it would give the bourgeois audience, would make it at once more interesting, amusing and acceptable. For unlike the *Lehrstücke* and *The Mother*, *Saint Joan* was intended solely for the theatre, not for working men's clubs and institutes. The parody and the poetry are, in fact, occasionally of a very high order, sometimes conveying character and furthering the action as well as mocking extremely cleverly the conventions of classical verse. In the first scene, for example, Pierpont Mauler, the Chicago meat king, having just been warned by letter (shades of how many Elizabethan plays!) to "get out of canning" begins the process of foisting an unwanted business off on his friend Cridle:

> Remember Cridle, how some days ago
> We crossed the stockyard as the evening fell
> And standing by the newest canning plant
> Remember, Cridle, how we saw that ox
> Great, blonde and sullen, looking at the sky
> As it received the deathblow. Oh, I felt

It had been meant for me. Oh Cridle, Cridle
Ours is a bloody business.*

And in a later scene Brecht neatly turns the tradition that Joan of Arc
recognized the disguised Dauphin thus:

Mauler: How do you know me?
Joan: Because you have the bloodiest face.

Cleverly and skilfully as he could handle poetry and parody, however, one must consider why Brecht found it necessary to use it at all.
His intention in *Saint Joan* was a propagandistic one: he wanted to show
the workings of capitalism, possibly a great "crisis of capitalism", in
theatrical terms which would illustrate the underlying simplicity of the
processes (as he understood them from his studies of Marxism) at the
same time as forcing his audiences to accept what he saw as the only way
forward — violent action by the downtrodden to overthrow the exploit-
ing class. Even given that he wished, as so often, to distance the events
by giving them an exotic setting against which they would show more
starkly, it is hard to escape the conclusion that he found it necessary to
use the conventions of "classical" characterization because the things he
required his "capitalists" to say could not be rendered believable on any
level except as a parody of some of the greater excesses of, say, the
Jacobean blood-drama. Sullivan Slift, for example, the broker who
plays Mephistopheles to Joan early in the play, is the "agent" by which
the whole of the capitalist system of the Chicago stockyards is made to
collapse. With Mauler, he makes up a double act of bloodthirsty lunacy
which could hardly be verbalized if it were not in language like this:

Mauler: This time I'll rip their skins off for good and all
                In accordance with my nature.
Slift: I'm overjoyed that you've shaken off
                Your weakness of the past few days. And now
                I'll go and watch them buy up livestock.
Mauler: It's high time this damn town had its skin ripped off. . .

The problem is akin to that which a modern audience has with a genuine
Jacobean play: despite its vigour and lustiness, the people and events
are somewhat unbelievable, to say the least. Sullivan Slift would not be

*The translation here is Martin Esslin's. See *Brecht: a Choice of Evils*, p.49

out of place in a tragedy of blood. But he certainly would be in a stock exchange.

That Brecht at this time believed that capitalists and the bourgeoisie in general were in reality some sort of savages or animals is possible. Joan says of them all: "Some day...you won't rate as human beings either, but as wild animals that...have to be slaughtered in the interest of public order and safety." That he thought the collapse of capitalism as a system was imminent is also possible. Certainly the state of Germany, America and the other industrialized nations in the late twenties must have led him to believe that a play explaining it all was needed, and his studies of Marxism must have led him to believe that underlying the disaster were some simple economic laws, being deliberately manipulated by a handful of immensely powerful and evil men; laws that were capable of being revealed. The real failure of *Saint Joan* is in this exposition. For economics is much more complex than Brecht understood, and the harder Brecht tried to simplify his story, the more bogged down he got.

One of the simpler acid tests of Brecht's mastery of story-telling is that almost all his plays, however great, can be boiled down to very few words of straightforward exposition. Even *In the Jungle of Cities* has a clear line when studied, although as we have noted it is fudged by many other elements in the writing. But the plot of *Saint Joan* is hard indeed to pin down, and even a very careful reading is unlikely to give one any clear idea of exactly what is happening. In performance the narrative "soup" is so thick that despite extensive use of placards, with the supplementary use of "newsboys" reiterating the salient economic facts, it is practically impossible to work out what is going on. There are many strands to the story, and several of them seem to be out of Brecht's control for much of the time. There are also ambiguities of character and action which are more accurately inconsistencies, and an almost overwhelming clash between Brecht's insistence that all the world's problems, and their solution, are blindingly simple and his awareness that it would merely sound naive to say so.

Joan Dark, the heroine, is a fine embodiment of this. We first see her in the early stages of the economic collapse, at the head of "the Black Straw Hat shock troop". She states that they are there, in "a world like a slaughter house":

> Summoned by rumours of threatening deeds of violence
> To prevent the brute strength of the short-sighted people

> From shattering its own tools and
> Trampling its own bread-basket to pieces —
> We wish to reintroduce
> God.

Her credo is that wealth and poverty, power and weakness, happiness and misery, are ordained, are like the rain (natural images, especially rain and snow, recur throughout) and she reveals a streak of almost comic naivety very soon afterwards when she insists to the starving workers that God's word is sweeter than whipped cream. Faced with the workers' insistence that their plight is man-made, she sets out to find out if this is so, which brings her into contact with Pierpont Mauler.

Somewhere at the back of Brecht's mind, here as in other plays, is an awareness of the possibilities of the historical/mythical character of Joan of Arc. (She is, after all, a *Verfremdungseffekt* in a man's world of military history.) Throughout her story, the main strand of the plot, she is seen as the Maid, bringing a purity and simplicity of mind to the complicated dealings and the moral sink of Chicago big business. She is faced with hurdles (presented in a quasi-religious fashion as three "descents into the depths") which she has to get across before she can reach full understanding — that is, the acceptance of violent revolution. But the simplicity and purity (which one can only sadly conclude are extremely close to Brecht's own political stance) lead her into situations in which the possibilities for bathos are endless. The best example is her "second descent" when Sullivan Slift shows her "the wickedness of the poor". This consists of a scene in which Joan sees a lady called Mrs Lucker-niddle, whose husband has been turned into bacon, give up the idea of causing trouble about it in return for three weeks' food. Another worker, Gloomb, tries to persuade Joan to work a dangerous machine which no one will man and which has cost him an arm, in return for a job. This, not surprisingly, only convinces Joan that Slift has shown her not the wickedness of the poor but their poverty. The scene skates so close to self-parody that Brecht is forced to end it on an openly ridiculous note:

> You've shown the evil of the poor to me:
> Now see the woes of evil poverty.
> O thoughtless rumour, that the poor are base:
> You shall be silenced by their stricken face!

But it does not alter the fact that the scene is a disaster for the play's "message". Is one meant to believe that Mauler and Slift would have been taken in by their own propaganda? When even Joan was not? It is merely silly. The silliness is compounded in the next scene, when Joan takes "the poor" to the livestock exchange — and Mauler faints at the sight of them! During her third descent Joan's naivety reaches its almost hilarious apogee when she still insists on Mauler's goodness to the sound of the army machine-gunning workers in the stockyards.

Pierpont Mauler, from the very start, is a character of great potential. He is reputed (and uses it as a cover for some of his nastiest dealings) to have a strange weakness — he cannot endure the thought of the suffering he brings to the beasts he slaughters. This pity does not extend to Mankind:

> On oxen I have pity; man is evil.
> Mankind's not ripe for what you have in mind:
> Before the world can change, humanity
> Must change its nature.

Joan, however, apparently moves him strangely. Throughout the long and complicated dealings and double-dealings he insists that he has a special regard for her, while she insists that he is "the one just man" even as we watch him, almost single-handed, wreck the livelihoods of himself, his partners, his competitors, and the working population of Chicago. Unfortunately, his great potential is never fully realized. By the time Brecht has him turning up repentant at the Black Straw Hats' mission, having lost all his money, then saving the situation for the capitalists all over again by the use of yet another letter from his mysterious friends in New York (an economic *deus ex machina* so unworthy of Brecht as to be hardly believable), he has become merely a cardboard tool of a hollow storyline. The end of Joan's story is equally unconvincing. Her journey from a naive belief that nothing can be changed, through a desire for change so long as force is not involved, to her famous "Only force helps where force rules" is blighted by the very fact of her naivety. If she was wrong to believe in a God who ordains (and her final speeches are more specifically aimed at religion than capitalism: "anyone...who says there is a God...should have his head banged on the pavement till he croaks"), if she was wrong to believe in Mauler's goodness (against absolutely overwhelming odds!), why should she be right in embracing the communists' message (which in any case has been hardly more than sketched in, although quite movingly in places)?

Beside Joan's and Mauler's there is a third strand in the story which is important to the message, but clumsily handled and equally unconvincing. This is the Black Straw Hat organization itself. So much weight is placed upon it that it is sometimes easiest to see the whole play as an attack on the Church, or at least the Salvation Army. The Black Straw Hats are portrayed as being, with foreknowledge and for selfish ends, interested not in religion but in keeping the poor quiet and under control for the capitalists. This they do by feeding them a subsistence minimum of food (all provided by the capitalists) and promises of happiness in the hereafter. Yet again, the very venom with which they are portrayed, plus the fact that Joan — desperately sincere — was a member of a church shown as irrevocably insincere, is self-undermining.

There is much in *Saint Joan* that is brilliant, funny and successful. The long verse description of the collapse of the market, for example, when we are told:

> An elephant might have wandered in
> And been crushed underfoot like a berry.
> Even the pageboys, seized with despair, bit one another...
> Unsalaried clerks, famous for lack of interest in business
> Were heard gnashing their teeth that day.
> And still we bought and bought; we had to buy.

Much of the final scene, too, when Joan, dying, is declared a saint because "by her philanthropic work in the stockyards, her championship of the poor, and even her speeches against us, she helped us over some really difficult weeks" is bitterly effective in performance. But this scene also contains loudspeaker announcements of terrible statistics about the collapse of the capitalist world, interspersed with a couple of pathetically thin (and with hindsight ludicrous) indications of communist successes: "Five year plan a success!"; "Five year plan in four years!".

As an explanation of capitalism, as an indication that Brecht understood his subject matter or had it under control, as a rallying cry for the use of force even, the whole play fails on almost every count. If it is meant to be taken as a believable representation of the actual workings of a finance system and the denizens of a real city or country it is madly unreal, and if it is meant to be schematized and symbolic (with Joan as nascent communism, perhaps, Mauler as capitalism, and the Black Straw Hats as the Church and/or liberal politics and piecemeal alleviation) it is merely too obscure. Brecht's communist revolution never came, but the use of force (with Hitler and Stalin at one time in unholy alliance) came soon enough. By the time he wrote *Mother Courage*, his view of force and what it might achieve had drastically altered. So, equally importantly, had his way of writing plays; the failure of *Saint Joan as a play* may well have been crucial there. One may only sadly reiterate that this piece, so complete an example of undigested material and so uncharacteristically single-faceted, is clearly the model for much political drama written since.

Throughout this era — which might be described as the passionate period of Brecht's love affair with communism — his writing was notable for a wild swinging between the extremes of austerity and didacticism on the one hand and a rich and anarchic theatricality on the other. At its best his writing was deeply ambiguous, at worst, deeply confused. The heart of the problem seems to have been the dilemma which at this time he could not resolve — because it was the communist dilemma. Stated at its simplest, it is the weird idea that the poor are good and the rich evil. In *Saint Joan*, Mauler — a rich man — states that man is evil and must change his nature; but *he* cannot change, even by becoming poor. Joan, who believes even Mauler to be good, is proved wrong. But the struggle which she would have led had she lived is directed at making the poor rich. What then? Presumably they cease to be good. (In the later *The Seven Deadly Sins*, Brecht demonstrates that even the *desire* to cease to be poor inevitably makes a person embrace evil.) But however frequently Brecht reiterated this simplistic equation — and during these years that was quite frequently — he clearly did not believe it; his confusion was between his own awareness of what might be called existential despair, and his belief that Marxism offered a way out. It was a tension that never apparently left him, and it became the dynamic of all his greatest plays.

Despite the wildness of these swings, despite the fact that he could be writing *The Threepenny Opera* and its successor *Happy End* at the same time as the early *Lehrstücke*, the view of Brecht as a straightforward political writer was, and is still, pushed to a grotesque degree. The opera *The Rise and Fall of the City of Mahagonny*, written in collaboration with Kurt Weill in 1928-1929, is a fascinating example of this process at work.

Mahagonny began its performed life at the Baden-Baden chamber music festival in 1927 as *The Little Mahagonny*. But when it emerged as a full-scale work at Leipzig in March 1930 it had a devastating reception.

The bourgeois audience — it was an opera, remember, not a play — tried to stop it, causing one of the noisiest "riots" in theatre history. From this point on, although it dropped out of sight fairly quickly, it has usually been seen as more successful *politically* than *The Threepenny Opera* in that it was instantly hated by the middle classes. The reason given for this "success" (which largely overlooks the fact of Brecht's reputation, by then, as being a communist and the very rapid build-up of the Nazi Party, especially among the middle classes) is that it is a much clearer attack on the bourgeoisie than the earlier work — in fact, an out-and-out didactic piece.

Despite the fact that, as so often with Brecht, the ambiguities are compounded by not inconsiderable differences in the available versions, the opera can still be far too neatly summarized as being the tale of a city in which everything is permitted. Jimmy Mahoney, who has come to live in Mahagonny with three friends after seven years' hard work in Alaska, is executed for the "greatest crime which exists on the face of the earth" — having no money. This is seen as adding up to a simple parable about a capitalist society founded and run on greed and its inevitable downfall. The trouble is that this summary ignores an absolute wealth of detail, much of which destroys the idea of a neatly-turned parable completely, as well as some broader elements in the story that make a communist reading difficult.

The more closely one looks at the opera, the more clearly emerges a distinct haphazardness in its story — a haphazardness which is not given any overriding political thrust, as it is in *The Threepenny Opera*, by a clear and solid intent embodied in the songs. The more clearly emerges, too, the fact that to a large extent the piece is made up either of material left over from plays Brecht had completed, or reworked scenes and ideas he had already tried and (possibly) wished to have another attempt at. What is more, he typically did not even change the names. The lady who founds Mahagonny, on the grounds that it is easier to get gold from men than by prospecting for it, is our old friend Leokadia Begbick; and Jenny Smith, the whore, has more in common with Jenny Diver than just a forename. Whatever else it might be, *Mahagonny* is the opposite side of the pendulum swing from the grimly attempted lesson of *Saint Joan*.

The oddest single point, perhaps, is that according to the "Speaker" the opera tells the story of Jim Mahoney, and indeed it is he who learns the lesson of poverty the hard way. But it is also he who instigates the golden rule: "You may do as you wish." For Jim, after a short time in

Mahagonny, finds the paradise of whisky, women, fishing, smoking —
boring. Instead of deciding that this is because there is too little direction in the life, that it is too aimless and undisciplined, he decides
rather:

> Ach, with your entire Mahagonny
> A man will never be happy
> Because too much peace reigns
> And too much harmony
> And because there is too much
> That can be depended on.

During a hurricane that springs up as if in answer to his prayer, and
which seems certain to destroy what the whole of the rest of the
inhabitants call "the city of joy", he discovers "the laws of human
happiness":

> In the interests of order
> For the best for the town
> For the future of Mankind
> For your own well-being:
> *You may!*...
>
> Therefore I call upon you:
> Do everything tonight that is forbidden.

This anarchic doctrine, which is accepted by the inhabitants after the
hurricane has miraculously (and hilariously, in the staging) missed
Mahagonny by doing a sudden detour, is recognized even by Leokadia
Begbick as being anti-society, anti-rationality, anti anything except the
unalterable laws of human nature. She sings:

> Bad is the hurricane
> Worse is the typhoon
> But worst of all is Mankind.

And Alaska-Wolf-Joe, one of Jim's companions and therefore not a part
of the Mahagonny criminal "establishment", agrees that neither hurricane nor typhoon is necessary, as man can create the same terror from
himself; an extension of Jim's equation of natural forces and man:

> Peace and harmony they don't exist
> But hurricanes they do.

(And typhoons when hurricanes aren't enough.)
Just like that is man.
He must destroy whatever exists.

Although Brecht represents the acceptance of Jim's doctrine as some sort of turning point, little changes in Mahagonny that one can put one's finger on. The play proceeds in a series of demonstrations (much in the manner of *The Seven Deadly Sins*) of selfish nastiness unbridled. Jakob Schmidt (another of the four from Alaska) immediately eats himself to death and is proclaimed "a man without fear" for having done it; a whore deals with a succession of men to a chorus of "Faster, boys, faster"; and Alaska-Wolf-Joe is killed in a boxing match with Trinity Moses, of the Mahagonny establishment, who is much bigger and stronger than he. This leads Jim to drink, and as he has bet all his money on Joe — he remains the only idealist in the piece, in that he is at least prepared to stay loyal to his friend — he cannot pay. This leads to his trial, his conviction on several points, and his execution for having no money.

Whether Brecht needed something to make the opera full-length or whether he wished to use good material because it was good material and had no place elsewhere, we cannot know. But it is at about this point that the story becomes so diffuse as to get any "message" hopelessly bogged down. The high-speed whoring scene ends with a duet between Jim and Jenny, totally out of place and achingly beautiful and, having lost his money, Jim decides to sail back to Alaska with his whore/lover Jenny and his only remaining friend Bill on an upturned billiard-table boat with a curtain-rod mast. They arrive at a dream Alaska, discover it is only Mahagonny, and the money is once more demanded. Jenny is asked if she will rescue him and her answer (largely because of the music, which has portrayed an even more powerful bond between them than the words) comes as a great shock. "Ridiculous", she says. "The things we girls are meant to do!" She then sings a song (again, of great beauty) which reinforces the feeling that Brecht was using *Threepenny Opera* material or exploring ideas about whores, rejection and love with very little relevance, or reference, to the theme of *Mahagonny*. Scene 6, in the first act, is equally clearly a thematically barely related song which Brecht wished to use, and the prolonged duet of farewell in the last act may be seen as an alternative to the "lovers' farewell" of *The Threepenny Opera*.

As the piece nears its conclusion the contradictions are piled on so thickly as to make detailed analysis unhelpful. The trial scene is a long (and highly successful) reworking of many of the ideas in both *Man Equals Man* and *The Elephant Calf*. The first person to appear before the court, Tobby Higgins, is even arraigned for "murder committed for the sake of testing an old revolver". The suspicion that Brecht is still talking about the evil inherent in man rather than in society is more than adequately demonstrated when Jimmy asks his friend:

> Please, Billy, give me a hundred dollars,
> So that my case is conducted humanely

and Bill replies:

> Jim, I feel close to you as a person,
> But money's a different matter.

Anything seems to be allowable in the writing (and the various versions reinforce this view) so long as it contributes to the overall operatic effect. Trinity Moses points out (rightly) that it was Jim who "conducted himself like the hurricane" and thereby "corrupted the whole city and destroyed peace and harmony", but the inhabitants respond by hailing Jimmy and shouting "Bravo". Then he is sentenced to two days' custody for the indirect murder of a friend (Alaska-Wolf-Joe, whom he bet on), a two-year suspension of civil rights (!) for destroying peace and harmony, four years' hard labour for seducing Jenny, ten years in the dungeons for singing forbidden songs during the hurricane, and for not paying for three bottles of whisky and a curtain rod: death.

Before the finale in the most commonly heard version there are two more "numbers" which can hardly be justified on any grounds other than that they existed and were well worth giving an airing. The first, like the whores' "Moon of Alabama" song, is in an English of considerable peculiarity and charm, and tells of the sad demise of Benares, "said to have been perished by an earthquake"! (What a German-speaking audience is supposed to have made of these two songs one can only imagine.) The other is a fine and bitter "play" (from the *Hauspostille*, Brecht's first book of poems) demonstrating how God came to Mahagonny "during a grey morning, in the midst of whisky" and tried to send the inhabitants to hell. They refuse to go on grounds which recall Marlowe's Mephostopheles: "You can't drag us into hell, because we always were in hell." It is introduced, oddly enough, by Jim, in the electric chair, asking Begbick if she is not aware that there is a God. And if it needed further undermining as part of the opera's message, it actually follows Jim's defiant affirmation that he does not regret that he has done whatever he liked.* He and the men sing:

> Don't let yourself be deceived
> That life means little.
> Drain it in giant swallows:
> You will not have had enough
> When you have to leave it.

The finale is an operatic triumph. With the city of Mahagonny burning in the background, a series of processions weave in and out carrying Jimmy Mahoney's possessions and clothes, as well as a number of contradictory placards: "For the natural order of things", "For the natural disorder of things", "For the freedom of the rich people", "For the freedom of all people" and so on. Begbick, Fatty and Moses reiterate that Mahagonny existed only because everything is so evil, and the men reiterate that mankind needs no hurricane because he can bring about his own horrors. A final "giant placard" reads: "For the continuation of the Golden Age"; and the whole cast sing the despairing lines:

> Cannot help ourselves and you and no one.
> Cannot help ourselves and you and no one.

The opera is, by any reading, no simple political message.

Because of its initial reception, as we have said, *Mahagonny* is almost invariably represented as being a political success in the way that *The Threepenny Opera* is represented as being a political failure. This is doubly peculiar in that not only is its message ambiguous, but it has actually been absorbed into the super-bourgeois world of opera. Its story has been over-neatly summarized so often that opera-goers are aware they are being excoriated and vilified (even though they are not), but because of the overwhelming effect of the music, plus the *social* convention of this specialized form of theatre, are able to wallow smugly in its glories, with the supposed left-wing cynicism and attack merely providing an added *frisson*. The bitterest song of all, in which Jenny and

---

*In the version published in *Gesammelte Werke*, Jim (called Paul) takes a different view of his fate — that the happiness he bought was no happiness and freedom paid for is no freedom. But the piece as a whole reveals broadly the same confusions of politics and intent.

Jim map out their relationship as whore and user to a hauntingly sentimental and lovely tune ("But what about underwear, my friend? Do I wear underwear beneath my skirt or go without?" "No underwear!" "As you like, Jimmy") is usually a show-stopper; part of a splendid night out at the opera with the added touch that even after all these years it may still be seen as a little *risqué*.

This area of failure for Brecht — as a performed writer — is brought home even more devastatingly in the last piece he and Kurt Weill completed together, the opera-ballet *The Seven Deadly Sins*. Commissioned by Georges Balanchine during the first year of their exile, it was probably written in haste and more in the specific hope of making money than anything. The idea is pleasant enough: Anna, a girl who is split into a "rational" persona, which is sung, and a "natural" one, which is danced, leaves her family in Louisiana to make her fortune, mainly to provide her mother, father and brothers with a big house. During the next seven years Anna I has to prevent Anna II from committing such deadly sins as Lust (having the man she loves instead of the man who pays), Pride (mixing up "art" with the business of being a cabaret showgirl) and so on, until they can return to the completed home.

As a small-scale attack on the values of the bourgeoisie it is unexceptionable, if not particularly impressive. Neither the words nor the music have anything like the bite and flair which the partnership usually achieved, except possibly in the section on Gluttony. But anyone who has seen it in performance can only wonder at the totality of Brecht's failure to break the complacency of a ballet audience. The obligatory ten or twelve minutes of adulatory applause, the bewigged flunkies presenting enormous bouquets to the principals, the middle-aged gentlemen in evening dress trotting down the centre aisles to toss roses onto the stage — all these are standard responses throughout the "civilized world". If the bourgeoisie had consciously sought a way to undermine everything Brecht fought for in the theatre they could hardly have come up with a better.

In a way, of course, it is odd that Brecht, who devoted an enormous amount of thought and energy towards achieving clarity of theatrical expression and an exactness of communication that would leave audiences free to consider and analyse, should have made these excursions into the (from the point of view of his technique and theories) murky worlds of opera and ballet, where an élite either does not hear the words or considers them of minor importance. But throughout this passionate period of his Marxism he was clearly fascinated by the possibilities of music, which plays a major part in almost everything he wrote. In exile he lost many things — deep collaboration with musicians being one of them and his apparent belief in the beneficial results of communist revolution another. From the mid thirties everything changed for him. In the most immediate sense he found a new target — Hitler.

5

Hitler and the Power of Force

The plays that will be considered in this chapter were written between 1931 and 1943 and are all (with the exception of *Senora Carrar's Rifles*) directly concerned with Hitler. They were not written as a straight-forward progression and they do not make up the full body of his dramatic works between these years. But they do give a fascinating insight into his view of the possibilities of human action and reaction in the face of unavoidable, and at times apparently irresistible, force. They also reflect a shifting awareness of the possibilities, even the dangers, of pacifism and/or appeasement, and a possibly subconscious but at times quite palpable distrust of (sometimes almost a disgust with) the "little man", the "masses" on whom he had for so long placed his political reliance and his hopes for the future. They are a peculiar mixture of the optimistic and the despairing, the pacifistic and the fiercely aggressive. Most important of all, they are almost exclusively a-political, not to say anti-political: where Marxism comes into the question at all it is tangentially, half-heartedly, often almost apologetically. One may reasonably conjecture that Brecht's belief in the people had at last been desperately shaken by events — the not-too-difficult equation of National Socialism with a genuine popular mass movement, the events in Russia under Stalin's dictatorship, finally the Russo-German military pact. Even outside these Hitler plays he never wrote another piece in which Marxism exists as more than an implicit way forward. Some of the Hitler plays clearly contain a call to arms; but the specific call to revolution was stilled forever.

The first play, *Round Heads and Pointed Heads*, not surprisingly comes nearest to being nakedly political. In fact it is close, in time, tone and construction to *Saint Joan of the Stockyards*. Started in Germany in 1931 as a free reworking of Shakespeare's *Measure for Measure*, it went through several major revisions before its first performance in Copenhagen on 4 November 1936. From Brecht's notes after the performance it is clear that he attached some importance to it in terms of his production methods, although it is possible that by this time he was aware to some extent of its political and historical shortcomings. He points out that the "parts were built up from a social point of view" and did not show the "eternally human" but what "men of specific social strata (as against other strata) do in our period (as against any other)"[1] which can be taken to mean that the behaviour of some of his characters would not be possible in a more developed (i.e. Marxist) world. He did not, however, make any major alterations to the play in later years, despite its many flaws of dramaturgy, political understanding, and prophecy. Perhaps he was satisfied to let it find its own level of theatrical obscurity; and indeed, it is nowadays extremely rarely performed.

The story (as in most of Brecht's failed plays) is much too complicated to be *accurately* summarized in a few words. But the main strand of the plot, and the one which has attracted the most contumely, concerns a Hitler figure, called Iberin, who is appointed dictator in the land of Yahoo when the Regent finds the social and economic problems besetting him are too difficult for him to handle. The Regent realizes that a war is what the country needs to bring new markets, reduce the corn glut and gain new industrial enterprises by sequestration, but because there is a popular movement at work in the country, the Sickle League (i.e. the German Communist Party), the populace would not stand for it. Against his better judgement he allows his privy councillor Missena to bring in the demagogue Iberin, as the "only man" who can pull the trick. Iberin was born into the middle class, from whom he draws most of his support:

> Both rich and poor alike he does condemn
> As money grubbers; for him the State's decline
> Is spiritual and reflects corrupted souls.

Further:

> Milord, this Iberin knows the people well.
> He knows an abstraction must be given face
> And form ere they can recognize it.
> Therefore he's given the spiritual ill a shape.

This "abstraction" is a racial theory at once absurd and pregnant with possibilities — that the true inhabitants of Yahoo have round heads and the "foreign" ones (a homeless and hearth-profaning race) pointed. Iberin will make the conflict one between these "races", and not between rich and poor. What's more he has his own private army and will crush the Sickle League without putting the State to the cost of providing soldiers.

The second scene, which is a very fine one, shows just how instantaneously effective this lunatic doctrine is. Almost overnight the moral degeneration in Yahoo has become far advanced and extremely vile. All the petit-bourgeois characters have a firm idea that they are going to benefit personally, preferably at the expense of others, and their pipe dreams are bolstered by one of Iberin's soldiers, who agrees with everything anyone says ("Rents are going to be lowered." *Soldier*: "Yes, that's right." "I've heard that they are going to be raised." *Soldier*: "Quite true.") A Tschichisch (Pointed Head) shop-keeper is denounced for not hanging out an Iberin flag, then beaten up and arrested by the dreaded Huas (*Hutabschlägerstaffel* or Hat-tippers; they check people's heads by knocking their hats off!) for attempting to rectify his mistake — "How disgusting; the Iberin banner in the greasy paws of a Tschich!". Meanwhile an Iberin soldier blackmails a Tschuchisch (Round Head) woman into buying a poster, and fails even to return her change after first overcharging her. Nanna, the prostitute daughter of the Round Head tenant Callas, approaches her former lover, the Pointed Head landlord de Guzman, and asks that her father be let off paying his rent. He says he cannot do it, because his sister Isabella is about to join a convent and her novice money has to be found, at which Nanna engineers his arrest by the Huas. In the climate of the times de Guzman's original seduction of the willing girl quickly becomes transformed into a racially unacceptable rape and the pivotal incident of the play. Overall the scene brilliantly demonstrates that not only is Iberin doing nothing for anybody except spreading fear and uncertainty, but that the general consensus is that a new era (a good one, inevitably) has begun.

Unfortunately, after this promising beginning, Brecht's own theory — and the Marxist one — of the reasons for Hitler's rise to power, forces him to veer away from the darkly fascinating and deeply convincing racial aspect of the story. For although Iberin is ambiguously characterized throughout as possibly believing his racial theory (a point which is almost always misunderstood or overlooked in discussions of the play) it is made clear that he has not only been put into power as the tool of the ruling class, but that he is prepared to accept money even from rich Pointed Heads when his army proves insufficient to crush the Sickle League. Moreover, in his Hitleresque speech after the League's apparently final defeat, he more or less dubs all those who joined — whether Round Head or Pointed Head — as unworthy of being Tschuchs. The poor, including the Round Head tenant Callas who has swallowed his racial nonsense more completely than anyone, are told: "If you are poor / It is because your work is insufficient. / Industry we need and not complaints." In the end the Regent, whose links with the wealthy have ensured a loyal army which Iberin could not hope to defeat, returns to power as the landlords try to persuade Iberin to reprieve de Guzman because he is a landlord first and only then a Tschich, and that although the racial ploy has served its purpose the landlords in fact run everything — including himself — by providing money. Iberin bows immediately to the Regent's right to take up government once more (his alacrity is presumably to ensure that he is allowed to retain a certain amount of authority; this is unclear) and is thanked because:

> It is no exaggeration if I say
> That your theory of the heads
> Has saved the realm.

With everything back to normal, however, the Regent admonishes: "Dear friend, no more Tschuch or Tschich", to which Iberin replies: "Jawohl, mein Fürst" — a way of saying "Yes, my Prince" which allows, in German, a certain ambiguity, in that *Jawohl* implies an emphasis beyond a mere *Ja*. (N. Goold-Verschoyle, in the Grove Press edition, cleverly translates it as "Good, Milord.") Whatever the ambiguity, however, the overall point is clear; essentially, Iberin is prepared to accept that his racial theory is most usefully and importantly a ploy, and is prepared to accept his role as the servant, not the master, of political power in the land.

Brecht's misreading of the course of history, and in particular the black pathological depths of Hitler's actual fear and hatred of the Jews (which were there, after all, for anyone to read in *Mein Kampf*) have been pointed out frequently enough. But there is another major strand in the fabric of this play which is even more fascinating and which is invariably overlooked. For the message of Marxist hope, embodied in the Sickle League which is represented in the two-dimensional and infrequently seen figure of the tenant, Lopez, works through the action of the plot on two individual members of the "mass" in particular (as well as most of the "little people" in general) who are treated by Brecht with a lack of warmth that borders on disgust. The tenant Callas and his daughter Nanna, at the end of the play, pour away the soup so patronizingly donated by the Regent, regret their mistake in not siding with the Sickle, and leave the stage converted and purged of what Marxists would call their "class treachery". But they are surely the most unsavoury and equivocal bearers of a communist message ever created.

From the very first scene in which he appears, Callas is characterized as being mean, vicious and untrustworthy. Having decided to throw in his lot with the Sickle League, he changes his mind as soon as he hears that his landlord de Guzman (a Pointed Head) has been arrested. The news of Iberin's accession to power, he says, is very good — "for us Tschuchs". And he refuses to let the Lopez family, until this moment his friends, shelter in his house when the news arrives that theirs has been burnt down because of their pointed heads. The news of the fire is significant; it reveals that Callas is not the only poor person who instantly and seriously embraces Iberin's doctrines and turns on his friends and neighbours. More significantly still, the Round Head village children immediately turn on their Pointed Head friends. Children appear in many of Brecht's plays, and hardly by accident; while he never expects them to be rational he clearly places great importance in them as the unsullied bearers of the future. In this play the children of the poor are universally and instantaneously corrupted; it is a deeply pessimistic point.

The relationship of Callas and Nanna to the new society is a shifting one, but it is always one of naked opportunism. Callas takes some not ignoble sentiments of Iberin's to mean he can steal horses from de Guzman because he (Callas) is a Tschuch and his landlord is not, and even when Iberin orders him to give up the horses again he is still so convinced by the racist claptrap that he visits de Guzman in the condemned cell to get his rent remitted. Nanna quite happily sees de Guzman condemned to death for the "rape" which gave her the wealth and independence (albeit as a prostitute) that she openly admits to enjoying, and, like her father, remains unrepentantly a racist even when Brecht is showing her to be an economic "victim". Thus, when she dons Isabella's novice habit to sleep with the secret police chief Zazarante and save de Guzman's life (a job for which her madame, the cafe-owner Cornamontis, will receive the payment) she comments:

> My latest job is to be guardian of propriety
> And keep sustained a pillar of society.
> A Tschuch must save a Tschich's repute,
> A nun's kept pure by a prostitute.

A piece of racist and economic sophistry (no one is forcing her to do anything, neither does anyone care that she and Isabella have differently shaped heads) which is not matched in the play until her father offers himself for hanging in de Guzman's place in return for two rent-free years and on the strict understanding that the hanging will not actually take place, and then comments:

> Tschuch or Tschich! Unjust or just,
> The poor man must die because his master says he must.

Like his daughter he argues a compulsion that is non-existent; like his daughter he has revealed himself as a racist.

Brecht is not everywhere in the piece so totally condemnatory of the "masses". Scene 9, in which the inexperienced Isabella goes to ask the advice of Madame Cornamontis and Nanna on how she should conduct herself in her sexual sacrifice with Zazarante, is in parts rich, ambiguous and moving. Cornamontis reveals a strange mixture of understanding, cynicism and depravity as she explains firstly that Isabella will find no difficulty in it ("There's less to know than you imagine, my child. That's the sad thing about it. It's our tragedy, as professionals, that the more we practise the less zest we can take — and give. You will be enjoyed all right. For these furtive enjoyments practically anyone will do.") and secondly that she ought not, and need not, do it anyway ("Why should you, in your position, make such a sacrifice? Why do anything for which you have no inclination? It would be unseemly for you, for whom other much less sensitive people earn money by the sweat of their brow, to do anything to lower yourself in these people's eyes...What would you say if one day the rain started falling from the ground to the sky?") There is then a bitter little set piece in which "The landlord's sister instructs the tenant's daughter in the three principal virtues — temperance, obedience and poverty" — all of which Isabella is taking on herself in the wealthy convent and which Nanna has had thrust upon her by birth.

In his note to the 1936 production, Brecht not only insisted that he is concerned to show how people act in *this* social situation *now*, but that contradictory behaviour in characters not only does not make them unbelievable but is essential in making them "come to life".[2] Callas and Nanna in particular both seem to vacillate wildly between being utterly hateful and being victims. But however hard Brecht tries to rehabilitate them at the end, it is extremely difficult, if not downright impossible, to get over the sheer weight of cynicism and despair about the poor he has laid upon them. And whatever he claims, they throw up time and time again the old opposition between his belief in the possibility of change and his doubts about the wolfish nature of mankind. Joan Dark, in *Saint Joan of the Stockyards*, was a goodhearted girl who learned the need, as Brecht saw it, for violent revolution; Callas is a man who is prepared to accept any expedient, however vile, that he thinks will make him materially better off.

In fact, it is hard to believe that Brecht genuinely hoped that at the end of the day Callas and Nanna would be accepted by an audience as representatives of a message of hope. For what he gives us in this peculiar play is a comprehensive portrait of two Nazis — ordinary, average, "decent" people who swallow hook, line and sinker both the racial and the financial nonsenses because they think they will benefit from them. The events demonstrate to and on Callas that the racial nonsense is a sham and the financial nonsense a trick; he ends up poorer than he began, and sees his former comrades, of both "races", being prepared for hanging. Does that really make him and his daughter fit candidates for Marxist conversion? They are totally believable examples of the type who could, and did, become race murderers. If Callas had joined the Sickle, he could easily have become its Joe Stalin. If Callas had joined the Sickle, most thinking members of an audience would have decided it was not for them. How aware Brecht was of the appalling implications inherent in this story it is impossible to know. But as we have said, Callas and Nanna are not the only members of their class portrayed as being greedy and brutish. Greed is, in fact, the driving force of everyone, even the Sickle League, who are prepared to die to bring about better things for all — that is, themselves. Did this, by Brecht's definition, not constitute greed? Or was he well aware of the ironies of the speech Lopez makes to Callas from the gallows, in which he points out that had he submerged his personal greed into the cause he would indeed have ended up with his heart's desire?

> You stole two horses on your own,
> Made off with them, like a thief, alone.
> Your fishing was a one-man affair,

Kuhle Wampe, the "engagement-party"

> You thought that way you'd secure your share.
> But you had your horses only as long
> As the Sickle army was whole and strong.

If you had joined us, says Lopez, you would have got away with your theft.

Brecht, like many of the middle classes who invented, or were converted to, communism, equated the masses in some mysterious way with nobility. It is not only in this play that this view clashes with his observation, or that his romantic love for the idea of the proletariat clashes with his knowledge of them. There are scenes in the film *Kuhle Wampe* (1931-1932) that are equally eerie in their combination of compassion and hatred, understanding and bafflement. We do not know exactly how much of it is directly his work, but we do know he shared the jubilation of the co-operative which made it in getting a left-wing viewpoint through the censorship system. And what does it portray? In detail, one of the most unsavoury pictures of the working classes at ease in their own element ever created, in the "engagement party" for a pregnant girl which degenerates into an oafish and disgusting display of drunkenness and selfishness, and in general, a truly remarkable parallel between the organized left in Germany in the early thirties and the organized right. The blond, handsome Aryan workers march, sing and take part in competitive sport "for victory", wear uniforms strikingly inappropriate to their age and supposed maturity, and even take part in some public badinage with a Jew which skates remarkably close to racism; all they seem to lack is a great leader. The makers of the film seem to be unsure whether they are for or against their characters, whether the masses are basically communist or fascist, or whether there is indeed any difference. In *Round Heads and Pointed Heads* it is time and again Iberin who is outraged by venality and greed, it is Iberin who insists, albeit in a twisted way, on a higher possibility in mankind than mere self. Which is not to say that Brecht was *for* Hitler; but may suggest that there is somewhere implied an uncomfortable recognition of the links between communism and fascism, idealism and greed, and of the danger of brutishness inherent in any code which postulates power as a legitimate weapon in the redistribution of wealth and justice. Is a fascist merely a communist who has taken a simple wrong turn and can be reformed? One would expect Brecht to say: Surely not; a communist is a Utopian lover of mankind, a fascist a murderous thug who will above all deny personal freedom. In this play it is hard to tell; he actually seems unsure of the difference — which is a dreadful position for a Marxist to find himself in.

Whatever Brecht's doubts about the knotty problem of the suitability of the masses as a vehicle for necessary social change, he was compelled (even while he continued to mull over *Round Heads* before its first performance) to face the fact that dictatorship in itself exercised a force that was all too effective in corrupting any body of people. Whether or not he quickly changed his view of Hitler as a puppet rather than a puppet-master we cannot know. Similarly, as far as we know, he never made a public pronouncement on the fact that Hitler deliberately murdered six million Jews. But as the bearers of hope, the masses undergo a profound and depressing change in the rest of the Hitler plays. In some of them they are there, but not as a political force. They exist rather as both the weapons of force and the victims of force. But force is the most notable ingredient, and it is seen as all-powerful, all-corrupting, all-pervasive. Any relief Brecht may have felt in turning away from the mighty intellectual problems of portraying communism as a real possibility rather than a dream was swamped in his recognition of the corrosive power of Hitler's machinery of terror. For Hitler, one may perhaps read any dictator.

In his exile, Brecht was an avid follower and collector of news items and hearsay stories, many of which he turned into a series of twenty-eight playlets and sketches gathered together under the general title *Fear and Misery of the Third Reich*. It was compiled between 1935 and 1938, and is one of those works which commentators seize upon as being "Aristotelian" or "un-Brechtian" with metaphorical sighs of relief that can almost be heard rising from the page. Brecht himself, with his usual propensity for responding to pointless challenges, refuted this view, and the proposed stage version, put together in America in 1942 and translated by Eric Bentley in 1943 under the title *The Private Life of the Master Race*, adequately proves his point. It consists of seventeen of the sketches, in themselves completely unconnected, but which add up to a cumulative picture of the Nazi terror, internal and external, that is at once distanced and frighteningly immediate. "On the stage at the beginning" (to quote Brecht's note to Bentley's translation):

stands a German Panzer (armoured troop-carrying truck), the classic Panzer which carried the Nazis to battle as victims of the New Order which they promoted, the Panzer which turned up in one country after another, in Poland, Scandinavia, France, the Balkans, and the Soviet Union. The seventeen scenes show the private life of the men in the Panzer, the environment they come from. The steel-helmeted soldiers crouch in the Panzer, their faces white as chalk, their guns between their knees. Each time the Panzer appears on stage — 4 times in all — military music is heard. The individual scenes are introduced or followed by a voice speaking out of the darkness and by the roar of the rolling Panzer. The roar of the Panzer is heard also during the scenes themselves every time the Terror sets in which has brought the Germans into the war.[3]

This description, as Brecht's of his own work so often are, is a brilliantly exact compression of what he achieves as a whole. Worth noting especially, however, are his own awareness of the pity he feels for the German people — even Hitler's soldiers — and his insistence on the colour of their faces. (It surely cannot be long before some enterprising student counts up the number of chalk-white faces in his *oeuvre* and questions more closely than Brecht has indicated what it says about his attitude to people. The same Panzer, incidentally, and the same pale villain/victims, roll past the quizzical eyes of Schweyk in *Schweyk in the Second*

World War as he trudges on his roundabout way to Stalingrad.) Here at last is a representation of a whole people — and class plays no measurable political part at all — as near destroyed as makes no difference by the power of force. Fear stalks Germany, then the rest of Europe, then Russia. And before it morality, courage, self-respect, humanity — all are attacked, bow, and at the very least go underground; more normally are shattered.

Cumulatively these sketches are the most telling theatrical picture of a dictatorship ever achieved, and the very fragmentation has its own part to play in the total effect. Short, often bitterly humorous pieces are mixed with longer portraits of more complicated miseries to give an overall impression of what life was like in Germany from 1933 to 1938, while the soldiers, who sing of how the internal horrors of the New Order were spread, through the agencies of discord and treachery, "from Norway down to the Alexandrian sands", operate with a disembodied voice and geographical sign-boards to provide a framework in which the Nazi vileness is seen creeping inexorably over the face of the earth. The Voice and the song, in fact, provide not only a framework, but a key to Brecht's view of how Hitler's terror worked. After we have seen (through the eyes of his neighbours) a man brutally arrested, for instance, the Voice tells us:

> Thus neighbour betrayed neighbour.
> Thus the common folk devoured each other
> and enmity grew in the houses and in the precincts.
> And so we went forth with confidence
> and shoved onto our Panzer
> every man who had not been slain:
> a whole nation of betrayers and betrayed
> we shoved onto our iron chariot.

The joint themes of betrayal and loss of trust recur time after time as ways in which Hitler provided himself with a master race whose private life is the iron chariot. "The common man dragged the common man onto our Panzer for us," we are told after an SA man has demonstrated how he marks the disgruntled unemployed by clapping them on the back and leaving a chalk cross on their shoulders from his marked palm: "With the kiss of Judas...with a friendly slap on the shoulder". And in the middle section of the play, where Brecht has moved on to deal with bourgeois Germans:

There is also a teacher on our Panzer
a captain now with a hat of steel,
Who teaches a bloody lesson to
French grapefarmers and fishermen of Norway
For there was a day seven years before
dimly remembered but never forgotten,
when in the bosom of his family he learned
to hate spies.

This playlet, "The Informer", makes possibly the most despairingly ironic point in the collection. For while in many of the pieces we see the characters on-stage abandoned by their friends as soon as they become targets of Nazi attention, in this one the "hero", a teacher whose son is in the Hitler Youth, is seen at the beginning abandoning his friend Klimbtsch "whose case is being looked into by the school-inspectors", and at the end in a lather of terror because he thinks his son is going to betray him for some remarks which might be considered insufficiently pro-Hitler. We know, poor fellow, that he is right — the Voice has told us. But the point is hideously made. In Hitler's Germany even one's children could betray; and parents were no longer the source of morals and attitudes in their own young.

Apart from "The Chalk Cross", an oddly clumsy piece (Brecht used the material much better in a twenty-five line poem with the same title), the bourgeois section contains the longest, and most deeply explored, playlets. "The Jewish Wife" comes nearest to criticizing overtly the middle classes for not standing up against Hitler, but Brecht — who saw the build-up of Nazi thuggery over several years — clearly understood the corrosive power of force too well to point the finger at any one class. In the piece, Judith Keith, who has decided to leave her Aryan husband so as not to lose him his job as head surgeon at a clinic, allows herself to berate him in her imagination:

What kind of men are you all? What kind of man are you? You people discover the quantum theory and let yourselves be bossed by half-savages; you have to conquer the world, but are not allowed to have the wife you want. . . You're monsters or the bootlickers of monsters...Let's not talk about misfortune. Let's talk about shame. Oh, Fritz!

But even in her imagination she has already answered her criticisms with an extraordinary depth of compassion and insight:

I'm packing because...already you can't sleep at night. I don't want you to tell me not to go. I'm going in a hurry because I don't want to have you tell me I *should* go. It's a question of time. Character is a question of time. It lasts for a certain length of time, just like a glove. There are good ones that last a long time. But they don't last forever.

She predicts in her imagination that her husband will hand her her fur coat, which she will not need until winter, although she is ostensibly only going away for a couple of weeks. When he actually helps her pack he does just that. She makes no comment.

In the next scene, "In Search of Justice", Brecht chooses to treat the predicament of a Judge less with compassion than an almost surreal humour. He has to reach a judgement on three SA men who have smashed up a Jewish jeweller's shop. The Jew's Aryan partner wants the blame laid on the Jew, for selfish reasons, the Jew's Aryan landlord, for equally selfish reasons, wants the SA men in trouble. The Judge is frightened of crossing not only the SA but also the SS, who will expect a different "interpretation" of the facts. All the advice a fellow judge can give is to "look out for himself" — to which he responds "I am looking out for myself. Only I don't know what advice to give myself." The prosecutor has already quoted the Justice Minister's edict, "Whatever's useful to the German Folk is just." But although he is prepared to follow this lunatic precept (like the Teacher in "The Informer", who would teach whatever was wanted if only he knew what it was) he is in the frightful dilemma of not knowing what is *required* (not desired) by the thugs who can, and will, break him for a "wrong" decision. This Judge's friends drop him (by telephone) even before he goes into court; they realize the case will destroy him. His attendant suggests he might have to conduct the trial from the dock, then "laughs absurdly" at his joke. It is a horrible, and horribly funny, play.

For the poorer classes the lessons of silence are learnt equally effectively. In "The Box" a young wife persuades an angry friend to leave unopened the zinc coffin in which the SA have returned her husband after he has complained about low wages; it is the only safe thing to do.*

*This, too, Brecht dealt with in a poem of 1933 with the opening stanza:

> Here in this zinc box
> Lies a dead person
> Or his legs and his head
> Or even less of him
> Or nothing, for he was
> A trouble-maker.(*Poems 1913-1956*, p. 216)

In "Winter Relief" a rambling old woman repeatedly screams "Heil Hitler" while vomiting, after a careless remark about food prices has led the SA to arrest her pregnant daughter. In "The Man They Released", the man, newly out of a concentration camp, agrees with his former political comrades that they are right not to dare trust him. The awareness, the compassion and the hopelessness were extended to all.

It must have been symbolically deeply important to Brecht that Hitler's armies came to grief in Russia, and at the end of the play we see the Panzer stationary and frozen on the Eastern Steppes "defeated in the poor man's land". (Although it is significant that the soldiers have "come alive" for the first time, at last aware, perhaps, of what being part of Hitler's New Order has cost them.) But the final sketch, "Plebiscite", offers only a very forlorn and muted message of hope, in the same way that the play as a whole pays only lip-service to communism. In the thirties, in Germany, it may have seemed the only oppositional possibility against Hitler (the rest of the world did precious little before the war, even in the way of understanding) but by this time Brecht knew very well what was happening in Stalin's Russia, and the play is a clear-sighted view of dictatorship that comprehends its realities outside Germany as well as inside. In "Plebiscite" two workers and a woman listen on the radio as Hitler enters Vienna in triumph in 1938, and they discuss the difficulties of getting out a leaflet opposing the idea of "One Folk, One Reich, One Führer". The older worker, listening to the "roar of victory", comments: "Doesn't that really sound like one Folk?" to which the woman (inevitably the woman) retorts: "It sounds like twenty thousand people drunk on someone else's money." She then reads a letter from a condemned communist to his son on the eve of his execution: "...Even if it looks as if I achieved nothing, that is not really the truth...Until [our task] is completed life has no value. If we do not always keep it in view, the human race will sink into barbarism." Inspired by this courage, they determine to publish a leaflet — containing the single word: NO! This particular moment of hope was already dead, of course, when Brecht wrote the sketch; that is not the point. It remained, and remains, a gesture of sorrow, warning and exhortation. He knew the roar of victory was not merely twenty thousand bribed and drunken people, and he had not shied away from portraying a whole population corrupted by fear. He did it, however, with remarkable compassion and a steadfast refusal to give up hope completely; if only for a distant future.

It has often been said of *Fear and Misery* that, as in *Round Heads*,

Brecht misjudged the fullness of the horror of Hitler's Germany, especially in relation to the Jews. This judgement obviously smacks of
hindsight, as one of the remarkable things that emerges from his plays
of this period as a whole is that even a man who hated Hitler as virulently
as Brecht did had absolutely no conception of the depths of his lunacy
and vileness. Pre-war concentration camps he knew about; extermi-
nation camps he never even dreamed of. But although the colours of the
piece are muted, it is none the less effective for that. Brecht had, of
course, seen the appalling growth of politics by thuggery up to 1933, but
chose not to depict it directly until *The Resistible Rise of Arturo Ui*, when
he did so satirically and humorously. There is no dramatic "overkill" in
Fear and Misery. It is a cool, clear and appalled look at a rotting society.

Notably less effective is the short play *Senora Carrar's Rifles*, which
was written in 1937 as a vehicle for Helene Weigel in exile, and makes a
remarkably emotional (for Brecht) and unconvincing point. Senora
Carrar, the widow of a Spanish fisherman, who had, in her view, much
too much of a taste for fighting, is determined that her two young sons
will not become involved in the battle against the fascist forces that cost
him his life. A succession of people try to convince her that theirs is a
righteous struggle, and that she should let her sons go, taking with them
the rifles she has hidden under the floorboards. But she totally rejects
the idea of spilling blood for blood, is clear-sighted about her husband's
penchant for violence, and believes that Franco and his generals are at
least well-intentioned. Those who are innocent — that is, do not fight —
will not suffer. At the end of the play her elder son, who has been out
fishing, is brought home dead; shot by some passing fascists in a
gunboat because he was wearing a worker's cap. Senora Carrar, convinced, collects the rifles, and leaves with her brother and remaining
son to join the fight. The generals *are* lying, there *are* times when the
rules of the Church must be broken; if a shark attacks, retaliation
cannot be condemned as violence. Politically, the point is made so
weakly as to be laughable (it is difficult to imagine how Brecht could
have allowed himself the worker's cap idea); and even taken as a
demonstration of the conversion of Senora Carrar to an awareness of the
existence of evil that must be resisted against any odds, it is unimpres-
sive. Ruth Berghaus' production for the Berliner Ensemble was usually
given for children, who in a performance seen in 1979 found plenty to
giggle about but apparently little to hold their interest. Even with
Weigel playing the lead, it is hard to imagine much value in the piece.

For this reason if no other it is a pity that two short plays Brecht wrote in 1939, *Dansen* and *What's the Price of Iron?*, are far less well-known. They are sharp, biting, topical plays in which the dangers of appeasement and the need to fight against Hitler are much more clearly seen, with the gangster element, that had been touched upon in *Fear and Misery* and was to be dealt with in detail in *Arturo Ui*, coming very much to the fore. In the first, Dansen the pig-seller (Denmark), watches cravenly as The Stranger (Hitler) murders his neighbours, some of whom have pacts with him, one by one. Finally Dansen also signs a pact, which The Stranger tears up as soon as it suits him, an action which involves the loss of Dansen's pigs and the key to his neighbour Svendson's iron store, which Dansen was looking after. In the second play, Svendson (Sweden) not only sells increasing numbers of iron bars to The Customer, but later accepts the goods of his murdered neighbours in lieu of payment. Finally, after he has refused to join Mr Britt and Mrs Gall in a pact, on purely commercial grounds (he is selling more and more iron bars to The Customer, by whom, he insists, he does not feel threatened), war breaks out. The Customer enters his shop, armed to the teeth, and asks him: "How much is your iron?" Svendson, broken, replies: "Nothing."

There is little sympathy for the plight of appeasers in these two pieces, which is fair enough when one considers how quickly their prophecy came to be fulfilled (as well as the plays' shortness and slapstick nature). But in a later, longer play the pity and understanding which Brecht extended to people under Hitler in *Fear and Misery* is more significantly absent. *The Visions of Simone Machard* was written, with Lion Feuchtwanger, in 1942-1943, underwent various small changes until 1946, and was first performed in 1957. It is a reworking of the Joan of Arc story, set in France in June 1940. Simone, a simple (almost simple-minded) young girl almost alone does anything positive to oppose the advancing German forces; her final act is to fire a secret petrol hoard which is about to be given to them. Betrayed by all about her, either directly or by cowardly default, Simone is denied the martyr's fate of her historical counterpart because the French capitulation means "it's peacetime now" — and to make sure the insurance money is paid, the Germans hand her over to the French to be treated merely as an arsonist and not a saboteuse. She is sent to a notorious mental home, inevitably run by nuns, "where they finish with their heads swollen up and spit running out of their mouths." Her parents abandon her, even those who were her friends do nothing, and the firing of the village hall by the refugees she had helped is a very pale symbol of hope compared with the utter bleakness of her fate.

A very effective theatrical piece which deserves more exposure than it receives, it is another play in which Brecht the pacifist not only recognizes that some evils of his time were so great that they had to be met with force, but actively exhorts armed resistance as the only remedy. In the early thirties, when he rightly or wrongly saw fascism as a product and function of capitalism, he perceived the need for resistance by force. When Hitler gained power, rearmed, then started to roll Europe up like a carpet, Brecht knew he had to be fought, in any and every way. However desirable peace might be, however vital to true humanity, without justice and honour it was a sham. In *Mother Courage* (1938-1939) he showed the total hideousness of a war, any war; but in the earlier *Senora Carrar* he accepted its inevitability in some circumstances and in the later *Simone Machard* he illustrated the moral consequences of avoiding it. Time and again in these years Brecht dramatically examined the realities and implications of force; the number of angles from which he approached it is fascinating.

The later play is, in fact, a mirror reversal of his approach in *Senora Carrar*. There he showed one act of atrocity converting a woman (and through her, he hoped, an audience) to the notion of justifiable violent reaction. In *Simone Machard* he shows the continuing atrocity of moral degeneration as a way of, as it were, *disgusting* an audience into the recognition of the need for retaliation. The French are portrayed as cowardly, greedy, shallow and cynical, and unprepared to fight for their country at almost any price. In the short term, of course, it saves them from a certain form of destruction; but they are morally destroyed in the process, and are drawn with a contempt that borders on disgust. (It is a measure of Brecht's skill that they remain entirely believable as characters and are not merely caricatures.) The Spaniards, on the other hand, brought death, bestiality and destruction on themselves and still (Brecht's faction) lost; with no allies eventually to save them, as had the French. But they were human, brave and tragic; odd that to make the view convincing, after the failure of *Senora Carrar*, Brecht had to approach it from the underside.

It is this oblique angle of attack that makes the oft-repeated objection that *Simone Machard* is "too-heroic" so easy to refute. For Simone's acts on behalf of "our beautiful France" are not greatly heroic in the event — more those of a normal person, one cannot help feeling, compared with the spinelessness of all about her. In any case, she is a silly, childish girl, and Brecht wanted her to be played by a child; the point is that such things cannot and will not happen. France was heroless and hopeless. The use of Simone as a pathetic Saint Joan was intended to emphasize the moral emptiness of those who allowed her — in some ways forced her — to adopt the role. It is a violent and bitter attack on an occupied country suffering in too much silence under the heel of the jackboot, and its message is not about heroism, but about the corrosiveness of cowardice.

This strange — and tremendously unorthodox — viewpoint, which in some real sense allows more compassion for the Germans than for their victims, was further tested in the last of the plays directly about the European disaster, *Schweyk in the Second World War*. Written in America in mid 1943 with half an eye very uneasily on the Broadway musical market, it is an attempt to pit Hasek's Czechoslovakian Good Soldier Schweik, as the epitome of the "little man", against Hitler and his henchmen, who are seen in the "Higher Regions" conducting their dreams of world domination in terms of gross pantomime. Schweyk, who claims to have been "officially certified an idiot by a medical board", is a dog thief by trade, and alternately gets himself into trouble and manages to survive it by a rich combination of irony and crawling. After various brushes with the occupying forces involving the theft of a dog and its transformation into a parcel of meat to satisfy the hunger of his fat friend Baloun — and thus save him from an overwhelming desire to join the German Army just to get a square meal — Schweyk ends up in the Army himself, quite cheerfully looking for Stalingrad after becoming detached from his unit. During his wanderings through the icy wastes he meets Hitler, also lost. For Hitler, the loss of direction is irrevocable. Schweyk, however, is indestructible.

Despite several scenes which are funny and even charming (the one in which Schweyk steals a dog while two girls sing a sentimental ballad in two-part harmony, in the Berliner Ensemble production, achieves a fusion of almost explosive intensity that it is impossible to imagine by merely reading the words) the play overall is not a great success. In *Fear and Misery* the black shadow cast by Hitler is almost palpable; in *Simone Machard* the French, although unforgiven by Brecht, are at least seen to be under an actual, physical threat. But in *Schweyk* the necessary sense of despair is somehow unachieved. The Germans, nasty as they are, are not sufficiently nasty — indeed much of their venom is directed at each other — and nowhere is there a suggestion that the occupied people have a moral obligation to rise against them. In *Simone Machard* the bitterness is wholly on the surface of the writing, and it is directed against the

French; in *Schweyk* it is buried, and emerges only occasionally in anti-German jokes, the Czechs being let off completely. (This can still have a strange effect; even given that in East Germany today the destruction of the country in World War II is officially blamed on the Nazis rather than the Allied forces, some of the things Brecht has the Czechs say about their occupiers sound frankly embarrassing to an Englishman sitting among a German audience.) The only genuinely moving scene, in which an armoured vehicle appears before a silent Schweyk, clustered with frozen, mummy-like German soldiers "with chalk-white or blueish faces" to the strains of the "German Miserere" ("The third year saw the Balkans and Russia both invaded. / We should have won, but something has delayed it. / God preserve us.") instils pity for the Germans alone, not the invaded Russians or the Czechs. It suggests once again the (for us) peculiar possibility that Brecht saw Hitler as being a worse disaster for Germany than for the world the Germans conquered and almost destroyed.

The play is rich in ambiguities of a different kind, which almost certainly do not emerge in performance. Hitler throughout places his reliance on "the little man", without whom he cannot win. In the end, of course, he loses — and "the little man" survives. But despite the odd reference to communism, and despite the fact that Hitler broke on Russia (but her winter rather than her politics), Schweyk and his fellow "little men" are not only a-political, but possibly even bourgeois, and happy to be so. Among many such references, one speech of Schweyk's, to the Gestapo agent Brettschneider, is worth quoting at length:

Great men are always unpopular with the common herd...And for why? Because the common herd don't understand them and find the whole thing unnecessary, heroism and all. The common man doesn't give a bugger for living in a great age. He wants to go down to the pub for a drink and have goulash for supper...The common herd's a thorn in the flesh of any great man.

Throughout the play, too, he preaches the doctrine of bending to the necessity of the times. Someone who has been arrested is categorized as "some awkward fellow who didn't crawl" and later he tells a woman who thinks the Czechs should resist more actively: "Don't ask too much of yourself. It's something to be still alive nowadays. And you're kept so busy keeping alive there's no time for anything else." Mrs Kopecka, a delightful character, yet another of Brecht's drink-providing ladies — although this time in a fixed pub — and a petty business woman, is even given a beautiful song pointing up the joys of her establishment, which can be obtained at a modest profit to her. The wonderful description of Baloun's sister's wedding feast is in stark contrast, as well, to the bestialities of the engagement party in *Kuhle Wampe*. Finally comes Schweyk's affirmation that "business as usual" is the motto to see one through. Just before he meets Hitler, he finds a dog in the wilderness. "We're going to Stalingrad," he tells it. "...If you want to get through the war in one piece, keep close to the others and stick to routine, don't volunteer for anything, lie doggo till you get a chance to bite. War doesn't last for ever, any more than peace does, and when it's over... there'll still be people wanting dogs, and pedigrees'll still have to be faked..." Quite apart from the light such attitudes throw on both *Mother Courage* and *Galileo*, not to mention Brecht's own quizzical amoralities, the awareness that "the little man" is uncrushable, and unforceable into any dictator's mould, cannot be overlooked. By no stretch of the imagination can Schweyk and his friends be seen as "workers"; a dog thief, a photographer, a pub owner, a butcher's son. Nor are they the stuff of revolution. But they are human, admirable — and invincible. How far Brecht meant the ambiguities to go we can only guess; but anyone who doubts their existence need only imagine the implications of a production of the play in Czechoslovakia today.

In *Round Heads and Pointed Heads* Brecht not only saw Hitler as the puppet of his capitalist "backers", but also showed little direct awareness of the concrete realities of war. Throughout the action victories and defeats are noted, but no feelings of pain, destruction or loss illuminate it. By the time he put together *Fear and Misery*, terror was recognized as a sufficient reality to corrupt, corrode and destroy the soul of a whole people; behind the terror was Hitler. And in *The Resistible Rise of Arturo Ui*, written in Finland in 1941, he was able to portray, through the vehicle of a single, simple, brilliant metaphor, an overwhelmingly convincing view of how a self-pitying mediocrity could establish himself with the connivance of his "backers", then use the power of force to wrest control irrevocably from their hands. Historians have been arguing for years whether this "Frankenstein and his monster" view is adequate to explain the rise of Hitler, in the same way that they continue to argue over whether he was a "great" man or not. Brecht's notes of the 1950s leave us in no doubt as to his view:

The great political criminals must be thoroughly stripped bare and exposed to ridicule. Because they are not great political criminals at all, but the perpetrators of great political crimes, which is something very different...If the collapse of Hitler's enterprises is no evidence that he was a halfwit, neither is their scope any guarantee that he was a great man. [1]

As an analysis, one may feel this is underwritten, less than adequate. But he did go on to say that *Arturo Ui* was a parable, written to destroy "the dangerous respect commonly felt for great killers", and in the play itself his analysis is deep, searching and extremely difficult to refute. It is the word "resistible" that seems to have stuck most firmly in the craw of most critics, but among other things the play is yet another horrified look (in the vein of *Dansen* and *What's the Price of Iron?*) at the blind policy of appeasement that allowed a political thug to reach the point where he could challenge the world.*

Using his vast knowledge of gangster books and films, Brecht transfers a potted history of Hitler's rise to power between 1929 and 1938 to his beloved mythical Chicago. Quickly written (in about three weeks), it is an almost orgasmic outpouring of a view which Brecht could, for once, hold simply and without need for questioning or self-doubt — his hatred for Hitler and the desire to see him destroyed. This lack of inhibition seems to have led him to excesses of throwaway humour which are an odd counterpart to the excesses of dreary tendentiousness in his other play dealing with economics and Chicago, *Saint Joan of the Stockyards*; oddest of all because the excesses this time never fail to work. Even the basic situation (and the story is too well-known to be outlined in detail) hovers just this side of lunacy: Ui rises to power on the backs of the Cauliflower Trust! It is this total ridiculousness, however, that makes the parable so successful. He "wants to sell / Our cauliflower with his tommy guns." says Flake, a director of the Trust. "The town is full of types like that right now / Corroding it like leprosy, devouring / A finger, then an arm and shoulder." It is such an extraordinarily apt way of summing up the ignorance, stupidity and *barbarity* of fascism. Hitler great? says Brecht. Why not point up the depths of his awfulness and sheer unlikeliness? Flake continues:

*In the same notes Brecht's explanation for a communist critic as to why "the People" are missing serves very well, also, for the Western critics who want included an examination of the Jewish question. "The play does not pretend to give a complete account of the historical situation in the 1930s. The proletariat is not present, nor could it be taken into account more than it is, since anything *extra* in this complex would be *too much*; it would detract from the tricky problem posed." It is an elegantly polite rebuff; fortunately Brecht was a better playwright than his critics!

No one
Knows where it comes from, but we all suspect
From deepest hell. Kidnapping, murder, threats
Extortion, blackmail, massacre:
'Hands up!' 'Your money or your life!' Outrageous!
It's got to be wiped out.

But Sheet, the shipowner to whom he is talking, notices that Flake suddenly bears a resemblance ("Not too pronounced") to the gangsters. Again the parallel is exact: not only did Hitler rise on the backs of respectable and powerful men, but organized crime survives, and thrives, through the stupidity and corruptness of law-makers and law-enforcers; with Prohibition in America being the most complete example.

Brecht's daring with humour in short speeches is almost outrageously successful.* "By golly, it's not often that the gravy train / Travels the straight and narrow." "Short-lived / is fame in such a place. Two months without / A murder and a man's forgotten." "He was carrying a Webster sub-machinegun and made a suspicious impression." "It's not in his character to start fires. He's a baritone." "No one, unless he has to, tolerates / Coercion." Longer speeches, too, work with extraordinary suppleness to create a comic effect, to characterize, and to further the story. Dogsborough, who has ruined a lifetime of honesty by accepting a country estate from the Trust, actually achieves in a soliloquy a *moving* explanation of corruption:

Those poplars are what tempted me to take
The place. The poplars and that lake down there, like
Silver before it's minted into dollars.
And air that's free of beer fumes. The fir trees
Are good to look at too, especially
The tops. Grey-green and dusty. And the trunks —
Their colour calls to mind the leathers we used to wrap around
The taps when drawing beer. It was the poplars, though
That turned the trick. Ah yes, the poplars.
It's Sunday. Hm. The bells would sound so peaceful
If the world were not so full of wickedness.

*The excellence with which Ralph Manheim's translation for Eyre Methuen captures this deserves mention here.

Unlike the language of *Saint Joan*, which, as we have shown, needed to be a parody of classical modes to handle the excesses of characterization, the Elizabethan/Jacobean elements here work perfectly in every way. The absurdity is not that of Mauler and Slift, totally unbelievable caricatures of "capitalists", but a believable absurdity, (a) because we know both Hitler and gangsters and (b) because the "capitalists" are shown as being normal not rapacious, devious but stupid, and victims as much as villains. They think they are using Ui because they underestimate the power of unleashed evil, and even Ui himself — evil enough — is given the foils of Roma and Giri, who display both naked force and naked psychopathy. The language, bitter and compressed, now becomes a perfect vehicle for the story, which it conveys with immense clarity and muscularity.

Brilliant as the language itself is, it must not be overlooked that the articulation of the story is also of a remarkably high order, even for Brecht. The placards which illuminate the stage events seem at first glance to tell a direct tale; but they do not. The first starts "1929 to 32. Germany is hard hit by the world crisis"; the third "In the autumn of 1932, Adolf Hitler's party and private army are threatened with bankruptcy and disintegration." From this in fact very diffuse historical framework, Brecht creates a story of extraordinary intensity, in which the illustrative events he deploys not only reflect history but illuminate it; his art mirrors, cuts through and throws a cold analytical light on highly complicated processes by showing extremely simple end products. The question posed time and time again is this: how *could* the Germans have been so stupid as to let Hitler rise? And each time the answer is provided: like this, my friends, like this. From a play rich in such details, one need only cite the trial scene, in which Fish, accused of burning down a warehouse (a crazy counterpart to the Reichstag) is subjected to the most complete statement in the *oeuvre* that justice is not merely an illusion, but a device by which the ruling class represses the ruled. Six short scenes, punctuated cinematically by blackout and music, convey with high humour and deep horror the total corruption of the judicial process that undoubtedly occurred in Germany under the Nazis. When Giri, fuming, runs short of breath on screaming at the judge "Just keep your trap shut if you want to live", the judge takes the opportunity to reply "Defence counsel will incur charges of contempt of court. Mr. Giri's indignation is quite understandable." Immediately after the trial, for the first and only time, Brecht injects a tiny piece of realistic horror. A woman climbs out of a shot-up truck and cries:

Help! Help! Don't run away. Who'll testify?
My husband is in that truck! They got him! Help!
My arm is smashed...And so's the truck. I need
A bandage for my arm. They gun us down
Like rabbits! God! Won't anybody help?

Nobody will, of course. And in the same scene, when the tired and broken old "honest Dogsborough" (Hindenburg) writes his true will and confession, in which he admits to acquiescing "in all the machinations of that bloody gang", it can only lead, inevitably, to the false will written by the cripple Givola, which contains such lines of Jacobean horror as "And I bequeath my son to honest Roma." Nowhere does Brecht come closer to acknowledging his debt to Shakespeare's portrayals of the politics of ancient blood, or the comic vilenesses of Marlowe's Jew of Malta and a host of Webster's villains. Where the play transcends its models is in its scope; for Brecht shows us the great soul of evil and makes us laugh at it, with increasing revulsion and nervousness.

That this play is a masterpiece — possibly the greatest masterpiece of serious black comedy ever written — should be in no doubt. The stumbling block for most critics, however, has always been the equation of the mighty Hitler with a "mere" gangster. This despite his history and the fact that his "greatness" only emerged when he had political muscle — thuggery — enough to steamroller a demoralized opposition. This despite the fact that gangsterism, in the hands of politically less ambitious men, has made organized crime the biggest "industry" in America. This despite the chilling authenticity of *Fear and Misery of the Third Reich*, which shows a country run by gangsters. Whatever others make of it as a point of view, however, Brecht refused to underestimate the power of force. After the suicide of his friend Walter Benjamin he wrote: "Empires collapse. Gang leaders / Are strutting about like statesmen."[5] He had come a very long way from his almost affectionate view of the gangster breed in *The Threepenny Opera*, and he recognized not only the folly of affection but the appalling danger of creeping admiration for such men. Hitler was a gangster; to treat him as anything else would have been obscene. Brecht's refusal to compromise on this is compounded by other refusals to bow to comfortable orthodoxy. The play is a comedy, a ruthlessly funny and vicious one, which mocks classical drama, perhaps, as well as Hitler, and which shows up politicians, some of whom we chose to call statesmen, as shallow, unserious, cowardly, stupid (and also which reveals, one may conjecture, one source of his distrust of the British: "When the first two came barging into / My store and threatened me at gunpoint, I / Gave them a steely look from top to toe / And answered firmly: I incline to force." Chamberlain's "peace for our time" was not to be forgotten). The play is in fact *revolutionary*, in an entirely disreputable way; totally without respect for Hitler, it portrays the people who fail to oppose him as equally unworthy: as venal, corrupt, revolting. As a view of the nature of politics it is the most despairing thing Brecht ever wrote; but to dismiss it as over-bitter, over-cynical, over-simple is to fail to recognize not only a poetic distillation of historical events, but its prophetic accuracy in terms of *real-politik* in America, in Russia and most of the rest of the world.

The last, but possibly the greatest, block to an adequate response to the play has been, sadly, the overall facility, the breathtaking ease, the sheer theatrical panache with which it is executed. In *Saint Joan*, Brecht took what he saw as a complicated theme and failed completely to control it. Here he takes a truly enormous theme and makes the execution seem too easy for many people to take really seriously — it is a phenomenon which has led to the underrating of *The Threepenny Opera* also. The line "No one, unless he has to, tolerates coercion" is a good example; its simplicity and humour can all too readily mask its profundity and fittingness within the text. For this question, one can only look to a theatrical solution; and it is happily true that the more the play is performed, the more its merits are being recognized. One might use Shakespeare's history plays to help the process along. The best of them, so admired and revered, are also often seen as *being* history, although they are the products of historic events and personalities filtered through one man's vision. They are clear, straightforward, simplified — and have the feel, four hundred years on, of absolute psychological truth. The psychological truth of *Arturo Ui* seems similarly likely to live on. From whichever angle later playwrights approach Adolf Hitler, they are unlikely ever to achieve so strange and convincing a truth about him. We marvel at the characters Richard III, the Jew of Malta and Flamineo as essential insights into a savage age. When Brecht provides us with a key to cataclysmic aspects of our own, we should not dismiss him lightly.

6

Brecht's Theory of Theatrical Performance

> I have been brought to realize that many of my remarks about
> the theatre are wrongly understood. I realize this above all
> from those letters and articles which agree with me. I then
> feel as a mathematician would do if he read: Dear Sir, I am
> wholly of your opinion that two and two make five. [1]

With that as an epigraph, this chapter treads gently into the contorted
world of Brecht's dramatic theorizing. He was a compulsive corrector,
driven constantly to explain what he had just done as if it were the same
as what he was about to do; and he retained for forty years a curiosity
about the theatre that gave him ample opportunity to test, attack, and
revise his own views as well as everybody else's. Confronted with what
looks so like confusion, some critics have taken refuge in ignorant
abuse. But that is not acceptable. As a theorist, whether you like his
theories or not, Brecht stands among the few undoubtedly influential
contributors to the international debate on the sources and resources of
theatrical performance. Indeed, in Britain, until someone provides a
theatre for Craig, Artaud, Meyerhold or Grotowski, he is the only viable
alternative to Stanislavsky for actors and directors (even designers and
musicians) alike. Account *has* to be taken of what he said.

Let us admit from the outset that not all of it repays the effort. It
would be astonishing if it did. But, though he did not always do so,
Brecht could write with wit and wisdom about the art he practised. He
criticized its abuse in the German theatre of the twenties, he justified his
own failures as a dramatist and attacked his own successes, and during
his long exile he found himself a superfluous man, full of vigorous ideas
but with hardly anywhere to put them to work. The final expression -
which is not to say that it was a finally satisfactory expression - of his

theatrical theories was not the "Short Organum" but the Berliner Ensemble, where his theories were neither much read nor much referred to. Or perhaps it was both; and certainly it was his plays as well. He thought in his study and he thought in the theatre, an embodiment of the falseness of the distinction between "academic" and "practical" work that has obstructed the free development of Drama Studies in universities and drama schools. The concern that a theatre should take a central place in its society was with him from the angry start, and his study of Marxism strengthened his conviction. An unshakeable belief in the ameliorative social role of an achievable form of theatrical performance provides the basic motivation for almost all Brecht's theoretical writing. "The means must be asked what the end is,"[2] he wrote in 1938, and in the "Short Organum" of 1948:

The attitude is a critical one. Faced with a river, it consists in regulating the river; faced with a fruit tree, in spraying the fruit tree; faced with movement, in constructing vehicles and aeroplanes; faced with society, in turning society upside down. Our representations of human social life are designed for river-dwellers, fruit-farmers, builders of vehicles and upturners of society, whom we invite into our theatres and beg not to forget their cheerful occupations while we hand the world over to their minds and hearts, for them to change as they think fit.[3]

Brecht often tries to nudge his readers, as he did his audiences, into approaching theatrical problems with the critical attentiveness appropriate to scientific or technological problems. An answer is needed, he says, and will be found.

In *Brecht on Theatre* John Willett has usefully brought together a selection of the many things Brecht wrote about the theatre during his forty years of almost ceaseless interference with it. Even so, it is a mistake to sit down and read it from cover to cover. For one thing, Brecht repeats himself for different audiences. For another, he does not write consistently well. Much of his theorizing was provoked, as were his plays, by customs, theatrical conventions, and ideas that he found repellent. As a result, it can exhibit the tendentiousness that is an unattractive aspect of occasional writing. In later life, Brecht modified some of his opinions, making the point that has been made by many innovative thinkers, that in order to get his arguments heard at all he had to overstate them. The journalistic essay of 1926, "Emphasis on Sport",[1] is an example of the method. The essay begins stridently:

We pin our hopes to the sporting public. Make no bones about it, we have our eye on those huge concrete pans, filled with 15,000 men and women of every variety of class and physiognomy, the fairest and shrewdest audience in the world.

A reader, in less hurry to make a point, might well question the fair-mindedness of the average sporting crowd; but Brecht, provoked by a contemporary theatre at once demoralized and complacent, is in search of improvement:

When people in sporting establishments buy their tickets they know exactly what is going to take place; and that is exactly what does take place once they are in their seats: viz. highly trained persons developing their peculiar powers in the way most suited to them, with the greatest sense of responsibility yet in such a way as to make one feel that they are doing it primarily for their own fun. *Against that traditional theatre is nowadays quite lacking in character.*

Half a century later, and in a different country, the words are not out-dated. Two abiding features of Brecht's theatrical theory and practice are already stressed; that theatre should have a sense of (social) responsibility, and that it should have a sense of fun (*Spass* again!). A third outstanding observation in this early essay is concerned with the prevailing acting style:

In his obscure anxiety not to let the audience get away the actor is immediately so steamed up that he makes it seem the most natural thing in the world to insult one's father. At the same time it can be seen that acting takes a tremendous lot out of him. *And a man who strains himself on the stage is bound, if he is any good, to strain all the people sitting in the stalls.*

The italics are Brecht's, so that he was clearly eager to stress his dislike of a feature that most of his contemporaries would have assumed to be admirable. This is an early inkling of what would develop into a brilliantly unorthodox idea, or group of ideas, about acting. It was not yet very far evolved. We shall have to return to it. For the moment it will be sufficient to underline Brecht's unhappiness about a method of acting that tended to reproduce in the audience the emotions felt by the actor.

The stridency of this early essay is a characterisitic also of much that Brecht wrote on "Epic Theatre". The idea of such a name probably reached Brecht by way of Erwin Piscator, who subtitled Alfons Paquet's *Flags* "Ein Episches Drama" when he directed it for the Berlin Volksbühne in 1924. Ronald Gray has cautioned us against the over-easy assumption that the German "episch" is synonymous with the English "epic". Distinct from literary modes that are full of tensions and conflicts, the "episch", he suggests, is "slower-paced, reflective, giving time to reflect and compare."[5] That may be so, but it will not do as a description of Piscator's productions. It was from Piscator that Brecht received the jolting assurance that theatrical realism was not a matter of disguising from an audience that it was really in a theatre but of making the audience insistently conscious of where it was. From 1925 onwards, Piscator consistently used film in his productions. Why? Because "drama is only important for us insofar as it can be documented by evidence."[6] He replaced aesthetic criteria with criteria of effectiveness, and he loved exhibiting technology. It was not a slow-paced, reflective theatre. In comparison with Brecht's theatre it is shallow, but Brecht never disguised his debt to Piscator. Christopher Innes has indicated that "modern stage-machinery gave Piscator the potential to make reality the object instead of the subject of drama."[7] It was a new access to reality that Brecht sought in developing his ideas of epic theatre. He seems first to have used the phrase in May 1927, when he looked forward to "the creation of a great epic and documentary theatre which will be suited to our period."[8] The association of "epic" and "documentary" here is evidence of the debt to Piscator. As we will attempt an analysis of Brecht's dramaturgy in Chapter 9, it is sufficient for our purpose here to say that the crucial innovation of epic drama is its design on the audience. Brecht emphasized this in an essay written in about 1936 but unpublished in his lifetime:

The dramatic theatre's spectator says: Yes, I have felt like that too - Just like me - It's only natural - It'll never change - The sufferings of this man appal me, because they are inescapable - That's great art; it all seems the most obvious thing in the world - I weep when they weep, I laugh when they laugh.
The epic theatre's spectator says: I'd never have thought it - That's not the way - That's extraordinary, hardly believable - It's got to stop - The sufferings of this man appal me, because they are unnecessary - That's great art; nothing obvious in it - I laugh when they weep, I weep when they laugh.[9]

It should be apparent from this that Brecht had the art of acting under scrutiny, and indeed, his proposals for a style of acting appropriate to the "new" drama occupy a central place in his theoretical writing.

One important step towards this was the development of the idea of *Gestus*, which became an essential link between Brecht's theory of acting and his practice as a playwright. It is not an easy word to interpret. One of Brecht's own definitions distinguishes it from gesture (*Geste*) by calling it "a number of related gestures expressing such different attitudes as politeness, anger and so on".[10] The imprecision is obvious, but the association of gesture and attitude brings us close to the centre of Brecht's performance theories. What problems arise result from the amount of work Brecht wanted the word *Gestus* (or *gest*) to do for him. Thus:

A language is gestic when it is grounded in a *gest* and conveys particular attitudes adopted by the speaker towards other men.[11]

Or:

The piece "In Praise of Learning", which links the problem of learning with that of the working class's accession to power, is infected by the music with a heroic yet naturally cheerful *gest*.[12]

Or:

The realm of attitudes adopted by the characters towards one another is what we call the realm of *gest*.[13]

The list could be considerably prolonged until definition became a nightmare. Many of the contexts in which Brecht employs the word *Gestus* suggest that it is no more than a new title for an old thing, for that intuitive grasp of an idea in action which carries that idea from the lyric to the dramatic mode. Such intuition belongs to all great dramatists and all great actors. Perhaps it is wiser to abandon *Gestus* short of definition, and direct attention to those analytical sections of the "model-books" (explored in the next chapter) in which Brecht shows how the word was *used* by the actors who worked with him.

Gestus never lost its place in Brecht's vocabulary, either in respect of writing or acting plays. An apparently perverse sidestep into Stanislav-skian theory will help in the making of a final point about it. Stanislavsky invites the students in *An Actor Prepares* to divide any play in which they are to perform into its basic "Units". For such a difficult task his guidelines are disappointingly approximate, but his real interest is in the next step. "At the heart of every unit," he explains, "lies a creative objective."[14] The *unit* is the dramatist's. The *objective* is the actor's. Despite its psychological overtones, Brecht might have understood the distinction between units and objectives, but he used *Gestus* to describe both. "Each single incident," he explained in the "Short Organum", "has its basic *gest*"; and though "Everything hangs on the 'story' ", that story is "the complete fitting together of all the gestic incidents."[15] Brecht's *units*, then, are *gests*; and the Brechtian actor's *objectives* are *gests* too. The actor's basic *gest* (best translated here as something like 'attitude made purposeful by intention') is the "*gest* of showing".[16] He stands in front of an audience because he has something to show, and he declares himself as one who shows. What he shows may vary, but the *gest* of showing is invariable. This is not to downgrade what is shown. Brecht knew that "Not all *gests* are social *gests*", but his own concern was with "the *gest* relevant to society, the *gest* that allows conclusions to be drawn about the social circumstances."[17] There is no political or social dilemma in Brecht that is not also, and clearly so, a moral dilemma. "The eye which looks for the *gest* in everything," he wrote, "is the moral sense."[18]

Brecht believed that gestic acting in the service of his gestic language would convey clearly to his audience the urgent realities of his plays, but he did not make the naive assumption that gestic acting would arrive overnight. Including even the years in East Berlin, he saw only a handful of occasions when actors got it right. He records some of them: Peter Lorre in *Man Equals Man*, Charles Laughton in *Galileo* (some of the time), Helene Weigel in *The Mother* and (usually) in *Mother Courage* — not many more. Actors were reluctant to abandon the familiar routes to public adulation. Brecht hurried to the defence of Peter Lorre after his performance as Galy Gay in the revised 1931 *Man Equals Man* had been met with hostility:

At first sight, admittedly, it was possible to overlook the truly magnificent way in which the actor Lorre delivered his inventory. This may seem peculiar. For generally and quite rightly the art of not being overlooked is treated as vital; and here are we, suggesting that something is magnificent which needs to be hunted for and found.[19]

From Brecht's point of view, Lorre had managed with superb discipline to indicate the gestic content of the lines. By deviating from conventional stress patterns, he had withdrawn certain key sentences from the spectator rather than bringing them home to him, so that *the spectator*

Scenes from the 1931 production of *Man Equals Man*

had to make his own discoveries. For an actor, such self-sacrifice is extremely unusual, but Brechtian plays demand it. His poem "On Judging"[20] begins like this:

> You artists who, for pleasure or for pain
> Deliver yourselves up to the judgement of the audience
> Be moved in future
> To deliver up also to the judgement of the audience
> The world which you show.

Behind almost all that Brecht wrote and said about the art of the actor is a socialist determination radically to adjust the relationship of actor and audience. Stanislavsky had commended to actors a series of exercises in on-stage concentration:

In a circle of light, in the midst of darkness, you have the sensation of being entirely alone...it is what we call Solitude in Public. You are in public because we are all here. It is solitude because you are divided from us by a small circle of attention. During a performance, before an audience of thousands, you can always enclose yourself in this circle like a snail in its shell.[21]

You can, Brecht would have admitted, but you had better not. He would have endorsed Piscator's criticism of Stanislavsky:

It is not true that your centre of attention lies in the middle of the stage. When you play before a public, the public must be the centre of your attention.[22]

Brecht could not tolerate the figure of the actor-deceiver, nor did he conceal his contempt for an audience that came to the theatre in order to be well-deceived.

Consider first the theatre to which he was antagonistic. At its centre is what used to be called, with more confidence than we can now muster, "naturalism". The dramatist writes a play which, all things considered, is remarkably like life. The actor studies his role and strives to "become" the character he is playing. The audience says, "How true!" which really means, "All things considered, how like the life we lead," and then everybody goes home. The angry young Brecht called this sort of theatre "culinary". Broadway, like London's West End, is still a culinary theatre and so, when financial pressures impose a safety criterion on the choice of plays, is "off-Broadway" (and repertory theatre in Britain). It is not, though, an artless theatre. The early years of the twentieth century had witnessed a new purposefulness in the training of actors. How (the "why" was not yet widely in dispute) do they learn to behave naturally in such artificial conditions? Brecht cites as typically "naturalistic" this description by the actor Rapaport of a method of work:

On the stage the actor is surrounded entirely by fictions...The actor must be able to regard all this as though it were true, as though he were convinced that all that surrounds him on the stage is a living reality and, along with himself, he must convince the audience as well. This is the central feature of our method of work on the part...Take any object, a cap for example; lay it on the table or on the floor and try to regard it as though it were a rat: make believe that it is a rat, and not a cap...Picture what sort of rat it is; what size, colour?...We thus commit ourselves to believe quite naively that the object before us is something other than it is and, at the same time, learn to compel the audience to believe.[23]

There is little here to startle a British or American actor of the eighties. Similar exercises would be part of his training. Brecht rejected it, and much of what is essential to his acting theory can be recognized in his rejoinder:

This might be thought to be a course of instruction for conjurers [sic], but in fact it is a course of acting, supposedly according to Stanislavsky's method. One wonders if a technique that equips an actor to make an audience see rats where there aren't any can really be all that suitable for disseminating the truth. Given enough alcohol it doesn't take acting to persuade almost anybody that he is seeing rats: pink ones.

Brecht was less outraged by the practice of naturalism than by the claim that naturalistic acting was an artistic pursuit of truth. If the beginning is a lie, how can the end be truth? If the prime endeavour of an actor in a theatre is to convince the audience that he is not an actor in a theatre, what has success to say to truth? There is, of course, a political point. An audience so willingly deceived in the theatre will be willingly deceived at the hustings. If the appearance of accuracy is accepted as "truth", then a capitalist government will be able to sustain itself by reminding the people of jam yesterday, and by creating vivid images of jam tomorrow.

Against a background in the German theatre of a deceiving naturalism, Brecht hoped to establish an informative realism:

Our conception of realism needs to be broad and political, free from aesthetic restrictions and independent of convention. *Realist* means: laying bare society's causal network / showing up the dominant viewpoint as the viewpoint of the dominators / writing from the standpoint of the class which has prepared the broadest solutions for the most pressing problems afflicting human society / emphasizing the dynamics of development / concrete and so as to encourage abstraction.[24]

This is from a particularly dogmatic essay, "The Popular and the Realistic"; it should therefore be approached with caution. The final phrase, though, is an outstandingly helpful identification of an essential Brechtian quality. Walter Benjamin records in a diary entry for 24 July 1934 that when Brecht was living in Svendborg:

On a beam which supports the ceiling of Brecht's study are painted the words: "Truth is concrete." On a window-sill stands a small wooden donkey which can nod its head. Brecht has hung a little sign round its neck on which he has written: "Even I must understand it."[25]

Mere abstraction was of no use to Brecht, but neither was mere concreteness. He liked solid words, and he liked solid stage properties. He liked them because they declared themselves frankly, and so did not impede the audience's freedom to speculate. Through concreteness he hoped to draw together the activity of the manual worker, the poet and the actor, as he does in the opening lines of his poem on "Weigel's Props":[26]

> Just as the millet farmer picks out for his trial plot
> The heaviest seeds and the poet
> The exact words for his verse so
> She selects the objects to accompany
> Her characters across the stage.

If you are going to change the world, you have first to recognize its ways. Brecht was almost obsessively aware of the tendency of what is familiar to protect itself from criticism by its unobtrusiveness. The *Verfremdungseffekte* were designed to expose the familiar, to combat its unobtrusiveness. His preference for concreteness was part and parcel of his design on the audience. His actors, like his plays, were to present things in their concrete reality "so as to encourage abstraction".

    A Brechtian actor says, implicitly or explicitly, that he and the audience are in a theatre, exploring as individuals a matter of general interest. For the purpose of the exploration the "actors" will do and say things on behalf of people other than themselves. They will *show* the audience what Grusha, what Simon Chachava, did, since that is information essential to the judgement that everyone in the theatre might later wish to make; but they will not pretend to "become" Grusha or Simon Chachava. They will have two aims: to present a story with social implications in such a way as to encourage the individuals in the audience to pursue those implications, and to present it as well, and therefore as enjoyably, as possible. They will hope for a response unlike the response to "culinary" theatre. Their aim is to hear from the audience not "How true!" but "How surprising!"; not "Just as I thought", but "I hadn't thought of that."

As we have seen, Brecht was aware of the disparity between his theory and the practice even of those actors with whom he worked. Martin Esslin might even be right that the major impact on English theatre of the Berliner Ensemble's 1956 visit to London was not on acting styles but on stage design, lighting and the use of music.[27] But there followed certainly a renewed attempt by actors and directors to understand and apply alienation effects. George Devine visited the Theater am Schiffbauerdamm early in 1956, and noted on his programme that the acting was "like film acting".[28] In his production of *The Good Person of Setzuan*, which opened at the Royal Court in October 1956, the actors reduced their general vocal range in quest of Brecht's supposed anti-emotionalism. This has been a tendency of many subsequent productions of Brecht in English, a result perhaps of mis-hearing German as a monotonous language. Some actors have even persuaded themselves that change of tone *in* a play will turn them from Stanislavsky towards Brecht. Brecht demands nothing less from his actors than change of attitude *to* a play. The greatest barrier to Brechtian acting in Britain and America is the anti-intellectualism of most actors, and for that matter of most audiences. You cannot achieve Brechtian acting through the mastering of a technique. Technique must be consequent on the mastering of an idea and any number of alternatives to that idea, as well as on the actor's eagerness to communicate his understanding to the audience. Brecht had more faith in the effectiveness of understanding than most of his non-Marxist critics have. He ends a poem,[29] in which he protests his understanding of America despite his never having visited it, with two lines that have the force of a motto for Brechtian actors:

> These people understand what they're doing
> So they are understood.

It may well be argued that communication is more hazardous than Brecht allows. He would probably have accepted the point. He was aware that a new audience is harder to train than a new actor - and harder to find. But he had some confidence that the new working-class audience would come, and that it would come to learn. The actors must, then, be able to teach. Something of the distance to be travelled from Stanislavsky to Brecht may be understood if, in an improvization session, one set of actors is invited to imitate an argument and the other set to win one.

"Mystery," wrote Stanislavsky, "is beautiful in itself and is a great stimulus to creativeness."[30] It would be hard to imagine a less Brechtian statement. The quest for clarity in the theatre made Brecht suspicious of the emotionalism of actors to which Stanislavsky had contributed a new seriousness. A Stanislavskian actor is provided with some brilliantly conceived resources for getting into a character. From a Brechtian actor, on the contrary, a spectator receives only what has been got out of the character. He receives the gist of a character. There are always some things being withheld from the spectator by the actor, in order to tempt the spectator into speculation. The actor does not pull out all the stops. Such a vast amount of nonsense has been written about Brecht's attitude to emotion in the theatre, a very small part of it by Brecht himself, that a mystery has been made out of something which is without mystery. It is obvious that an actor's emotions may contribute powerfully to "naturalistic deception". In his iconoclastic early writing Brecht sometimes polarizes emotion and reason, but as early as 1927 he recognized publicly that emotion could not be denied in the Epic Theatre. "It would be much the same thing as trying to deny emotion to modern science."[31] The extent to which his attitude to emotion developed during the years of his exile can be inferred from the contrast between the handling of maternity in *The Mother* (1930-1931) and in *Mother Courage* (1938-1939). His mature position is stated in the *Messingkauf Dialogues*:

Neither the public nor the actor must be stopped from taking part emotionally; the representation of emotions must not be hampered, nor must the actor's use of emotions be frustrated. Only one out of many possible sources of emotion needs to be left unused, or at least treated as a subsidiary source - empathy.[32]

One of the Appendices to the "Short Organum", discovered among Brecht's papers after his death, takes the point even further, allowing that the actor's attempt *not to* empathize will be in useful tension with his inevitable temptation *to* empathize, and seeming almost to claim that it was to produce this tension that he objected to empathy in the first place.[33] However, Brecht was by then envisaging the "sizeable transformation" from an epic theatre to a "dialectical theatre", and so could be expected to strengthen the losing side of an argument. His opposition to empathy was a consistent and well-based one. The effect of empathy is to remove the distinction between actor and audience, allowing the audience to experience the action rather than to criticize it. Brechtian theatre is never working as it should when actors and audiences are experiencing simultaneously the same emotions. The point is made precisely in the short poem "The Moment before Impact":[34]

> I speak my lines before
> The audience hears them; what they will hear is
> Something done with. Every word that leaves the lip
> Describes an arc, and then
> Falls on the listener's ear; I wait and hear
> The way it strikes; I know
> We are not feeling the same thing and
> We are not feeling it at the same time.

An actor who sets out to empathize will tend to isolate himself in his role, shutting himself in the play instead of standing outside to criticize it. The task of a Brechtian actor is to understand and to communicate, not to empathize and be transformed:

A typical kind of acting without this complete transformation takes place when a producer or colleague shows one how to play a particular passage. It is not his own part, so he is not completely transformed; he underlines the technical aspect and retains the attitude of someone just making suggestions.[35]

Wherever emotions might obscure or interrupt the audience's critical awareness, the Brechtian actor must shun emotion. In empathizing, he will always be surrendering the necessary control.

There remains for consideration the *Verfremdungseffekt*. Once again the ideas themselves are clearer than criticism has made them. For English-speaking students of Brecht, the problem begins with the translation of *Verfremdung* as "alienation". *Verfremdung* is virtually a Brechtian coinage, but the kindred word *Entfremdung*, also translated as "alienation", has a lively philosophical, economic and political history.

Brecht would have known its important place in Hegel's work, and its application by Marx to the condition of the proletariat under capitalism. Many of Brecht's plays concern themselves with alienation in this sense. There is a danger of confusion here. If the alienation of the proletariat had been obvious, Marx would not have needed to expound it. It was not obvious because it was taken for granted, just as a Victorian industrialist took for granted that a woman's place was in the home despite the fact that he employed women in his mill. If, like Marx or like Brecht, you do not believe that it is "natural" that the majority of the world's population should labour mindlessly to fill the pockets of the minority, you will wish to establish, against the interests of that sophisticated minority, that it is not natural. You will want to have *recognized* as strange what you already believe *is* strange. That is to say that you will want to alienate alienation. Brecht's *Verfremdungseffekte* were theatrical devices, some literary, some technical, some histrionic, deployed in order to bring audiences to recognize the strangeness of social conditions that they took for granted. The failure of *The Threepenny Opera* to do this in exactly the way he wanted deepened Brecht's thinking about effective theatre, but the word *Verfremdung* itself did not enter his vocabulary until after his visit to Moscow in 1935. He encountered there the phrase, used by a Russian critic, Victor Shklovsky, "priyom ostranyeniya", *a way of making strange. Verfremdungseffekt* may be a translation of Shklovsky's Russian into Brecht's German. He used it almost at once in the title of an important essay on Chinese acting.

In most of the plays that annoyed him Brecht watched actors responding to the challenge of making events that are absolutely extraordinary seem comparatively explicable. Brecht's anxiety was contrary, to make the ordinary *in*explicable:

Who mistrusts what he is used to? To transform himself from general passive acceptance to a corresponding state of suspicious inquiry [a man] would need to develop that detached eye with which the great Galileo observed a swinging chandelier. He was amazed by this pendulum motion, as if he had not expected it and could not understand its occurring, and this enabled him to come on the rules by which it was governed. Here is the outlook, disconcerting but fruitful, which the theatre must provoke with its representations of human social life. It must amaze its public, and this can be achieved by a technique of alienating the familiar.[36]

Before familiarity can be excited into awareness, the familiar must be stripped of its inconspicuousness. The Philosopher of the *Messingkauf*

Pieter Brueghel the Elder, "The Fall of Icarus"

Dialogues states with surprising confidence that:

Anyone who has observed with astonishment the eating habits, the judicial processes, the love life of savage peoples will also be able to observe our own eating customs, judicial processes and love life with astonishment.[37]

But the confidence is an ironic masquerade. Brecht knew only too well the right hand's studied ignorance of the left hand's labour. "True A-effects," he wrote, "are of a combative character."[38] Any *Verfremdungseffekt* has the basic aim of drawing attention to events, ideas, principles, motives or comparisons that would normally be ignored or, at least, skimpily observed, and of drawing attention to them so that they can be altered. Brecht found the jolting into new focus splendidly exemplified by the painting of the elder Brueghel:

Anyone making a profound study of Brueghel's pictorial contrasts must realize that he deals in contradictions. In *The Fall of Icarus* the catastrophe breaks into the idyll in such a way that it is clearly set apart from it and valuable insights into the idyll can be gained. He doesn't allow the catastrophe to alter the idyll; the latter rather remains unaltered and survives undestroyed, merely disturbed.[39]

The violent but "unimportant" fall of Icarus scarcely diverts our attention from the strangely placid activity that surrounds it. That the ploughman should go on ploughing and the fisherman should fish still is a silent criticism of Icarus's extraordinary *hubris*. That they should ignore, or perhaps not see, the boy's death-plunge throws the activities of ploughing and fishing into strange focus. Similarly,

Whenever an Alpine peak is set down in a Flemish landscape or old Asiatic costumes confront modern European ones, then the one denounces the other and sets off its oddness.

Brecht's advice to actors is by no means as comprehensive as Stanislavsky's. It would be surprising if it was. Stanislavsky was temperamentally autocratic, and his books on acting are the literary aspect of his autocracy. Brecht was temperamentally collaborative, and he recorded his own ideas only when the occasion arose. He certainly did not expect the members of the Berliner Ensemble to consult his theoretical writings when rehearsing a play. Why should he? He was working with them. Even so, there is a lot of detailed advice, and sufficient concrete proposals to provide the basis for a training programme. *Brecht on Theatre* includes an undated list of twenty-four "Exercises for acting schools", which range from the bland "Cat playing with a hank of thread" or "Eating with outsize knife and fork. Very small knife and fork" to the purposefully Epic "Modifying an imitation, simply described so that others can put it into effect" or "The street accident. Laying down limits of justifiable imitation". [10] The last of these refers to what is probably Brecht's most famous acting exercise. He considered it important enough to write both an essay and a poem about it. It takes as exemplary of epic acting the case of an eye-witness demonstrating how a traffic accident took place:

The bystanders may not have observed what happened, or they may simply not agree with him, may "see things a different way"; the point is that the demonstrator acts the behaviour of driver or victim or both in such a way that the bystanders are able to form an opinion about the accident. [11]

There are two features of particular significance. The first is that "the demonstrator should derive his characters entirely from their actions. He imitates their actions and so allows conclusions to be drawn about them." That is to say that he does not do the bystander/spectator's work for him by filling in the gaps of motive and psychology. The second is that "Wherever he feels he can the demonstrator breaks off his imitation in order to give explanations. The epic theatre's choruses and documentary projections, the direct addressing of the audience by its actors, are at bottom just this." The street scene raises, of course, much simpler issues than many that will confront the actor of Brecht's plays. That is its advantage. "The object of the performance is to make it easier to give an opinion on the incident." Actors and directors at work on a complex scene should test the effectiveness of their work against this simple model, remembering that:

> ...even if you improved upon
> What the man at the corner did, you would be doing less
> Than him if you
> Made your theatre less meaningful - with lesser provocation
> Less intense in its effect on the audience - and
> Less useful. [42]

The orthodoxly trained actor who is chasing a Brechtian style has some unlearning to do. He will have absorbed exercises in observation and concentration, but he will have been praised almost exclusively for those performances in which he has seemed most completely to lose himself in the character he is playing. Against this, Brecht is interested in both the actor and the role. A Brechtian actor does not forget that he is a showman:

He has just to show the character, or rather he has to do more than just get into it; this does not mean that if he is playing passionate parts he must himself remain cold. It is only that his feelings must not at bottom be those of the character, so that the audience's may not at bottom be those of the character either. The audience must have complete freedom here. [43]

There is some wishful thinking in this notion of the audience's complete freedom. We are constrained by the showman as well as by the impersonator. Nevertheless, there is a measurable difference in the degree of constraint. Brecht's admiration for Charles Laughton was based partly on the fact that "the showman Laughton does not disappear in the Galileo whom he is showing", and he offers an illustration that might be of assistance to a lesser actor than Laughton:

...we find a gesture which expresses one half of his attitude - that of showing - if we make him smoke a cigar and then imagine him laying it down now and again in order to show us some further characteristic attitude of the figure in the play.[44]

All the training is designed to produce "an actor who is fully capable of leaving us to our thoughts, *or to his own.*"

We have italicized the final phrase to emphasize the respect Brecht had for his actors. He was opposed to the kind of hierarchy that dominates the theatre still. After the 1935 production of *The Mother* in New York, he complained that the excellent designer Mordecai Gorelik was given no say in the "grouping and positioning of the actors".[45] English designers would not expect to be asked. The kind of collaboration Brecht envisaged and, to a notable degree, practised in the Berliner Ensemble would alarm most actors, too. Current orthodoxy requires the director to take responsibility for every aspect of the staging of a play. That Brecht expected much more participation from his actors will emerge from a careful reading of the list of "Common tendencies for actors to guard against" printed in *Theaterarbeit*:[46]

Gravitating to the centre of the stage.
Detaching oneself from groups in order to stand alone.
Getting too close to the person addressed.
Always looking at him.
Always standing parallel to the footlights.
Getting louder when increasing speed.
Playing one thing out of another instead of one thing after another.
Blurring over contradictory traits of character.
Failing to explore the playwright's intentions.
Subordinating one's own experience and observation to what one imagines those intentions to be.

The hardest skills to acquire are certain of those aimed specifically to produce a *Verfremdungseffekt*. Certain exercises may help. Brecht suggests one in which two women calmly fold linen whilst feigning a violent quarrel for the benefit of their eavesdropping husbands. But there are not, I think, many actresses who could be persuaded to *understand* (they might "agree") that they are learning, not only to contradict the voice with the body, but also about folding linen. When Mother Courage haggles whilst Swiss Cheese is being prepared for death off-stage, it is the nature of business transactions as well as the horror of war that is under scrutiny. The monetary *gest* coincides with the military *gest*, which it alienates and by which it is alienated. Grouping will help the actor to realize the complexity of the scene — Brecht several times recorded the importance of grouping to the effective presentation of a *gest* — but he must also work by himself to encourage the audience to make comparisons. How does an actor indicate to a spectator that what happens in the play is not the only thing that could have happened? How does he allow for the footnotes as well as playing the text? The Philosopher of *The Messingkauf Dialogues* is uncompromising on the need to do so. One important exchange ends with the Dramaturg asking for confirmation, "You mean play all the scenes with reference to other potential scenes?" and the Philosopher answering simply "Yes".[47] No technique can do it. It requires a strenuous effort at understanding. Actors are generally too conditioned to emotional personalization. They tend to mock what they cannot impersonate. The only time we have seen the "Not...But..." exercise employed by an English group, it soon developed into a frivolous listing of sexual adventures and/or disappointments; and yet it is, perhaps, Brecht's most concrete illustration of acting that alienates:

The very simplest sentences that apply in the A-effect are those with 'Not...But'; (He didn't say 'come in' but 'keep moving'. He was not pleased but amazed). They include an expectation which is justified by experience but, in the event, disappointed. One might have thought that...but one oughtn't to have thought it. There was not just one possibility but two; both are introduced, then the second one is alienated, then the first one as well. To see one's mother as a man's wife one needs an A-effect; this is provided, for instance, when one acquires a stepfather.[48]

One further piece of advice requires our notice:

The actor should refrain from living himself into the part prematurely in any way, and should go on functioning as long as possible as a reader (which does not mean a reader-aloud). An important step is memorizing one's first impressions...Before memorizing the words he must memorize what he felt astounded at and where he felt impelled to contradict. For these are dynamic forces that he must preserve in creating his performance.[49]

Such memorizing of first impressions is calculated to keep the actor at an emotional distance from the character he impersonates. It is part of the historicizing process to which Brecht devoted some of his most careful thought.

If we ensure that our characters on the stage are moved by social impulses and that these differ according to the period, then we make it harder for our spectator to identify himself with them. He cannot simply feel: that's how I would act, but at most can say: if I had lived under those circumstances. And if we play works dealing with our own time as though they were historical, then perhaps the circumstances under which he himself acts will strike him as equally odd; and this is where the critical attitude begins.[50]

The spectator will only criticize if the actor himself has criticized. Rehearsal practices recommended to advance this criticism include:

1. Transposition into the third person.
2. Transposition into the past.
3. Speaking the stage directions out loud.[51]

There is no doubt that an actor's relationship to his words will be affected if he prefaces them with "He smiled, and said with forced nonchalance..." or if in a late rehearsal he has to answer for his first impressions of the role. For those who wish to explore the relationship between Stanislavsky and Brecht, the contrasting approaches to "Emotion Memory" on the one hand and "Memorizing one's first impressions" on the other provide a fruitful starting-point. Stanislavsky's street scene, for instance, is a world away from Brecht's:

...At my feet lay an old man, poorly dressed, his jaw crushed, both arms cut off. His face was ghastly; his old yellow teeth stuck out through his bloody moustache. A street car towered over its victim...[52]

Enough said. There are points where the twain shall never meet.

7

Mother Courage: Brecht's Staging

Mother Courage and Her Children is the play which has most consistently tested, in performance, the durability of Brecht's theories of "epic acting". The emotional intensity of at least three scenes — the death of Swiss Cheese and his mother's refusal to identify his corpse (Scene 3), the drumming and the death of dumb Kattrin (Scene 11) and the final sight of Mother Courage, alone now, but still hauling her wagon across Europe (Scene 12) — has been matched only rarely in the whole history of drama. If the audience is not to empathize with Mother Courage, it must be because the actress has discouraged such empathy by the way in which she has played the less traumatic scenes. In the original Berlin production, Angelika Hurwicz introduced a comic-critical element into her portrayal of Kattrin that may, too, have reduced the tragic impact of Kattrin's death. But a tragic impact remained, and Brecht acknowledged it:

Members of the audience may identify themselves with dumb Kattrin in this scene; they may get into her skin by empathy and enjoy feeling that they themselves have the same latent strength. But they will not have experienced empathy throughout the whole play, hardly in the opening scenes for instance.[1]

There would be no need to concern ourselves with this issue if it had not become so well-worried a bone of contention. *Mother Courage* provides vivid circumstantial evidence that Brecht could have written poignant tragedies in the western "psychological" tradition. But such tragedies, whilst they may often depict individual greatness, have tended to reinforce a sense of human limitation, to confirm that individuals are trapped by circumstances that they cannot change except by personal sacrifice. Brecht was opposed both to Western individualism, and to the view that the world is unchangeable because it is ultimately unknowable. Taking its themes and images from war and from trade, *Mother Courage* demonstrates the way in which "little" people collaborate with those who exploit them, the "big" people; but it does so in order to invite its audience to put a stop to the collaboration. Sympathy, even empathy, with Mother Courage must be tempered by criticism of her equivocation. She is, after all, a provider of fodder to cannon-fodder, and her "motherhood" is extremely unreliable. No production of *Mother Courage* is going to bring about the fall of capitalism in the West, but that is not an argument for muzzling its trenchant criticism of dog-eat-dog working-class collaborators by sentimentalizing its leading character, or by foisting onto the story of her survival and the death of her three children an excusing tragic inevitability that it does not have.

We ought to be alerted to the distance between this play and the Elizabethan tragedies which, in some ways, it resembles, by an episode in the opening scene. In order to protect her children from the insistent attentions of two recruiters, Mother Courage persuades first the sergeant and then her three children to test their fate by drawing slips of paper. Those slips marked with a black cross predict death in the war. Everyone has drawn a black cross. It is a trick, and the audience knows it is; but it is also a parody of a stock scene from "star-crossed" tragedies. The fact that Mother Courage's prophecies are as accurate as those of Macbeth's "secret, black and midnight hags" is a conscious irony. The mood and context of the scene resist supernatural interpretation, for anyone less comically gullible than the sergeant. The "tragedy" of *Mother Courage* is going to be man-made. It is also going to be without rhetoric. To Kenneth Tynan, familiar with English performances of high tragedy in the post-war period, the 1949 Berlin production of *Mother Courage* seemed "light, relaxed, and ascetically spare", and he celebrated its "new kind of theatrical beauty, cool and meaningful".[2]

That first Berlin production has been carefully documented with photographs and accompanying commentary in one of the several published "model-books" by which Brecht hoped to preserve "standard" productions. The idea of the "model" production is not easily acceptable in the British and American theatre, where directors and designers have a dominant role. Brecht goes some way to reassure the doubters in his introductory observations on the *Couragemodell*. It is intended, he explains, "not to render thought unnecessary but to provoke it; not as a substitute for artistic creation but as its stimulus...The model must not be pressed too far.''[3] At the very least, though, he would have expected subsequent directors to consult the model, and not to "break away from it at once". Since the model is so informative, the expectation is a fair one.

Two examples of stage-detail, preserved in the photographs of the Berlin production, may illustrate both the value of the model and the ways in which Helene Weigel criticized the character she was playing. They are not stipulated in the stage directions of the published text. The first comes at the end of Scene 6. Kattrin has just returned to the wagon, with a disfiguring scar running from high on her forehead, over her right eye and down to the base of her right cheek. Weigel runs to her aid, bends to put down the basket she is carrying as she holds her up, and then guides her to an old chest upstage left. Kattrin slumps down. Weigel bandages the eye, all the while talking to the Chaplain. There is then a sequence of photographs that significantly amplifies the information in the text. That text provides us with two stage directions to frame the episode. The first describes Mother Courage's promised treat for her injured daughter: *"She fishes Yvette's red shoes out of a sack."* The second follows her outstandingly clumsy attempt to please her daughter by giving the shoes to her: *"Kattrin leaves the shoes where they are and crawls into the wagon."* The essence of the scene is clear enough. Mother Courage is treating her daughter like a baby, who can be distracted from pain by the offer of a toy. The gesture is both endearingly maternal and offensively patronizing. It is also carefully timed. The whore's shoes have been established in Scene 3 as images of Kattrin's erotic fantasies. Mother Courage promised then to return them to Yvette, but three scenes and three years later she has neither returned nor sold them. Perhaps she has stored them for the safer days of peace. That is to say that she may be deluding herself as well as Kattrin with promises of Kattrin's marrying when the war is over and the choice of a husband is no longer restricted to soldiers. If so, like all her motherly gestures, this one would probably be diverted by the promise of a quick sale. Why can the shoes be offered now? Because Mother Courage realizes that Kattrin's scar makes her safe from the lust of soldiers, utterly unmarriageable. It is a cruelly pointed generosity. The photographs show the wagon broadside on to the proscenium in Scene 6. Downstage right sits Erwin Geschonneck as the Chaplain, big, disconsolate and ludicrous. Weigel goes to the front of the wagon to get the shoes, crosses back towards the sagging shapeless heap of the bandaged Angelika

Hurwicz and holds out the prize. Hurwicz turns away. Weigel thrusts the shoes at her. Hurwicz stands up and shuffles the four or five steps to the back of the wagon, groping her way in. She knows what the offer of the shoes implies. Weigel follows her with her eyes, but her legs are so still that the folds of her skirt do not move. She is still holding the shoes. Instead of following Hurwicz into the wagon, she walks to the chest and puts the shoes away into it. Weigel's Mother Courage knows the value of a pair of red shoes. The second detail is recorded in the commentary as well as the photographs. The play is about to end. Mother Courage has admitted that her daughter is dead. She accepts the peasant's offer of a decent burial, and gives him something to cover the cost. The stage direction states simply that *"She gives the peasant money."* Weigel did more:

Even in paying for the burial, Weigel gave one last hint of Courage's character. She fished a few coins out of her leather bag, put one back and gave the peasants the rest. This did not in the least detract from the overpowering effect of desolation. [1]

The *Couragemodell* is both a valuable historical document, and, wisely used, a stimulus to any future actor, director or designer. The aim of Brecht's mature dramatic work was the "depiction of reality for the purpose of influencing reality".[5] The idea of the model-book is all of a piece with this active view of history. The depiction of the past reality of a valued production is intended to influence every subsequent "present" production. The exegesis of history to alienate (make strange) present social conditions and encourage people to change them is as Brechtian as it is Marxist. There are times when Brecht uses "historicization" as a synonym for *Verfremdung*. *"Historicizing"*, he wrote in the second appendix to *The Messingkauf Dialogues*, "involves judging a particular social system from another social system's point of view." The play *Mother Courage and Her Children* does that. The *Couragemodell* transposes the process from the social to the theatrical sphere. Some further examination of it will illustrate the play's life in the theatre.

Mother Courage and Her Children, written when the war was imminent but not yet declared, was first staged in Zurich in April 1941, when Brecht was in Finland. The director was Leopold Lindtberg, and the cast included a number of fine German anti-Nazi actors, most notably Therese Giehse as Mother Courage and Wolfgang Langhoff as Eilif. The scenery was by Teo Otto, and some attempt must be made to describe it. We can begin with a bare stage, backed by a permanent framework of huge screens "making use of such materials as were available in the military encampments of the seventeenth century".[6] Coloured projections were thrown onto these screens, and there was a revolve in the centre of the stage, which came into use whenever the scenes began or ended with the wagon in motion. The performance begins and ends on this bare stage, but the intensity of the play has intervened, and what we see is only literally the same:

> ...the actors can suggest at the start that here is a wide horizon lying open to the business enterprise of the small family with their canteen, then at the end that the exhausted seeker after happiness is faced with a measureless devastation.[7]

On the empty stage at the start of the play stand two recruiting soldiers. "How can anybody get a company together in a place like this?" is the play's first line, and there is no doubt that the *mise en scène* mocks the attempt. How can you recruit soldiers in a ghost-town? And then, onto the empty stage trundles the wagon, and business begins. Only once more before the end will the stage be empty. That is in Scene 7, when Mother Courage is at the height of her success, and the world is her oyster. (There is a photograph of Weigel, in the Berlin production, arms akimbo, a chain of silver talers round her neck, prancing as she sings in derision of those who try to evade the war. The wagon is being pulled diagonally across the revolve by a characteristically dejected Geschonneck and by Hurwicz, hunched, one eye still bandaged and the other focussed on nothing. It is an image of Mother Courage's destructive obsessiveness.) For the camp scenes (3, 6 and 8) smaller screens, stretched canvas, poles and so on were used to create and vary the environment. For those scenes (2, 4, 5, 9, 10 and 11) which required set pieces, Otto provided three-dimensional structures, "using realistic building methods and materials, but in the form of an artistic indication, giving only as much of the structure as served the acting."[8]

When, eight years later, Brecht and Erich Engel staged the play at the Deutsches Theater in Berlin, they historicized the Zurich production. In the previous year under the management of Wolfgang Langhoff - the creator of Eilif in Zurich - the Deutsches Theater had staged a ceremony in honour of Brecht's fiftieth birthday. Brecht and Helene Weigel were delayed, and did not reach Berlin until the end of October 1948, but this gave them time for over two months' rehearsal of the play, which opened on 11 January 1949. It was the success of this production that allowed them, with Langhoff's active support, to establish their own Berliner Ensemble, whose performances, until the move to the Theater am Schiffbauerdamm in 1954, were staged at the Deutsches Theater. The cast was new, the music was new (Dessau instead of Burkhard), but the scenery (and, therefore, the staging) was greatly dependent on Teo Otto's Zurich design. The projections were dispensed with; in their place, much starker, Heinrich Kilger suspended above the stage in large, black letters the names of the countries in which the scenes took place. It was also decided to fly in a musical emblem above those songs that "did not arise directly out of the action" or arose from it but none the less remained clearly apart. The emblem consisted of a drum, a trumpet, a flag and a number of electrical globes that lit up. Brecht defends the idea on the grounds that it was a visible sign of the shift to another artistic level - that of music; but it is a clumsy device, unredeemable even by the humorous touch of presenting the emblem in Scene 9 as a victim of the war - shot to pieces. Kilger's task was to adapt Otto's designs for the new production. The abandonment of the projections, together with the decision to use lighting that was "white and even and as brilliant as our equipment allowed" removed from the Berlin production much of the Zurich "atmosphere". But the records of Otto's original designs served as a model for Brecht and Engel. Nowhere was their application of his plans more crucial than in the positioning of Mother Courage's wagon during the ten scenes (1, 3, 5, 6, 7, 8, 9, 10, 11 and 12) in which it is a major scenic element. Brecht found Otto's solutions "admirable", and retained them. This imitation is not a small or incidental piece of flattery. The position of the wagon affects the whole progress of the play. Mother Courage's possessive concern for the wagon is a direct cause of Swiss Cheese's death, and a prominent feature in the lives and deaths of Eilif and Kattrin. The wagon is a part of the family, almost a fourth child, whose dilapidation mirrors the decline of Kattrin, but survives it. More specifically, the positioning of the wagon determines the stage groupings.

It is as well to understand where Brecht's attitude to grouping relates to that of other major directors, and where it differs. The idea of "grouping" includes the inert tradition of "blocking" by superseding it. No serious director would quarrel with Brecht's insistence that "the arrangements of the movements and groupings must follow the rhythm of the story and give pictorial expression to the action." An extra emphasis begins to declare itself in the commentary on Scene 1 in the *Couragemodell*:

Positions should be retained as long as there is no compelling reason for changing them; and a desire for variety is not a compelling reason. If one gives in to a desire for variety, the consequence is a devaluation of all movement on the stage; the spectator ceases to look for a specific meaning behind each movement, he stops taking movement seriously. But especially at the crucial points in the action, the full impact of a change of position must not be weakened. Legitimate variety is obtained by ascertaining the crucial points and planning the arrangement around them.

Again, a serious director would agree, though he might be surprised by the forcefulness of Brecht's insistence. The first three items to which Brecht draws attention in a list of "Common tendencies for actors to guard against" are all concerned with grouping:

Gravitating to the centre of the stage.
Detaching oneself from groups in order to stand alone.
Getting too close to the person addressed."

These are points which he is prepared to apply in detail, and with a hard-headed recognition of the problems. For example, he devotes a section of the commentary on Scene 1 to the actors of the recruiting soldiers:

There will be some difficulty in persuading the actors playing the sergeant and the recruiter to stay together and in one place until Mother Courage's wagon appears. In our theatre, groups always show a strong tendency to break up, partly because each actor believes he can heighten audience interest by moving about and changing his position, and partly because he wants to be alone, so as to divert the attention of the audience from the group to himself. But there is no reason not to leave the military men together; on the contrary, both the image and the argument would be impaired by a change of position.

In the Berlin *Mother Courage*, no one was to move unnecessarily. It becomes increasingly clear, as one reads Brecht's own analysis of the structure of each scene, that a regrouping of the actors is a signal to the audience that one instructive incident is over and a new one about to begin. We can refer again to the two crucial sections (65 and 66) of the "Short Organum". "Each single incident has its basic gest" and the whole story is "the complete fitting together of all the gestic incidents". But we can add now the concluding sentence of section 66:

The grouping of the characters on the stage and the movements of the groups must be such that the necessary beauty is attained above all by the elegance with which the material conveying that gest is set out and laid bare to the understanding of the audience.

It is here that Brecht's attitude to stage grouping differs from that of other directors. Grouping and movement must, for him, declare, or at least reinforce, the *social* meaning of each incident. The *gest* reveals itself in the grouping.

Critics and commentators have habitually denied or ignored Brecht's commitment to collaboration in theatrical affairs. For instance, Carl Zuckmayer, who was a fellow-dramaturg at the Deutsches Theater in 1923-4, boosts his psychological speculation with the apparent authority of anecdote:

For all his seemingly conciliatory nature, he had a strong craving for power; not raw power, but the power of the mind, which does not command but guides.

In the late twenties, when the concept of literary and theatrical "collectives" became fashionable, especially in Berlin, I once said to him "For you the collective is a group of intelligent people who contribute to what one person wants - that is, what you want."

He admitted, with his peculiar sly smile, that I might not be so far wrong at that. [1]

To such an account, there are several possible responses. In the first place, a collective from which any individual withholds his strongest opinions is diminished by that withholding; in the second place, it would be naive to confine Brecht to a view he may have accepted in his twenties; and in the third place, the recipient of a sly smile from Brecht should be more wary than Zuckmayer is about interpreting it. The records of the Berliner Ensemble provide rich evidence of the seriousness with which Brecht approached his collaborators. We have seen how much Teo Otto's design predetermined grouping. It is clear that the actors, too, were allowed to make a creative contribution to the evolution through rehearsal of the final production. The concluding points in the list of "Common tendencies for actors to guard against" exemplify the kind of respect accorded to the actor's intelligence in the working atmosphere of a Berliner Ensemble rehearsal. The actor should avoid:

Playing one thing out of another instead of one thing after another.
Blurring over contradictory traits of character.
Failing to explore the playwright's intentions.
Subordinating one's own experience and observation to what one imagines those intentions to be.

As a director, Brecht was prepared to learn from his actors.

The Berlin production of *Mother Courage* began with an overture, played by four musicians only, but still "a reasonably ceremonious preparation for the confusions of war". The musicians were visible, placed in a box beside the stage from which they had access to the stage proper or to the wings. There was also a Prologue, showing Mother Courage, her family and her wagon on their way to the war. The song from Scene 1 was transposed to the Prologue. Brecht and Engel, recognizing the strain on Helene Weigel if she were required to sing over the rumbling of the revolving stage, had the first stanza recorded, and relayed to the darkened auditorium as the wagon was drawn onto the empty stage. The second stanza was sung by Eilif and Swiss Cheese:

We had conceived of the song as a dramatic entrance, lusty and cocky — we had the last scene of the play in mind. But Weigel saw it as a realistic business, and suggested that it be used to picture the long journey to the war. Such are the ideas of great actors.

The setting out of the commentary on Scene 1 in the *Couragemodell* is broadly adhered to in the subsequent scenes. It begins with a sentence encapsulating the basic *gest* of the scene: "The business woman Anna Fierling, known as Mother Courage, encounters the Swedish army." There is then a brief synopsis of the whole scene, in six or seven sentences. Under the heading of "Over-all arrangement", these sentences are then treated one at a time, with appropriate descriptions of the stage action of the Berlin production fleshing out the bare bones of each incident. It is in this section, with its brief description of every element in the narrative sequence, that Brecht analyses the gestic composition of the scene in the theatre: "one thing after another" rather than "one thing out of another". The commentary then concludes with a series of observations, often illustrated by accompanying photographs, on details appropriate to the playing of the particular scene.

Brecht isolates the pivotal point of Scene 1. Professionals of commerce have met professionals of war. Eilif and Swiss Cheese are harnessed like horses, and the soldiers assess them as they would assess horses, thumping their chests, feeling their calves, testing their muscles. In another context, Mother Courage's assessment would be equally professional. She is open for business: "...now gentlemen, wouldn't you need a nice pistol, or a belt buckle, yours is all worn out, sergeant." But the sergeant's reply alerts her to the conflict of professional interests which is the *Grundgestus** of the scene:

I need something else. I'm not blind. Those young fellows are built like tree trunks, big broad chests, sturdy legs. Why aren't they in the army?

Brecht's direction highlighted this crisis by delaying the move of the recruiters over to Eilif and Swiss Cheese. The first three sentences of the sergeant's speech were spoken from stage left (wagon and children were stage right), where Mother Courage had joined the two recruiters in pursuit of a quick sale. The soldiers then cross to the wagon to take stock of its "horses". Weigel gave the audience a momentary glimpse of maternal pride as she watched the appraisal of her sons' physique. But when the sergeant returns to Mother Courage to confront her with the question, "Why aren't they in the army?", she runs over to thrust herself between the recruiter and Eilif. It is, Brecht explains, a detail worked out "painstakingly and inventively in accordance with the principle of epic theatre: *one thing after another*." Much can be inferred about the practice of the Berliner Ensemble from the associated suggestion that:

The pace at rehearsals should be slow, if only to make it possible to work out details; determining the pace of the performance is another matter and comes later.

One further detail from Scene 1 illustrates the undemonstrative style, in conventional terms even "undramatic", of the Berlin production. When Mother Courage draws her knife, she does so without savagery. She is quite simply showing how far she will go in defence of her children. Brecht's instruction is that "the performer must show that Mother Courage is familiar with such situations and knows how to handle them."

* *Grund*, literally translated, means "ground". *Gestus* is discussed on pp. 146–147 above.

The pivotal point of a gestic incident is expressed through significant movement. In the opening dialogue of Scene 2, Mother Courage and the Cook dispute the value of a capon. The sentence that Brecht uses to summarize this incident is made up of two provocative parts:

Mother Courage sells provisions at exorbitant prices in the Swedish camp before the fortress of Wallhof; while driving a hard bargain over a capon she makes the acquaintance of an army cook who is to play an important part in her life.

There is no room to doubt that Mother Courage charges exorbitantly. The audience must draw the inferences from that. What Bildt (Ernst Busch took over the part in 1951) and Weigel established in the Berlin production was the pleasure that each took in the bargaining. The movement came only on the Cook's question, "You know what I'm going to do?", and represented the initial failure of Mother Courage's attempted blackmail. But this is not a defeat that depresses the businesswoman:

Courage…was amused at the way the cook fished the chunk of rotten beef out of the garbage barrel with the tip of his long meat knife and carried it, carefully as though it were a precious object — though to be kept at a safe distance from one's nose — over to his kitchen table.

If the whole scene, to use Brecht's ironic description, presents "War as a business idyll", this opening exchange gives it an obliquely affectionate aspect.

The writing of the Cook's part gave Brecht some trouble. The earliest typescript records a change of name and nationality. Originally a Swede with the plausible name of Feilinger, he becomes a Dutchman incongruously called Lamb. Brecht was a marvellously mischievous inventor of names, but he makes surprisingly little of this one. The evolution of Jessie Potter, first to Jeanette and then to Yvette Pottier is, rather, from incongruity to plausibility. It was the relationship of these two characters that caused the trouble - and the rewriting. Yvette appears in two scenes (3 and 8), the Cook in four (2, 3, 8 and 9). Their story is a small cautionary tale, inset in a play which is almost as inattentive to it as history always is to such tiny tremors. What is unusual, though, is the Aristotelean treatment Brecht gives it. The technique, that is to say, is of conventional "suspense" drama in which one thing leads to another, rather than that of epic drama, in which one thing simply follows another. We will have noticed, but not remarked on, the Cook's smoking his pipe during Scene 2, but we have no great reason to connect it with the story of Yvette's seduction. It was in Flanders, she explains in Scene 3, and she was sixteen when she fell for a skinny, Dutch army cook. A callow crush, obviously, but how was she to know he had a brunette at the same time, that he was well known to girls as Pete the Pipe, and that his habit of continuing to smoke his pipe while he made love wasn't normal? Now, five years later, she is whore to the soldiers, as ruined a maid as any in Europe. Regine Lutz's singing of the Song of Fraternization was emotional, and her exit "conspicuously whorish". No one on stage openly puts two and two together. There is no indication that Brecht thought of conveying recognition through Kattrin, though Hurwicz almost certainly thought of it herself, as any Kattrin would. Scene 3 is a high point in her dreams of sex. The actual meeting of the Cook and Yvette is delayed until Scene 8, by which time Yvette's vindictiveness has a war-worn irrelevance. A horrific transformation has taken place, though. *Theaterarbeit* contains adjacent photographs of Regine Lutz in the two scenes.[11] In the first, she is flamboyantly *décolleté*, young and attractive. In the second, as the widowed Countess Stahremberg, she is plastered with make-up, obviously bald underneath a black wig, bloated, twisted, and she walks with the aid of a stick. And she is twenty-four years old. It is true that Brecht had several shots at giving Yvette an accurate age, the earliest of which would have made her thirty-nine by Scene 8, and it may be that he was careless of her particular chronology. Even so, the inset story of Pete the Pipe and the ruined maid is not complete until the hideous "old" woman has limped off-stage. But this Aristotelean melodrama is undermined before it even begins. It is undermined in Scene 2 by the mature and knowing relationship struck up between the Cook and Mother Courage as a by-product of business.

Brecht was dissatisfied with the playing of the Swedish general in Scene 2 because it showed too little about the ruling class. The general is drunk. There is a characteristically crafty observation on this. "It need not be clear whether the general drinks in order to honor the soldier or honors the soldier in order to drink." His interest in Eilif is, by implication, homosexual. "It would have been better," Brecht argues in retrospect, "to make him an effete Swedish aristocrat." The idea of inserting a sabre dance as well as a song for Eilif came to Brecht during the rehearsals, and he gives a lot of attention to it in the *Couragemodell*. The carefully composed stage picture has Eilif dancing at the downstage apex of a triangle whose upstage base line joins a crouchingly attentive Mother Courage outside the tent and a decadently lolling general inside it. There is at least a suggestion that if decadence is good business, Eilif is prepared to be decadent. The dance must be performed "with passion as well as ease." Mother Courage's "brave, intelligent son" has the mental and physical agility of a predator. As Mother Courage explained to the recruiting sergeant, "he inherited his father's intelligence; that man could strip the pants off a peasant's arse without his knowing it." We will see Eilif only once more, on the way to his execution. Brecht's eye for indicative *transition*, as distinct from dramatic *development*, is evident in a costume note:

Eilif has a cheap, dented breast plate and is still wearing his frayed trousers. Not until scene 8 (the outbreak of peace) does he wear expensive clothing and gear. He dies rich.

The playing of the scene in the tent involves a third character. It is an inglorious introduction for the Chaplain, who remains stubbornly a minor force in the play, despite the fact that he has the second largest speaking role. It is Eilif whom the general invites to the table, it is with Eilif that he drinks, it is in contrast with Eilif's effectiveness that he jeers at the Chaplain's ineffectiveness. The reasoning is clear: "The general's treatment of the Chaplain is meant to show the role of religion in a war of religion." It is a definitive statement of Brecht's attitude to the holy protestations of Gustavus Adolphus and of his Catholic antagonists. The Chaplain is disregarded in his first scene, and remains in abeyance almost throughout the play. As we shall see, though, he has his moments.

Scene 3 is much the longest in the play, which is almost half over by its end. The wagon is stage right, and it is important that those who stand to the right of it cannot see or be seen by anyone elsewhere on the stage. The rhythms need to be carefully established:

In scene 3 a camp idyll is disrupted by the enemy's surprise attack. The idyll should be composed from the start in such a way as to make it possible to show a maximum of disruption. It must leave room for people to run back and forth in clearly laid-out confusion; the parts of the stage must be able to change their functions.

One other general observation is of significance not only to this scene, but also to the play at large:

Courage's unflagging readiness to work is important. She is hardly ever seen not working. It is her energy and competence that make her lack of success so shattering.

Kattrin takes after her mother. When the scene opens, they are folding washing. (The folding and putting away of linen was one of the exercises Brecht recommended to trainee actors.[12]) At the same time, Mother Courage is haggling with an ordnance officer over the price of black-market bullets. (The exercise has variants in which the actors continue to fold linen whilst feigning a violent quarrel, and even when coming to blows. As we suggested in Chapter 6, the business of folding linen is made strange by its unlikely association with, in this instance, black marketeering, which is, in its turn, alienated by the ordinariness of the domestic actions that punctuate it.) The corruptness of the bargain is as matter-of-fact and almost as regular as household washing: and Mother Courage is unaware of any inconsistency in her following a crooked deal with an admonition to Swiss Cheese to be honest.

There follows one of the three-character episodes of which the play is unusually full. The commentary indicates that Mother Courage took her sewing and sat downstage with Yvette whilst Kattrin removed washing from the makeshift line slung between the wagon and a cannon which has evidently been commandeered and "made strange" as a clothes-prop. Yvette is drinking brandy, an image for Kattrin of sexual indulgence and luxury, and for the audience of sexual disease and desperation. If Kattrin did not already have romantic fantasies, Mother Courage's determination to divert her from them would create them in her. Such protectiveness is provocation. Now Kattrin works and listens to the story of Yvette's downfall. The subsequent episode is further provocation. Brecht's descriptive sentence links the physically separated groups. "While Courage flirts with the cook and the chaplain, mute Kattrin tries on the whore's hat and shoes." This is, in fact, over-compressed. The sexual banter takes place on the main stage, and ends with the Chaplain's randy reference to Kattrin as "this delightful young lady". It is at this point that Mother Courage leads her guests off to the unseeing section of the stage, stage right of the wagon. If it is possible to describe the conversation there as a flirtation, that is only because sexual commerce for Mother Courage is as combative as any other kind of commerce. The Cook's long, sarcastic speech about Gustavus Adolphus and Mother Courage's astonishing counter-attack are among the play's most challenging observations on the war. It was essential that they should be heard, without the distraction of Kattrin's pantomime with boots and hat. To meet this, an addition unrecorded in the published text was made in performance. Yvette's story and the attentions of the Cook and the Chaplain have helped to focus Kattrin's attention on the red boots and the hat. While Mother Courage serves brandy to her guests behind the wagon, Kattrin moves downstage to sit beside the barrel that serves as a table. Mother Courage has meanwhile made her attack on the Poles for butting in when Gustavus Adolphus was marching his army across their landscape, and the Chaplain has reinforced the point with his party-line description of the Swedish King's mission to "free" the people of Poland and Germany from the Emperor's yoke. It is at this point in the published text that the Cook makes his long speech. Not so in performance, where he said no more than, "I see it this way, your brandy's first-rate, I can see why I liked your face, and this war is a war of religion," [13] before breaking into the Lutheran hymn "Ein' feste Burg ist unser Gott". Brecht notes that:

> They sang it with feeling, casting anxious glances around them as though such a song were illegal in the Swedish camp.

It was during this singing that Kattrin tried on hat and boots. A sequence of photographs shows Hurwicz, skirt hoisted and hat plonked on her head like a mob-cap, testing and admiring the boots which comically fail to transform her. She would let the audience laugh at her, though she didn't force it. By the end of the hymn, Kattrin has reduced her activity, and the Cook continues, "…but we were talking about the king." There is scarcely a speech that could be more firmly called "Brechtian" than Mother Courage's reply to his withering dismissal of Gustavus Adolphus. "He can't be defeated because his men believe in him," she says, and continues *earnestly* (the adverb is a masterstroke of ironic genius):

> When you listen to the big wheels talk, they're making war for reasons of piety, in the name of everything that's fine and noble. But when you take another look, you see that they're not so dumb; they're making war for profit. If they weren't, the small fry like me wouldn't have anything to do with it.

"That's a fact," says the Cook as Kattrin gets up and begins her futile imitation of a whorish strut. Behind the wagon, Mother Courage affirms that "We're all good Protestants here! Prosit!" She lifts her glass, and the Catholic attack begins.

The effect on the Chaplain of this turnabout is fascinating. In the episode Brecht entitles "The surprise attack" he is "the fixed point amid all the running and shouting". He "stands still and gets in everybody's way." Scene 3 changes the Chaplain's life. However underrated, he left the General's tent as an accredited priest. When the Catholics attack, he becomes a displaced person. As a hewer of wood or peeler of vegetables, he is clumsy and dependent. A shift of military fortune has forced him to take refuge. As Roy Pascal has shrewdly indicated, there are some contradictions in Brecht's interpretation of the Chaplain. [14] We have to reconcile the statement that the Chaplain "shows no exaggerated involvement in the tragedy of the honest son" with his singing of the beautiful *Horenlied*. In the 1949 production, when Hinz played the part, the *Horenlied* was omitted, but Brecht restored it when Geschonneck took over from Hinz in 1951. He tells us in a note that Geschonneck sang it "quietly and bitterly", [15] but however it is sung, the implied comparison of Swiss Cheese's imminent suffering with Christ's passion indicates the Chaplain's involvement in "the tragedy of the honest son". The same note refers to Geschonneck's "extraordinarily gentle, embarrassed gesture" of protest when Mother Courage tells Kattrin not to howl like a dog because it gives the Chaplain the creeps. Pascal is probably right to relate Brecht's confusion to his simultaneous condemnation and recognition of the ethic of human charity (*Menschlichkeit*). The Young Comrade of *The Measures Taken* was similarly beset by goodness, and certainly the Chaplain's way is not going to improve the human condition. Brecht intends the portrait to be critical, but the compassion of this defeated priest extends the play's emotional range. There is no gainsaying Pascal's conclusion that "when he drops out of the play it is one of those irreparable losses that by the end leave Courage bare." The brief "conversation" between Swiss Cheese and Kattrin is another moment of triumphant humanity. Brecht's note proclaims its purpose and describes its provenance:

The short conversation between mute Kattrin and Swiss Cheese is quiet and not without tenderness. Shortly before the destruction we are shown for the last time what is to be destroyed.

The scene goes back to an old Japanese play in which two boys conclude a friendship pact. Their way of doing this is that one shows the other a flying bird, while the second shows the first a cloud.

The last half of the scene is dominated by the tracking down and killing of Swiss Cheese. The text draws our attention to parallels from the Crucifixion — the *Horenlied* does so openly, but there is also Mother Courage's triple denial of her son and the fact, bluntly stated by Swiss Cheese himself immediately after the mid-scene time-gap, "This is the third day..."; and the notes add, almost gratuitously, another when Brecht describes how Yvette, delighted at the prospect of gain, gives mother Courage "the kiss of Judas" before crawling avidly into the wagon. Helene Weigel's most famous single piece of business, her silent scream when she hears the off-stage volley that signals Swiss Cheese's death, brings that moment into parallel with the horrific instant when the veil of the Temple was rent in twain. This is the only time in the play when Mother Courage reaches an Aristotelian *anagnorisis*. For the rest, as Brecht said, she learns no more from her tragic experiences than a guinea-pig learns from the experiments in which it participates.[16] A superb sequence of photographs captures this extraordinary incident. Weigel is sitting to the left of the barrel-table, and Geschonneck to the right. Four-square to the audience, and almost moronically bewildered, he is drying glasses. In the first photograph, Weigel is leaning forward, mouth wide open, hands scrabbling at the lap of her skirt. In the second, she has thrown her head back as if baying silently to the moon. Her fingers are still tense. Geschonneck wears the puzzled look of a schoolmaster who has just sat on a drawing pin. In the third, Weigel holds the same position, though her fingers are beginning to relax. Geschonneck has gone. Another photograph, out of this sequence, shows him lumbering helplessly across to the wagon. The final picture is of Weigel steadying herself for the next crisis. Her hands lie loose in her lap, her body is slightly hunched, her eyes are closed, and her bottom lip pouts sullenly from a downturned mouth. It is with an expression not unlike this that she will deny any knowledge of the corpse:

When the soldiers come in with the dead boy and she is asked to look at him, she stands up, goes over, looks at him, shakes her head, goes back and sits down. During all this she has an obstinate expression, her lower lip thrust forward. Here Weigel's recklessness in throwing away her character reaches its highest point.

Brecht's admiration for the way in which Weigel defied the audience's wish to see her as Niobe is clear. The actress is here embodying the playwright's intention. The silent scream provides a more technical insight into the actor's craft:

Her look of extreme suffering after she has heard the shots, her unscreaming open mouth and backward-bent head probably derived from a press photograph of an Indian woman crouched over the dead body of her son during the shelling of Singapore. Weigel must have seen it years before, though when questioned she did not remember it. That is how observations are stored up by actors. — Actually it was only in the later performances that Weigel assumed this attitude.

The effect of the superficially incongruous linking of Swiss Cheese's death and Christ's passion is not deflationary. On the one hand it makes the Crucifixion as matter-of-fact as a minor military execution in a nameless village, on the other it augments our sense of loss. That is to say that the audience may evade the Brechtian inference that Christ's self-sacrifice was quite as ineffective as Swiss Cheese's. The wonder is not that he cut the *Horenlied*, but that he had the nerve to restore it.

One final production detail from Scene 3 will show the way in which Brecht the director was able to reinforce the determination of Brecht the writer to give each incident its separate, and often contradictory, status. Yvette's Colonel is a figure of farce, a lustful *senex* out of a *commedia* scenario. "His only function," Brecht explains, "is to show the price the whore must pay for her rise in life; consequently he must be repellent." The actor Pilz used a stick as an image of his lechery:

In his passionate moments he pressed it to the ground so hard that it bent; an instant later snapped straight — this suggested loathsome aggressive impotence and produced an irresistibly comic effect. Considerable elegance is required to keep such a performance within the limits of good taste.

This is the man who might save Swiss Cheese.

Scene 4 is dominated by the Song of the Great Capitulation. Its shape is very clear. Mother Courage begins with a determination to make a complaint. She will not be put off by the clerk. The young soldier begins with a determination to make a complaint. He will not be put off by his older friend. Mother Courage sings her song of capitulation, during which she *learns* what she *teaches*. Neither she nor the soldier makes the complaint. It is evident from the photographs that the young soldier looks remarkably like Eilif. That may, but need not, have been a coincidence. In his notes, Brecht affirms the social significance of the scene:

In no other scene is Courage as depraved as in this one…Nevertheless Weigel's face in this scene shows a glimmer of wisdom and even of nobility, and that is good. Because the depravity is not so much that of her person as that of her class, and because she herself at least rises above it somewhat by showing that she understands this weakness and that it even makes her angry.

The dangers of a Mother Courage who invites the audience to identify with her are vivid in this scene. The intention is not to "increase the spectator's own tendencies to resignation and capitulation" but to "put him in a position to feel the beauty and attraction of a social problem." Actors will overplay this scene unless they understand its social purpose.

In Scene 5 we encounter for the first time a significant event in the Thirty Years War. The sack of Magdeburg was an almost unparalleled atrocity, and a dramatist of pacifist inclinations might have been expected to make much of it. Brecht does no such thing, as the laconic final sentence of the scene's title vividly demonstrates. This may be a famous foreign field, but we are to be confined to some corner of it. "Tilly's victory at Magdeburg costs Mother Courage four officers' shirts." Keith Dickson has brilliantly analysed the historical and geographical background of *Mother Courage*, observing the implication that "the familiar division into 'periods', 'phases' and 'spheres of influence' is a mere textbook convenience which has little to do with the reality of war."[17] Having begun in remote Dalarna (Scene 1), and followed Gustavus Adolphus through an ill-defined Poland (Scenes 2, 3 and 4), the play picks at the hem of Magdeburg in Scene 5, nods towards the skirmish in Ingolstadt made significant only by the death of Tilly (Scene 6), passes along a highway somewhere in Europe (Scene 7), acknowledges *en passant* the death of Gustavus Adolphus at Lutzen (Scene 8), takes Mother Courage through Germany (Scenes 9 and 10) to Halle, "which changed hands so many times that historians do not bother to keep the score"[18] (Scene 11), and ends with the highway to nowhere-in-particular opening up again.

With the mortgage on Magdeburg's life foreclosed, Mother Courage fights to retain her own property interests, and in Scene 5 she ends fairly even — four shirts down and one fur coat up. The scene is a whirl of movement which leans heavily on farce conventions. Consider, for instance, Brecht's description of the gestic composition of two central sequences. The first comes under the sentence heading, "Kattrin threatens her mother":

With the help of one soldier the chaplain has carried a wounded woman out of the house, then an old peasant whose arm is dangling. Again he calls for linen and all look at Mother Courage who lapses into silence. Angrily Kattrin seizes a plank and threatens her mother. The chaplain has to take it away from her. He picks Courage up, sets her down on a chest, and takes some officers' shirts.

Kattrin's rage is real, but the Chaplain's treatment of both her and Mother Courage is deflationary. There are many such moments in early film comedies, moments, say, when the fury of two "little" men is easily quelled by the muscle power of the "big" policeman. The second sequence is more telling still. It comes under the heading, "At the risk of her life Kattrin saves an infant":

Still struggling with the chaplain, Courage sees her daughter rush into the house that is threatening to cave in, to save a baby. Tugged both ways, between Kattrin and the officers' shirts, she runs about until the shirts are torn into bandages and Kattrin comes out of the house with the infant. Now she runs after Kattrin to make her get rid of the baby. (Movements: Kattrin with the baby runs counter-clockwise around the wounded, then clockwise around the wagon.)

The chase routine is a time-honoured staple of farce, but the snatched prop here is a baby, and the obstacle round which they have to manoeuvre is a severely wounded peasant woman. There is a splendid photograph which shows Kattrin centre-stage, wrapped in a swirl of skirt about to weave round the wagon (clock-wise), and Weigel downstage right in hot pursuit. Just opening up to her view is the Chaplain, plodding away from the wagon tearing a shirt. It is Weigel's suddenness of lithe action, the spring of a tigress, that emerges vividly from the photographs of this scene. For the unknowing Kattrin, this baby foreshadows death, but at the moment she is triumphant, as Brecht indicates in a powerful note:

At the end of the scene Kattrin lifted the baby into the air, while Courage rolled up the fur coat and threw it into the wagon: both women had their share of the spoils.

It is in Scene 5 that the smouldering relationship of mother and daughter blazes for the first and only time. There is no doubt that Brecht invested more emotion in this continuing portrait of hostile dependence than he intended. It was probably to counter it that he claimed, in a note to Scene 5, that "it is necessary to show an intelligent Kattrin from the start." It is not, he insists, her infirmity but the war that breaks her. The note is contentious and question-begging. It may be "wrong", but it is certainly possible to play Kattrin as a dumb idiot with a golden instinct. To say she is "intelligent" is to say too little. Intelligent in comparison with whom? Not, surely, with even the Chaplain, who shows surprising resolution in this scene. Brecht calls him, in another retrospective note, "part scoundrel, part superior intelligence". We would expect some criticism of his "heroism" here, knowing something of Brecht's attitude to heroism. What we get is that certainly, but also a startling insight. "He acts in a spirit deriving from the realization that in the last analysis he himself was one of the oppressed. When he helps the injured, it becomes clear that he too is to be pitied."

There is nothing more surprising in Scene 6 than the bitter eloquence with which the Chaplain explains the longevity of war. If Brecht intended cynicism to dominate, he cannot deny us the suspicion that such cynicism is mixed with despair. There are two notes about the Chaplain's marriage proposal. The first is characteristically insistent on the fact that Mother Courage changes from scene to scene:

Mother Courage has changed. Increasing prosperity has made her softer and more human. Both qualities attract the chaplain and he proposes to her. For the first time we see her sitting briefly at rest, not working.

The second is one of those curt pieces of deceptive blandness with which Brecht's prose is enriched:

He chops clumsily, complaining that his talents are lying fallow, and, probably with a view to avoiding physical labour, asks her to marry him.

It ought to be made clear in the playing that the proposal is a commercial speculation. The Chaplain wants to share the profits instead of merely providing the labour. But that is not all. The sight of Mother Courage pulling at the Cook's pipe excites a latent rivalry in the man of God. He longs for security, no doubt, and a status higher than that of a labourer, but there is sexual attraction too. No actor worth his salt will miss the opportunity of demonstrating this as he chops wood whilst reviling the "scheming Don Juan" to whom the pipe originally belonged.

The folding of linen in Scene 3 is paralleled in Scene 6 by the taking of the inventory of stock. Off-stage, Tilly is being buried. "The pause during the funeral march must be long," says Brecht, "otherwise the funeral scene will not produce the right effect." Weigel added a line of her own to the funeral "oration" Brecht wrote for Mother Courage. The text has: "...conquer the world, for instance, that's a nice ambition for a general, he doesn't know any better"; and Weigel, still taking the inventory, inserted, "Jesus Christ, the worms have got into my biscuits." Brecht accepted the extra sentence, knowing that the worms would soon be getting into Tilly as well. Weigel was responsive to the technique Brecht noted in Brueghel's "Fall of Icarus". The big event goes on in the background, criticized and alienated by the small event in the foreground. In the Berlin production, the stage picture was given added tension by having the catholic Clerk stand to check that Mother Courage said nothing traitorous during her mourning for Tilly. It is a nice example of Brechtian irony that he finds nothing to which he can take exception.

At the end of Scene 6, Mother Courage curses the war, but in Scene 7, exultant beside the bandaged Kattrin and the dejected Chaplain, she sings a song in spirited defence of it. Brecht notes that "in this short scene Weigel showed Courage in the full possession of her vitality, as previously only in scene 5;...in scene 5, however, she was gloomy; here she was cheerful."

The year is 1632 — that is to say that eight years have elapsed since the opening scene — and the unlocated highway of Scene 7 brings the wagon, in Scene 8, towards Lutzen. The brutal significance of distance and time in a world where communications are slow is a central issue in this scene. It takes three weeks for the news of Gustavus Adolphus' death to reach Mother Courage's wagon. On the Chaplain's advice - or so she claims - she has stocked up for continuing war. Now she learns that there has been peace for three weeks. But what does "peace" mean? The skirmishes and the pillaging have continued along Mother Courage's route. In one of them, Eilif has killed a peasant woman and stolen her cattle. A similar deed made him a hero in Scene 2. In Scene 8 he is to be shot — because news of the peace had not reached him in time, and because peace, unlike war, gives to murder its real name. The irony, though, is taken even further. Mother Courage returns with the news that war restarted three days ago. Eilif is shot in the ten minutes of ignorant peace; but he is innocent of the atrocity for which he is punished, because "in fact" (although what has fact to do with the little victims of the war?) the truce was over when he killed the woman. In a technical sense Eilif dies a hero, but no one will ever notice. Mother Courage does not even know he is dead. Talking happily to the Cook as she readies the wagon for departure, she wonders whether she will see her son tonight, not knowing that "she is going to ride over his grave." That is Brecht's note on this poignant exit. He makes no comment on Mother Courage's reference to Eilif, surely in the hearing of Kattrin, as "my favourite", but he does record a production detail that says a lot about Kattrin's increasingly pitiable state:

While they are packing, Kattrin appears. She sees the cook staring at her scar, covers it with her hand and turns away. She has come to fear the light.

Again in scene 11, when the soldiers drag her out of the wagon, she holds her hand over her eye.

The Chaplain, of course, worries her less, but the Cook is a sexual force. When the Chaplain, with pathetic optimism, goes behind the wagon to put on his clerical robes, Mother Courage and the Cook sit on the wooden bench in front of it. "Amid the ringing of the bells they sit there almost like lovers." Yvette's attempt to discredit Pete the Pipe is counter-productive, as Mother Courage suggestively assures him:

It hasn't lowered you in my estimation. Far from it. Where there's smoke there's fire. Coming?

The invitation is unambiguous. The Chaplain has lost his cockfight with the Cook. His time is over. Brecht has a graphic note on his return in priestly dress:

When the chaplain comes back — he stands in the middle of the stage like a last incisor in a toothless mouth — the cook begins to demolish him.

The Chaplain makes a last bid for attention, during which he dubs Mother Courage "a battlefield hyena", and then surrenders:

Hinz as the chaplain obtained a powerful and natural effect when, suddenly throwing all his arrogance to the winds, he begged the cook not to squeeze him out of his place with Courage, because, having become a better man, he could no longer practise the clergyman's profession. His fear of losing his job lent him a new dignity.

Some of that dignity asserts itself again when he accompanies a snivelling Eilif to his drab death. We will see neither again, and the whole effect of Scene 8's emotionally complex conclusion is to draw attention to Mother Courage's incapacity to learn the truth about loss.

Two years later, in Scene 9, Mother Courage and the Cook are reduced to begging for food, though they beg from the strength of words rather than the weakness of avowed hunger. The constant shifts in fortune should be vivid in production. Brecht is not a reticent writer, nor is he recording gradual progress. It is an exceptionally severe winter, and the Cook and Mother Courage are in shabby sheepskins. The Cook unharnesses himself "morosely" and puts it to Mother Courage that they should go to Utrecht. He ignores what we cannot fail to notice, that this is a *three*-character scene again. In fact, Kattrin dominates the scene for the audience. A shrewd note insists:

In this scene the cook must not under any circumstances be represented as brutal. The tavern he has inherited is too small to keep three people, and the customers cannot be expected to put up with the sight of the disfigured Kattrin. Courage does not find his arguments unreasonable.

Nevertheless, she rejects them. Weigel made it plain, during the begging song, that she was thinking things over. Her sexual partnership with the Cook is at risk, and she is ready to lose the wagon, or to sell it. Her cogitation is "desperate", but by the end of the song, she has decided to decline the Cook's offer, and she goes into the presbytery just for the sake of the soup. It is now that Kattrin, through the lewdly symbolic placing of the Cook's trousers over Mother Courage's skirt, provides her own interpretation of the scene. It is a combination of altruism (she "decides to spare her mother the need to make a decision") and disgust. Hurwicz accompanied it with a barely stifled "uncanny, malignant giggle". The motherhood of Mother Courage is once again fully exposed; there is a degree of truth in her disavowal, although it cannot be taken completely at face value:

...don't go thinking I've given him the gate on your account. It's the wagon, I'm used to it, it's not you, it's the wagon.

On the first of those sentences, Weigel pushed a spoonful of soup into Hurwicz's mouth. Brecht's note on the final moments of the scene gives a vivid indication of the careful pacing of the Berlin production:

Scenes of this kind must be fully acted out: Courage and Kattrin harness themselves to the wagon, push it back a few feet so as to be able to circle the presbytery, and then move off to the right. [stage left] The cook comes out, still chewing on a piece of bread, sees his belongings, picks them up and goes off to the rear with long steps. We see him disappear. Thus the parting of the ways is made visible.

We will have noted that, for the first time, Mother Courage is sharing the job of pulling the wagon. Ernst Busch as Cook underlined the sexual significance of her departure by letting his pipe fall out of his mouth.

The text of Scene 10 consists simply of the two stanzas of the "song of Home", sung off-stage by a solo voice. It is a song of comfort and of staying still. Its emotional reference is to the tavern in Utrecht where Mother Courage might have taken refuge, or to Kattrin's lost dreams of a home, and the visual image contrasts the still facade of the peasant house with the two silent women pausing momentarily in their weary trudge to Halle. "They hear the voice from the peasant house, stop, listen, and start off again. What goes on in their minds should not be shown; the audience can imagine." In his Munich production of the play Brecht admitted a variant that amply illustrates his fondness for irony. "...the song was sung with unfeeling, provocative self-assurance. The arrogant pride of possession expressed in the singing turned the listeners on the road into damned souls."

Brecht was probably unwilling to admit the extent to which the fortunes of Kattrin had gripped his imagination. We have noted, in the commentary on Scene 5, his questionable insistence that "it is necessary to show an intelligent Kattrin from the start." He was fearful of the psychological speculations her mute heroism inspired in audiences and hoped to cast some intellectual doubts on them:

The whole point is missed if her love of children is depreciated as mindless animal instinct. Her saving of the city of Halle is an intelligent act. How else would it be possible to bring out what must be brought out, namely, that here the most helpless creature of all is ready to help?

The question is not an honest one. Brecht must have known that the point he is stressing makes itself in performance, regardless of "intelligence". If Kattrin appears intelligent at all, it is only because of the stupidity of the Catholic soldiers whom she "outwits". Kattrin's death is, by any reckoning, an emotional climax, and Hurwicz played it to the full. There is a photograph of the melodramatically splayed death-gesture, and Brecht's commentary records that "Kattrin falls forward, the drumsticks in her drooping hands strike one full beat followed by a feeble beat." What he does not stress in his observations is the near-knockabout comedy that magnificently threatens the solemnity of the scene. Elevated on the small roof-structure stage right, Kattrin is physically as well as emotionally out of reach of the ridiculous soldiers and pathetic peasants. The idea of knocking her off with a pine tree is daft enough, but the decision to prevent the drum from waking Halle by drowning it with *more* noise is dafter. Brecht's note, whilst recording honestly a directorial decision, is disingenuously po-faced:

Such scenes as the one where the peasant tries to drown the noise of Kattrin's drumming by chopping wood must be fully acted out. As she drums, Kattrin must look down at the peasant and accept the challenge. In tempestuous scenes the director needs a certain amount of stubbornness to make miming of this sort last long enough.

In general, the notes on this scene display Brecht's anxiety, and conceal his pride. But pride there was. He knew he had outplayed the traged-ians at their own game, and was embarrassed, merely, to take home the prize.

For the play's final scene, the set pieces of Scene 11, the house and barn, were removed. On an otherwise empty stage stood the wagon, with the three peasants standing uncomfortably in front of it, and Mother Courage on her knees, pillowing the head of her dead daughter. The lullaby was sung "without any sentimentality":

By slight emphasis on the "you", Weigel portrayed Courage's treacherous hope of bringing her child, and perhaps hers alone, through the war. To this child who had lacked even the most ordinary things, she promised the most extraordinary.

The businesswoman will make even a lullaby competitive, and though she learns that Kattrin is dead, Mother Courage learns nothing else. When the peasants have gone, she "goes to the wagon, unrolls the cord which Kattrin had until then been pulling, takes a stick, examines it, pulls the loop of the second cord through, wedges the stick under her arm and moves off." The stage is as it was in Scene 1, and the off-stage voices sing a third stanza of the song Mother Courage had sung at the beginning. The revolve turns and Mother Courage describes a full circle on it. "Of course the audience would understand if it [the wagon] were simply pulled away. When it goes on rolling there is a moment of irritation...But when it goes on still longer, a deeper understanding sets in." Michael Morley interestingly compares this conclusion with the tear-jerking walk-offs of Charlie Chaplin at the end of so many of his films, but he fails to allow that such an allusion may be critical.[19]* Brecht is not aiming to celebrate the brave and beaten life of a great woman, but to expose the dependence of the exploiters on the collaboration of the exploited. He could accept that the part may be played in more than one way — his Munich Courage was Therese Giehse, heavy, big-breasted, an image of motherhood against the spare, lithe figure of Helene Weigel — but he consistently inveighed against interpretations that turned Mother Courage into a Niobe weeping for her lost children. In an observation made during the sixth year of the Berliner Ensemble production, he emphasized a point that any actress of Mother Courage would be wise to bear in mind. "Weigel's way of playing Mother Courage was hard and angry; that is, her Mother Courage was not angry; she herself, the actress, was angry." Performed as Brecht wished it to be performed, this is not a play about an individual but about society. "If lives are worth anything," says the Philosopher of the *Messingkauf Dialogues*, "it is for and by means of society."

*In *Plays and Players* (February 1978), Sally Aire records an occasion when Peggy Mount, playing Mother Courage at Birmingham, abandoned her wagon on-stage because the revolve broke. Of the alternatives open to an actress, this was not, we take it, the most "Brechtian". But what is?

8

In Search of a Theatre

Brecht begins his short poem, "Understanding",[1] written in about 1928, with a ringing stanza:

> I can hear you saying:
> He talks of America
> He understands nothing about it
> He has never been there.
> But believe you me
> You understand me perfectly well when I talk of America
> And the best thing about America is
> That we understand it.

The idea of America, of course, is one thing. The other thing, the feverish actuality of America, Brecht first experienced in 1935. Earlier in the same year he had visited Moscow, where he had not only discussed plans for the publication of the German language periodical *Das Wort*, but also witnessed and been affected by the performance of the Chinese actor Mei-lan-Fan. Not that the visit had been a wild success. Living through his third year of exile in Denmark, Brecht found his morale threatened by a lack of recognition and a lack of theatrical outlets. The news from New York that the Theatre Union proposed to produce *The Mother* was a tonic; but the adaptation, when it reached him, seemed to him a naturalistic betrayal of his epic intentions. It was also a political betrayal by what he believed to be a workers' theatre, promoted by the American Communist Party. Brecht stormed off a verse letter correcting the bias of the adaptation, and challenging the actors to have faith in the worker-audience. Shortly before, he had written for Ruth Berlau's small company of amateurs about to embark on a production of the same play the long poem "Speech to Danish

Working-Class Actors on the Art of Observation". He was not to know that the Theatre Union was a very different organization, not all of whose members were communists and the majority of whose audience was liberal middle-class. His attempt, by personal intervention, to change the style and intention of the performance ended in violent confrontations and led to his being banned from the theatre. Brecht could plausibly assume that the production's disastrous failure was a result of culpable misconception by lily-livered American professionals with a blind faith in culinary theatre. If he did so, his experience at the Riddersalen Theatre in Copenhagen exactly a year later must have been a rude shock. Despite one bitter disagreement,[2] Brecht had no fundamental quarrel with Per Knutzon's carefully non-Aristotelian staging of the world premiere of *Round Heads and Pointed Heads*; but it was another flop. There could no longer be much doubt that what Brecht conceived of as concrete social realities communicated themselves to his audience as abstract social proposals. The American debacle suggested that *The Mother* would forfeit its political integrity if the actors gave it a concrete humanity, and its theatrical future if they did not. The communist critics had raised disturbingly similar objections to the 1932 production in Berlin. Together with the Copenhagen disappointment, it was sufficient to bring to an end the most pedagogic phase of Brecht's writing. Like Ezra Pound's Florealis, on whose soul nine adulteries, twelve liaisons, sixty-four fornications, and something approaching a rape "rest lightly", Brecht had agreed to mask his temperament and "pass for both bloodless and sexless".

The new phase, the one which includes all Brecht's greatest plays, was mischievously intimated in June 1935, when Brecht let it be known that he was working with Hanns Eisler on an operetta about a woman pirate, with an eye to persuading Mae West to take the lead; but *Senora Carrar's Rifles* was the first actual product. It may have been the work on this play that Brecht had in mind when he wrote to Karl Korsch:

I could not help being very pleased, after *Roundheads*, that my residence permit was renewed. And, moreover, I have friends enough who tell me that I must choose either a reactionary content or a reactionary form; both together would be too much of a good thing. And a prominent communist said, "if that is communism, I am not a communist". Perhaps he is right.[3]

Certainly the form of *Senora Carrar's Rifles* is reactionary; far more reactionary than Synge's *Riders to the Sea*, which provided the incentive

Charles Laughton as Galileo, 1947. "What attracted L. about Galileo was not only one or two formal points but also the sheer substance." (Willett, *Brecht on Theatre*, p. 164)

for the play. It is not, after all, the arguments that convince Senora Carrar to join the fight against the Generals, but the death of her son. The debate has a sputtering life in the attempts of the Priest to defend his passivity, but for the Senora herself, and through her for a majority of the audience, it is so much wasted breath. Her change of heart is as unconnected to the play as any in an eighteenth century sentimental drama. This is the least affecting of Brecht's studies of motherhood, a step back from Pelagea Vlassova before the massive advance to Mother Courage.

Such an advance could only be made when Brecht had checked his head-long preparedness to compromise too far with a sentimental theatre. His long struggle with *The Life of Galileo* marks off the phases of his mature concern with concrete theatrical realities. In that respect, as well as others, *Galileo* is the centrepiece of Brecht's work. To follow its metamorphoses from the first draft, written in three weeks in November 1938, through the version prepared in collaboration with Charles Laughton for its American opening in July 1947, to the form in which it was presented by the Berliner Ensemble five months after Brecht's death is to watch at work a playwright who never rested on his laurels.[4] It is also to observe that peculiarly Brechtian balance of power between the right word and the right stage business. Galileo is one of the great battlefields of a conflict Brecht could not resolve. Instead, he came to accept it as the dialectical aspect of his dramaturgy. On the one hand was the reactionary theatre, with its love of crisis and climax; on the other was the epic theatre, where each verbal transaction, however "cool", illustrates the social *Gestus* that is its *raison d'être*. Brecht was always unwilling to acknowledge in print his own mastery of the pregnant moment, preferring to emphasize in the staging of such moments the means whereby their social significance could be pointed. Even in so short a scene as the second of *Galileo*, when Venice receives its telescope, there are ten distinct *gests*. In rehearsal, Brecht would bring them out lingeringly. His vigorous endorsement of Charles Laughton's habit of worrying at the meaning of Galileo's words is typical: "One has to rehearse as if the play could go on for twelve hours."[5]

The text of *Galileo* exists in three distinct versions. In the first, which was used for the performance in Zurich in 1943, Galileo's recantation is not emphatically "criminal", nor is the harshness to his daughter inexcusable. The collaboration with Charles Laughton began in 1944, and encouraged a fuller development of Galileo's bodily self-indulgence:

> All of them, the way they carry their bellies around
> You'd think it was swag with someone in pursuit of it
> But the great man Laughton performed his like a poem
> For his edification and nobody's discomfort.[6]

They had been working for many months when, on 6 August 1945, the atom bomb was dropped on Hiroshima. "Overnight," wrote Brecht in his preface to the American edition, "the biography of the founder of modern physics read differently." It is a sensational overstatement, though not to overstate at that time would have been shameful, and it misleadingly suggests that Hiroshima rewrote the play. What is certain is that the Laughton Galileo carries a heavier burden of historical guilt than the 1938 original. But Laughton's Galileo ran to tend Virginia when she fainted at the realization that her hopes of marriage were dead. The Galileo of the final version works on while Andrea and the Little Monk rush to her aid. Brecht's determination to obstruct simple admiration of Galileo is wholly in line with his anti-heroic, anti-empathetic ideas of both theatre and politics. Hiroshima provides one explanation of the progressive hardening. The intervening awareness that even Helene Weigel's abrasive Mother Courage could be met with love and tears by a preconditioned audience provides another. There are many more. Spotting the variations is not an idle task when the subject is so rich, but the abiding qualities should not be ignored.

A theatre out of touch with the great movements of its time was anathema to Brecht. For him, the task of the sister arts of drama was "to entertain the children of the scientific age, and to do so with sensuousness and humour."⁷ *Galileo* is the only major play by Brecht that avowedly takes a historical figure as its central character, but it does so because that figure is a scientist and because ours is an age of science. Through Galileo, Brecht asks questions about the scientific attitude. Galileo is *dissatisfied* with the present state of knowledge. He is a specialist in the very art of *observation* which Brecht commended to the Danish working-class actors. Through the telescope he sees mountains on the moon, whereas the Venetian senators, inward-looking, fail even to observe "a common pedlar on the next corner hawking that same tube for a song". Unlike the scientist Galileo, the senators take things for granted. But the scientific attitude requires *doubt*. In his confession to Andrea, the old and almost blind Galileo insists that "Science trades in knowledge distilled from doubt." Dissatisfaction, observation, and doubt – the animators of scientific progress – are the animators of social progress too. And they are the essential ingredients of *Verfremdung*. So it is that Brecht's theatre of a scientific age is also a theatre of social revolution. The historical Galileo was not a champion of the people, but neither was he unaware of the threats to the established order of things that his discoveries represented. Not surprisingly, Brecht has pressed the point a lot further. The labourers in Ludovico Marsili's vineyards, the peasants of the Campagna among whom the Little Monk grew up, the Florentine artisans, "all Italy, down to the last stableboy, is prattling about the phases of Venus and thinking at the same time of many irksome things which are held in our schools and elsewhere to be immutable." The quotation is from the critical Scene 12, in which the Inquisitor alerts Pope Urban VIII to the menace of the new astronomy. The carnival scene, 10, has provided us with the evidence already, for the song of the ballad-singer and his wife is a call to social disobedience. Brecht's revisions make the point with increasing vehemence, giving substance to Keith Dickson's indignant riposte: "It is hardly playing fair with a historical character to invent a social revolution and then blame him for betraying it." And yet, why not? As with his adaptation of *Coriolanus*, Brecht is not concerned to dramatize history, but to X-ray it. His Galileo, not history's, is conscious that he has betrayed the people. "The battle to measure the sky was won by doubt; but credulity still prevents the Roman housewife from winning her battle for milk," he confesses to Andrea. That is one aspect of Galileo's criminal recantation. The crime against science is not dissociable from it, though Galileo does not realize the association until the penultimate scene. To his conforming pupil Filippo Mucius, he says in Scene 9, "Not to know the truth is just stupid. To know the truth and call it a lie is criminal!" Such scientific absolutism is of a piece with his submission in Scene 4 that "as scientists we have no business asking what the truth may lead to." Hiroshima (and poison gas) has destroyed human confidence in the disinterested pursuit of knowledge, and the Galileo who delivers his recognition speech to Andrea "in lecture style" accepts a terrible guilt:

As a scientist I had a unique opportunity. . .If I had held out, scientists might have developed something like the physicians' Hippocratic oath, the vow to use their knowledge only for the good of mankind.

To confuse this view with Brecht's would be a mistake. Such power never lay within the grasp of the historical Galileo. But what we are looking at is a play, not a tract. From the standpoint of supreme intelligence, Brecht's Galileo, like Goethe's Faust, makes decisions that are, for mankind, exemplary. Through him, the theatre audience is offered the chance to observe, to doubt, and to be dissatisfied.

The subject of the play is so urgent, and its mode of argument so beguiling, that criticism often surrenders to it. Most of what has just been said, and much of what has been written about *Galileo* over the years, might equally well have been said about an historical novel, a political essay, or a scientific apology. Whilst this is a fault, it is an understandable one. *Galileo* is a doctrinally fascinating debate play, threatened in the theatre by an audience's impatience with other people's conversations. This is not to say that Brecht's Galileo could ever fall as flat as does the Isaac Newton of Shaw's *In Good King Charles's Golden Days*, a play written at much the same time and with some of the same concerns. But the play is both wordy and static, and its dramatic energy is not infrequently squandered by Brecht's willingness to exploit Galileo as a Socratic instigator of doubt, somewhat after the manner of the Philosopher in *The Messingkauf Dialogues*. Laughton's cuts are not difficult to defend. The saving theatrical grace is the superbly realized portrait of Galileo's appetite. In the opening scene, stripped to the waist, he washes himself with pleasure. His instruction to the boy Andrea is, "Put the milk on the table, but don't shut any books." Good milk amid good books. The association is maintained and enriched throughout the play. Cardinal Barberini, transformed before our very eyes into Pope Urban VIII, speaks a truth we have experienced when he tells the Inquisitor in Scene 12 that Galileo "gets pleasure out of more things than any man I ever met. Even his thinking is sensual. He can never say no to an old wine or a new idea." Such zest for life, such ungentlemanly gusto reincarnates Baal and forecasts Azdak. Like Azdak again, Galileo protects his appetite with peasant cunning. His monomania is tempered by fear. If the culmination of the argument is Scene 14, the culmination of the play is Scene 13, that magnificently sparse cliff-hanger, slung between Andrea's furious despair, "Unhappy the land that has no heroes!", and Galileo's dialectical counterthrust, "No. Unhappy the land that needs a hero." If the play ended there, its Aristotelean strength would be greater, its tragic hero, like a blinded Oedipus, dwindling towards death. The remaining scenes, in effect a kind of epilogue, shift the focus outwards. Even so, the dominance of Galileo is undeniable, and Brecht was obviously disturbed by it. He described the first draft in his *Arbeitsjournal* as "opportunistic" (he was, after all, still hungry for theatrical success), deceiving himself as well as later critics.

There is a superficial opportunism also in the writing of *Mother Courage and Her Children*. With characteristic discretion, Brecht had inconspicuously crossed from Denmark into Sweden in early 1939. The Swedish actress Naima Wifstrand, who had translated *Senora Carrar's Rifles*, offered Helene Weigel some teaching in her acting school. With a whiff of hope in his nostrils, Brecht wrote *Mother Courage* in about five weeks. Had Wifstrand completed a translation, she would presumably have created the role, with Helene Weigel supporting her as the necessarily "dumb" Kattrin. The composition of *Mother Courage* interrupted work on *The Good Person of Setzuan*, a project for which Brecht had higher hopes. "When writing for one's store cupboard,"he noted, "there is no need to make concessions."[9] As early as 1927 he had recorded the idea of writing about a prostitute, Fanny Kress, who disguises herself as a cigar merchant in order to be of economic assistance to others. A few years later came a slightly more detailed sketch for a five-scene piece in which the prostitute's male disguise as proprietor of a cigar shop does not interrupt her profitable night-trade. On the contrary, it allows her scope as her own pimp. The proposed title of the play is a potent oral pun. *Die Ware Liebe* sounds like "True Love" (*wahr* meaning "true"), but means something more like "Love is a Commodity" (*Ware* meaning "goods, wares"). The idea is a pleasing one, offering space to the comic spirit that is surprisingly sporadic in *The Good Person*. Some of Brecht's enthusiasm for the play may have been swallowed by the work he did with Weill on the ballet of *The Seven Deadly Sins* in 1933. The seven deadly sins may bring Anna and others happiness, but the need in the jungle of the seven cities is to commit the bourgeois virtues. The paradox survives in the Courtroom of the final version of *The Good Person* when the policeman steps forward to explain:

Miss Shen Teh was a young lady who wished to be nice to everyone, who lived and let live as they say. Mr. Shui Ta on the other hand, is a man of principles.

Western literature has had a long-lived interest in the split personality, to which Germany contributed the Gothic *Doppelgänger*. Its healthy aspect is reflected in countless comedies about the adventures of identical twins, but the nineteenth century's concern with psychology had given it a morbid turn. Poe's *William Wilson* and Stevenson's *Dr Jekyll and Mr Hyde* stand out from a mass of mediocre work intended sensationally to polarize good and evil in a single personality. Both on the continent and in England, the comedy of identical twins had descended into the melodrama of *The Corsican Brothers* and *The Lyons Mail*, and the notion of the disintegrating personality had been accorded a word of its own in 1912, "schizophrenia". From such a tradition Brecht wished emphatically to dissociate himself, and the shift of setting from the Berlin of *Die Ware Liebe* to the semi-mythical Chinese city of Setzuan is an element in that dissociation. *The Good Person of Setzuan* is imprecisely in debt to oriental modes of performance, a debt which can be broadly inferred from Brecht's essay, "Alienation Effects in Chinese

Acting". [10] Over one incident, the correspondence between the essay and the play is exact. In the essay Brecht recalls a performance at the New York Yiddish Theatre of a play which Eric Bentley has identified as *Haunch, Paunch and Jowl*. The incident concerns a woman's complaint that the compensation for an injury done to her leg in a traffic accident has been bungled, and now "It's started to heal up":

Working without the A-effect, the theatre was unable to make use of this exceptional scene to show the horror of a bloody epoch. Few people in the audience noticed it; hardly anyone who reads this will remember that cry. The actress spoke the cry as if it were something perfectly natural. But it is exactly this – the fact that this poor creature finds such a complaint natural – that she should have reported to the public like a horrified messenger returning from the lowest of all hells. To that end she would of course have needed a special technique which would have allowed her to underline the historical aspect of a specific social condition. Only the A-effect makes this possible.

The injury to Wang's hand in *The Good Person* is a reworking of the incident, and it is Brecht's aim to call attention, not to the particular helplessness of Wang, but to the fact that Wang finds that helplessness natural. His acceptance illustrates the general inability of society to serve its own best interests under capitalism. Shen Teh splits off Shui Ta from herself when she recognizes that general inability. In the western psychological tradition, the mask of Shui Ta would be a mask of evil. But Shui Ta is not evil, he is *respectable*. That is Brecht's ironic masterstroke. Shen Teh will commit perjury to bring Wang his compensation, but Shui Ta knows that she "was not present when the trifling incident took place", and is confident that Wang "wouldn't want her to ruin herself completely by telling anything other than the truth."

This is one of the incidents in which the whole action of the play is embedded. The gods are by instinct conservative, but they have the kind of tired commitment to ethics that keeps every conservative government in touch with the middle classes. Unless they can find a good person, they will have to change the world. They will have, that is to say, to recognize that goodness is overwhelmed in the prevailing condition of society. Their discovery of Shen Teh prevents a world revolution. Shen Teh discovers, on the contrary, that goodness is the very thing that demands a world revolution. Her compassion for the common man is not shared by the common man. If it were (or when it is) the world must be changed. Until then Shui Ta, the man of principle, the counter-revolutionary, must protect her. A possible version of the parable would have Shen Teh trapped for ever in the body of her "murderer" Shui Ta. But in Brecht's version, a fugitive Shen Teh escapes continually to perpetuate altruism; and those fugitive acts are sufficient to satisfy the undemanding gods. As they vanish slowly from the courtroom on their incongruous pink cloud, she plays her desperate last card: "But I need my cousin!":

The First God: Not too often!
Shen Teh: At least once a week!
The First God: Once a month: that will do!

No better resolution is offered by the play. With a sly devotion to his principles, Brecht leaves the next step to the audience.

With that as its action, and with Brecht to write the plot, *The Good Person of Setzuan* ought to be a better play. It starts superbly, with the borrowed simplicity of oriental story-telling, and direct addresses to the audience are confidently handled throughout. It is in the middle scenes, from 4 to 7, that Brecht's control of his material slackens. The plotting becomes fussy, the transitions from Shen Teh to Shui Ta are handled with surprising gracelessness, too much is expected of minor characters like Shu Fu the barber and Mrs Mi Tzu the householder, and even the love of Shen Teh for Yang Sun falters towards the merely conceptual. In June 1940 Brecht commented that "No play has ever given me so much trouble." Perhaps, as a result, he abandoned it a stage too early, failing to prune what he had planted. There is a descriptive sentence in the essay on Chinese acting that may be relevant: "He acts in such a way that nearly every sentence could be followed by a verdict of the audience and practically every gesture is submitted for the public's approval." The middle scenes of *The Good Person* are full of gestures and sentences that demand from the audience a response on behalf of human society. For the sake of the play, several of them should have been cut. For the sake of politics, they were left in. It is questionable whether the political points are strengthened. Ronald Gray speaks for many English-speaking critics in arguing that "the play does no more than state the basic problem underlying all politics: how to create a just society out of a crowd of largely unjust individuals."[11] The fact that Gray is wrong is less significant here than the fact that he can get away with it. Part of the problem is that Brecht has been too clever. According to the play's notional pattern, and certainly in the surface responses of the audience, Shen Teh's polar opposite is Shui Ta. In the event, Shui Ta's function is absorbed by Yang Sun. The kind of intellectual satisfaction that an audience gains from recognizing a pattern cannot be slighted, and the fact that our first encounter with Yang Sun is a sympathetic one makes the adjustment even harder. There are times in the tender wooing dialogue of Shen Teh and Yang Sun when Brecht seems emotionally committed to the willow pattern. The change from the soft-spoken lover of Scene 3 to the ruthless individualist of Scene 5 is too bad to be true, and the play never recovers its dialectical balance. How much can be won back in performance will depend on the intelligence of the actors.

Brecht completed a first draft of *The Good Person* in Finland, to which he had fled when the *Wehrmacht* entered Denmark and Norway in April 1940. Almost at once he embarked on a new and unique project, a play which was eventually titled *Mr Puntila and his Man Matti*. Puntila himself has a family resemblance to the gluttonous Galileo and a split personality less optional and more extreme that Shen Teh's, but the play is not very much like any other by Brecht. Its peculiar provenance is a major reason for that. Hella Wuolijoki, on whose estate in Kausala Brecht was living, had written a play about a Finnish landowner who when he was drunk was very very jolly, and when he was sober was horrid. She now proposed that she and Brecht should rewrite it as an entry for a Finnish folk-play competition. It may be that Brecht's initial involvement in this manifestly opportunistic undertaking was half-hearted. Certainly he thought little of Wuolijoki's play, which he proceeded totally to rewrite. A homely, conventional comedy was turned into a gargantuan farce with a rough edge of class conflict, a coarse line in sex-talk, and more openly poetic prose than Brecht had ever allowed himself. It is, of course, incongruous that a German, after a stay in Finland of only a few months, should have composed a Finnish folk-play, and yet *Puntila* is undeniably local. The Finnish summer of 1940 was the happiest period of Brecht's exile, and the texture of the play is enriched by the strength of his feeling for particular places. This Finland is real, not a representative locale like the London, Chicago, Mahagonny, or Setzuan of other plays. Brecht is celebrating a country briefly but vividly experienced. Völker quotes, probably from Brecht's *Arbeitsjournal*, an indulgent note:

These clear nights are very beautiful. Just before 3 o'clock I got up, because of the flies, and went outside. The cocks were crowing but it had never been dark. And I do so love to urinate in the open. [12]

The sentiment is handed over, almost *verbatim*, to Puntila when, in Scene 10 during one of his frequent bouts of extravagant mateship, he and Matti are pissing in the yard. Brecht's delight in Finnish landscapes reaches its height in Puntila's paean of possessive patriotism during the "climb" up Mount Hatelma in Scene 11, where the rhetoric satirizes the sentiment without damaging the descriptions. But, though set solidly and finely in Finland, the play is not about Finland. Its serious concern is with the unalterable enmity of the dominated and the dominators, and Matti is the spokesman, the cool corrector of his hot master. In the words of Red Surkkala's song, "such is the love between vixen and cock."

Brecht's already-quoted comment, "*Puntila* means almost nothing to me, the war everything; I can write almost anything about *Puntila* but nothing about the war", may have contributed to a critical undervaluing of the play which is only now being adequately challenged in the English-speaking world. Michel Saint-Denis' controversial production for the Royal Shakespeare Company in 1965 seems unfairly to have deterred other English theatrical managements. It may also be that the elaborate political disguise of Brecht's own disingenuous commentary on the play has shaken off adherents. The fact remains that this was the play that Brecht chose as the opening performance of the Berliner Ensemble, and it demands attention.

The Prologue is a shifty piece of writing. Brecht was over-defensive about the play's relevance in a country where the landowner was a thing of the past. "Not only the struggle but the history of that struggle is instructive," he reminded his East German critics, "because the class struggle demands that victory in one area of conflict be exploited so as to promote victory in another."[13] The Prologue prejudges Puntila. He is a prehistoric monster, a plague, useless, and the play is comic only because "laughter too can help to win the day." In 1940, Brecht had had this to say:

Puntila is far from being a play with a message. The Puntila part therefore must not for an instant be in any way deprived of its natural attractiveness, while particular artistry will be needed to make the drunk scenes delicate and poetic, with the maximum of variety, and the sober scenes as ungrotesque and unbrutal as possible.[14]

Ten years later, the tune had changed. At Zurich, Leonard Steckel had played Puntila without special make-up, and he seemed to most of the audience "a likeable man subject to the occasional nasty turn when in a state of sobriety, which state being tantamount to a hangover the turns seemed excusable." Without changing his text, Brecht now decided to change the play by altering Steckel. When he played Puntila in Berlin, Steckel was given "a foully shaped bald head and made himself up with debauched and debased features". This, Brecht decided, was the right approach, and any performance on the Zurich model was a mistake. "Only now did [Puntila's] drunken charm seem menacing and his sociable approaches like those of a crocodile."[15] This is a wretched misjudgement of his own play: worth trying as a theatrical experiment but not worth endowing with scriptural authority. Not only does it restrict the actor of Puntila, but, more seriously, it downgrades Matti. It is the fact that Matti sees the sinister aspect of his master's drunken charm and a reptilian slime in his sociable approaches that distinguishes him from the other characters *and* from the audience. To make that insight available to everybody is to turn Matti into a mere time-server and make his opposition to Puntila a matter of routine. This is the only play of Brecht's which might genuinely be better performed against his own instructions.

It was, characteristically, the play's form that occupied Brecht most. Once he had that right, he wrote quickly. Four drunken scenes are followed by four sober scenes. Scene 9, the *scène à faire* of conventional dramaturgy, begins sober and ends conclusively drunk. Sobriety does not return during the play, but Matti's departure in the final scene promises a deadly spell of it in a notional future. "This play's satire," wrote Brecht, "is of a poetic kind. The director's task therefore is to translate its poetic features into memorable images."[16] There is no real hardship there. The images are present from the beginning. Before a word has been said, a judge falls off his chair in a drunken stupor while Puntila drinks on. Matti's entrance, mistrustful and observing, establishes the play's controlling relationship. His anecdotes point out the realities of the social law that Puntila splendidly repudiates when he is drunk. A responsible man, a man like Shui Ta or like Puntila when he is sober, is "a man who's capable of anything. For instance, he loses sight of his own child's welfare, he has no feeling for friendship." Matti is a responsible man, but in the present state of society he is responsible for very little. If Puntila recalls the gross Merchant of *The Exception and the Rule*, Matti recalls the Guide. When he was working in a paper mill, he tells Eva in Scene 2, "the porter quit because the boss asked him how his son was getting along." The sober Puntila has pushed his daughter Eva into an engagement with a spineless diplomat. Everyone will accept the drunken Puntila's verdict that the fiancé is not a man, but Matti asks, "What is a man anyway?" The same question is answered by the Merchant of *The Measures Taken*, "I don't know what a man is. I only know his price." The relevance of this to the hiring market of Scene 4 is obvious to Matti and to the audience, though not to the drunkenly benevolent Puntila. It is the diplomat's lack of virile interest in Eva which foils her attempt, in alliance with Matti, to get him to break off their engagement. The episode of the feigned seduction in the sauna is another of the play's memorable images. This could have been the *scène à faire*, but the bloodless diplomat's compliance aborts it. What it initiates, however, is a surprisingly powerful and uneasy series of sexual encounters between Matti and Eva, culminating in his testing of her fitness to be a chauffeur's wife, in Scene 9. Played honestly, the relationship will carry almost into the world of Strindberg's *Miss Julie*. Brecht was concerned that the actors should give to it a poetic reality. He counselled that the compromising sauna scene should not be played farcically, and that Scene 9 might benefit if the actors bore in mind the casket scene from *The Merchant of Venice*. It would falsify his social vision if Eva were to get off too lightly. His particular affection went out towards the women of Kurgela. Scene 8, in which they tell their tales, is one of the best he ever wrote, a superbly resourceful way of incorporating Hella Wuolijoki's Finnish anecdotes. Brecht found it difficult to do these "noble" characters justice in performance, and his view is that Caspar Neher's artistry solved a problem which a literary or even a dramatic intelligence could not. The costuming of "real" people who get involved in a fairy tale is bound to raise problems, and it was Neher who found the solution both to this and to the crucial question of their grouping in Scene 8. Brecht defines the key to their presentation with a typical "not. . . but" instruction: "It would be completely wrong to portray them as comic; rather they are full of humour".[17] Puntila and the gentry were "masked" for the Berlin production. Matti, the maids, the workers, and the women of Kurgela were not. Neither was Eva, for reasons that Brecht is unwilling to define. It is a fair assumption that he was fonder of the "naturalism" of her relationship with Matti than could be wholly reconciled with his dominant staging theory.

The productive year in Finland was rounded off by the writing of *Arturo Ui* and a further worrying at the text of *The Good Person*. In May 1941, the long journey across Russia to America began the last, and in many ways the saddest, phase of Brecht's exile. The encounter in actuality with a country that had so far existed largely as a potent personal image was perilous enough. The need to earn a living that took him almost immediately to Hollywood was worse. In a sense Brecht was lucky. Friends rallied round him. A house in Santa Monica had been rented in advance of his arrival. Notable German actors — Peter Lorre, Oskar Homolka, Elisabeth Bergner, Fritz Kortner — spoke up for him in the studios of Hollywood, and not without effect. According to Völker, Brecht worked on over fifty film projects during his six years in America. The outcome was pitifully small. His greatest contribution was to Fritz Lang's *Hangmen Also Die*, and that led to bitter wrangles. The money that bought Brecht off may have helped him to write *Simone Machard* with Feuchtwanger, *Schweyk* and the adaptation for Elisabeth Bergner and Paul Czinner of *The Duchess of Malfi*; and when Feuchtwanger sold film rights for the novel he had based on *Simone Machard*, Brecht received a sufficient share to allow him the peace of mind to write one of his greatest plays, *The Caucasian Chalk Circle*. He was in his mid-forties, though, threatened with a sense of failure, and living a broken-backed life a long way from home. For him the purge of the reds under Hollywood beds was probably a blessing in disguise. His appearance before the House Un-American Activities Committee on 30 October 1947 was a Galilean exercise in dramatic deceit. It provides a not inglorious courtroom scene, with one of the great dramatists of courtroom confrontation slyly contriving to play the main part almost as if he were a spear-carrying extra. No wonder he laughed when he heard recorded extracts on the radio that evening. There was no shortage of people to blame Brecht for his failure to take a stand against the House Committee. When the tigers of moral courage are rampant, they will always expect the leopard to change his spots. Brecht was rarely immaculate and his biography, particularly where it concerns women, is not a noble one; but his rejection of martyrdom, both in October 1947 and after the East Berlin rising of 17 June 1953, is consistent with his intellectual dislike of western individualism. In *Man Equals Man*, Bloody Five castrates himself because the seductiveness of women threatens to soften him. Such monstrous self-pride exacts too high a price for Galy Gay, as it would for Galileo, Schweyk, Azdak or Brecht. Temperament colludes with conviction in encouraging them to sacrifice heroic individuality and keep their testicles.

The day after his Washington interrogation, Brecht flew to Paris *en route* for Zurich. The Zurich Schauspielhaus had retained a unique faith in Brecht's plays during the war years, staging the world premieres of

Galileo (1943), *Mother Courage* (1941) and *The Good Person of Setzuan* (1943). Reunited with Caspar Neher, Brecht had legitimate hopes of re-establishing a theatrical life for himself. The first chance came in early 1948, when he adapted Hölderlin's translation of *Antigone* for performance at Chur. This was the production that led to the publication of the first *Modellbuch*, issued in the Russian sector of Berlin the following year, but the staging was an unsatisfactory struggle against untidy odds. Brecht's adaptations are, of course, revealing, and the study of them is not arid, but they are at the business end of a career too varied to be explored in every detail. Like the earlier verse play, *The Trial of Lucullus*, *Antigone* has a mechanical air when translated from the German. The staging of *Puntila* in Zurich in June 1948 gave him more scope as a director, but also pointed up more clearly the impossibility of achieving committed performances from uncommitted actors. Brecht wanted rehearsals that were also discussions, and he was concerned to re-establish his investigation into the kind of acting that might follow discussion rather than replace it. The invitation to direct a play of his own at the Deutsches Theater in East Berlin was timely. *Puntila* had been well received in Zurich. So, now, was *Mother Courage* in Berlin. There was a prospect, though not a guarantee, of his being allowed to form a company of his own in the Russian sector of his native Germany. With his eyes open, Brecht travelled cautiously, but he travelled with hope.

Leaving Helene Weigel in Berlin, as formal head of the proposed Berliner Ensemble, Brecht returned to Zurich and set about writing what proved to be his last original full-length play, *The Days of the Commune*, which he hoped would provide the first original production of the new company in the autumn of 1949. It is an unwelcoming play, as lacking in the familiar Brechtian *Spass* as any but the most rigid of the *Lehrstücke*. Even so, its critical neglect is surprising. Nowhere else has Brecht exhibited so much of the painful awareness over which his political faith had to triumph. It is a very honest play which documents without vainglory the war of the ragged trousers against the stuffed shirts. That is not to say that it is without bias. Brecht does not pretend to a generosity towards Thiers and Bismarck that he does not feel. They are caricatures, the only "masked" actors in a play which otherwise employs the traditional understatement of the slice-of-life. A German audience is almost bound to be reminded of Hauptmann's *The Weavers*, not only because of its assumed class-antagonisms, but also because it is without a hero or a plot. In a series of short scenes, it depicts the rise and fall of the Paris Commune of 1871, alternating for the most part between meetings of the Central Committee of the Commune and a group of disaffected National Guardsmen who find themselves logically committed to an unexpected revolution. [18] Hesitating on the brink of a move to East Berlin, Brecht is reviewing the apparently unfavourable disparity between the vigorous ideals that precipitate a people's revolution and the unholy opportunism needed to preserve it. His clear conclusion is that the Communards, who may have lost if they had marched on Versailles, lost anyway because they did not. The long-lived conflict in Brecht's thinking between pacifism and revolutionary realism is apparently resolved dialectically; but how real is such a resolution? He was fifty-one by the time he moved back to Berlin; if there was going to be a war, he would be a non-combatant. And a war, let it be remembered, was far from being a remote possibility. It was in October 1949 that the Socialist Unity Party established the German Democratic Republic in reaction to the election of Adenauer and the establishment of the Federal Republic. Brecht, having accepted that *The Days of the Commune* was too raw politically, was rehearsing in East Berlin for the opening of *Puntila*, destined to be the first production of the Berliner Ensemble.

It is certain that, if a performance had been in prospect, Brecht would have made alterations to *The Days of the Commune*. When the play was eventually staged at the Theater am Schiffbauerdamm in 1962, Brecht's suggestion that the same actor should double as Bismarck and Thiers was adopted. During the last seven years of his life, his finest creative perceptions were often of that sort; recognitions, that is, of the way in which a text *grows* into a performance. In the form in which we have it, *The Days of the Commune* is something, but not a sufficient something, more than an articulated skeleton. Its possibilities, if more fully fleshed, were beautifully indicated by a British theatre group in 1976. For Brecht's Thiers the faceless mass of Parisians are scum, and *Scum* was the title chosen for Monstrous Regiment's lively amplification of the conflicts adumbrated in *The Days of the Commune*. Can you destroy the guillotine if you spare the bank? Can the internationalism of the socialist movement (the captured German cuirassier of Brecht's play has an important dramatic role) overcome the opportunistic nationalism that resists it? What is the role of women in a people's revolution? How much should be risked in order to protect a gun? or an apple tree? To compare *Scum* with the Royal Shakespeare Company's pedestrian production of *The Days of the Commune* in November 1977 is to re-enter fruitfully into a debate about the status of Brecht as a "classic" dramatist. Monstrous Regiment had tampered with Brecht for the same positive reasons that made Brecht tamper with *Coriolanus*. The company's strongest commitment was to the role of women in a people's revolution, and the play was rewritten to suit the number of actors the company could afford and the lively concerns that they wished to communicate. There is no doubt that Brecht is better served by such irreverence than by the routine reverence of a still-culinary theatre. But the argument is not so simple. *Scum* is triumphant, but irreverence can lead to a poor result as surely as reverence can lead to a good one. Brecht's own combative response to a given text can be seen from *Baal*, his earliest *Gegenstück*, through to *Turandot*, his last adaptation. It is still preferable to stage Brecht's plays unaltered *and* with his own commentaries in mind, but the rehearsals must be combative. If the actors passively accept Brecht's text rather than answering it back, it will not finally be Brecht's text that they perform.

9

Brecht's Dramaturgy

In May 1979 Michael Billington, in a *Guardian* review of David Zane Mairowitz's play *Landscape of Exile*, wrote a sentence which encapsulates some of the key problems in understanding Brecht. After describing Mr Mairowitz as "a passionate Brechtian" he continued:

I feel he has written a scrupulous Brechtian play, full of strong dialectic and well-sketched background, without the one ingedient that makes Brecht a great dramatist: the readiness to betray his theories for the sake of a throat-grabbing scene.

Michael Billington, it must immediately be said, is one of Britain's more sympathetic critics of Brecht. Mr. Mairowitz is another, as well as being influenced by him as a writer. Furthermore, on the evidence of their writings, there are few, if any, academic critics who would disagree with Mr Billington's rule-of-thumb definition of Brecht's dramaturgical method — that he was always willing to "betray his theories" for the sake of dramatic effect. That they are utterly wrong is at least partly due to Brecht himself. Aristotle, who was not a playwright, wrote an aesthetic which set out certain points that came, rightly or wrongly, to be seen as rules. Brecht, who was, wrote a great deal of commentary on drama in general and his own work in particular, but hardly in a form sufficiently fixed and final to be called an aesthetic. While it is true to say that Aristotle recommended the imitation of an action and Brecht the *interruption* of an action, nowhere did Brecht suggest that *parts* of that action should be, for want of a better word, dull.

The base problem lies in the fact that Brecht's writings about his own work were almost always from hindsight, almost always indicated a future direction that was not necessarily inherent in the piece he was describing and which he very often did not then go on to adopt, and frequently contained downright lies about both his intention and his achievement. But while this provides difficulties of interpretation enough concerning the staging and acting of the plays, it is their dramaturgy, the actual techniques that make them different from those of other writers, which has raised the thorniest problems of all. Billington's assessment of the theories which underpin those techniques — at once supremely confident and almost diametrically opposed to the reality — is a case in point: many writers have isolated the elements of his dramaturgy to their own satisfaction; none, so far as we know, has even approached an adequate gloss.

One of the major stumbling blocks is terminology. From very early in his theoretical writings Brecht used the word "dramatic" as the opposite of the sort of play he was sure had to be developed if theatre was to have any relevance to the age in which he lived. This obviously emerged from his belief in the mid twenties that the "only approach" that suited the "dramatic form" was a simple setting down of what happened, "epic theatre" which brought out "the material incidents in a perfectly sober and matter-of-fact way".[1] By 1927 he was writing that the "new school of play-writing lays down that the *epic theatre* is the theatrical style of our time"[2] (and incidentally, in the same article: "It would be quite wrong to try and deny emotion to this kind of theatre") and by February 1929 that "the traditional major form, dramatic form, isn't suitable for present-day subjects."[3] By 1930 the schism was complete and enshrined in his famous list in the *Mahagonny* notes which label "epic" theatre as the alternative to "dramatic" theatre. There are three reasons for not printing that list here. The first is that it is easily available since it is included in almost everything that has been written about Brecht. The second is that its compressed language can make the theory of epic drama seem more complicated than it is. The third is that, with our blackboard training behind us, we are dangerously trustful of lists. This one is extremely early and, despite its fascination, should not be allowed to speak for the totality of Brecht's work. A useful note at the end of *Brecht on Theatre* reminds us that, towards the end of his life, Brecht was ready to replace the label "Epic Theatre" with one which laid less stress on the narrative element, "Dialectical Theatre".[4] Another essay, unpublished in his lifetime, presents a clear image of the episodic emphasis of epic drama:

The epic writer Döblin provided an excellent criterion when he said that with an epic work, as opposed to a dramatic, one can as it were take a pair of scissors and cut it into individual pieces, which remain fully capable of life.[5]

The offence to Aristotelian unity is conscious. Brecht used the name "Aristotelian Theatre" as well as "Dramatic Theatre" to categorize the tradition against which his "Epic Theatre" was set.

What this has led to, and why, is clear to see. Any dramatist who uses the word "dramatic" in an apparently pejorative sense, and then in his staging and acting proposals seeks to make both his audiences and his practitioners look upon the theatre as a place of instruction and a tool for social change as well as a place of entertainment, is at the very least inviting misunderstanding. That he was so overwhelmingly and universally misunderstood, even by sympathetic critics, is interesting, and part of the phenomenon that we examined in Chapter 1. The key words, of course, are "as well as a place of entertainment". Brecht wanted even his *Lehrstücke* to entertain,[6] and by the time of his later theoretical writings insisted that entertainment is an absolute basic of theatre. But he used the word "dramatic" purely to describe a way of *telling* a story in theatrical terms and for a purpose he disagreed with. "Culinary" was his contemptuous word for it. He did not intend, by attacking "dramatic theatre", to indicate an opposition to story — the very stuff of drama — in itself. Again, from his earliest theoretical writings to his last, the word "story" recurs with extraordinary regularity, often linked with the idea of narration; and in an appendix to the "Short Organum"[7] he stated with the utmost clarity the way of narrating a story that he considered vital if one was not to slip into the failings and excesses of the theatre practitioners he despised:

For a genuine story to emerge it is most important that the scenes should to start with be played quite simply one after another, using the experience of real life, without taking account of what follows or even of the play's overall sense. The story then unreels in a contradictory manner; the individual scenes retain their own meaning; they yield (and stimulate) a wealth of ideas; and their sum, the story, unfolds authentically without any cheap all-pervading idealization (one word leading to another) or directing of subordinate, purely functional component parts to an ending in which everything is resolved.

What Brecht is insisting on, quite simply, is not a story that is "undramatic" as the word is normally understood (flat, dull) but a story that is unfalsified. He had an abiding hatred of the "well-made play" but not of the well-wrought story; in a note published after his death he listed some of the elements that could be learnt from classical plays:

The invention of socially significant stories, the art of narrating them drama-tically, the creation of interesting persons, the care for language, the putting forward of great ideas and the support of all that leads to social progress.˄

It is hard to resist the feeling that Brecht was in fact giving a pocket definition of his own dramaturgical techniques here. Certainly he has put his finger on some of the essential features: and *still* they are generally overlooked.

The idea that "throat-grabbing scenes" are a betrayal of Brecht's theories, for instance, is absurd. From the beginning of recorded history and clearly beyond, the art of the story-teller has been metaphorically to grab the throat of his listener or reader. From the beginning of Brecht's theoretical writing (and clearly beyond!) his intention was to entertain and instruct his audiences by narrating stories. The fact that he evolved a series of theatrical devices to modify the immediate effect of some elements of the telling, to obviate from the very start any danger of an *overall* emotional effect blinding an audience to the importance — including the *emotional* importance — of indivi-dual *parts* of a story which he intended to be rooted in reality, is to some extent irrelevant. At the heart of each of his plays is a story, and it is the quality of the story — as we have seen throughout this book — which is the most immediate key to the success or failure of most of his works. There are, of course, other elements; but the story, the well-wrought, clearly narrated, "throat-grabbing" story, is the very essence of Brecht's dramatic art. If the plays are examined, this becomes almost ludicrously obvious; but until it sinks in, it seems inevitable that the cover-all word "Brechtian" will continue all too frequently to be a synonym for boring or, at least theatrically, deadly dull.

One of the great wellsprings of Brecht's creative drive was the strength of his reactions to the works of writers who were his contem-poraries, and to the theatre which he attended and criticized. The way of telling a story which he saw on stage — whether it was the well-made play of the bourgeois writers or the emotionally intense outpourings of the Expressionists — made him determined to do better. But whether he understood it or not, at the heart of the form of theatre which he was trying to create, and which he insisted, and probably believed, was new, was a very ancient form of story-telling indeed. In theatrical terms, it had been exploited to great effect by only one writer in one play. The form was the ancient ballad, and the play was Büchner's *Woyzeck*.★

On the face of it, this is hardly a startling or original point to make. But while other writers have noted Brecht's debt to the ballad (and indeed it is another of those words which recur frequently in his own writings) it has not been realized (nor perhaps did Brecht realize) just how basic the connection is, nor indeed just how complete a key it provides to many of the ambiguities and complexities of his work. First and foremost, before he ever became a playwright, Brecht was a poet. He was always, even as a very young man, a poet of great diversity. In some poems he tried (usually succeeding) to achieve a complex emotional effect through a simple, limpid word-picture, but in many more he set out to tell a story. Some of the most remarkable of these story-poems come very close to reproducing the weird, ambiguous effect of the ancient ballad.

Raw and dreadfully simply-told tales of human beings behaving with great ferocity towards one another abound in all western cultures. Many of them crossed frontiers, and centuries-old ballads recorded all over the continent of Europe also crop up in the English, Scottish and Irish traditions. What has not been sufficiently noted is the strange fact that the ancients who wrote, made, transmitted, and transmogrified these ballads almost always ignored aspects that nowadays would be considered of paramount importance in telling a story: most noticeably the question of motivation. When Boccaccio wrote down his tale of Lisabetta he almost certainly added to the original ballad not only more detailed *reasons* for her brothers' inhuman action, but also the gruesome circumstance of the unhappy girl's cutting off her lover's head and putting it in a pot of basil. Keats' version is a full-scale romantic attempt to illuminate character and motive as well as a retelling of the remarkably sickly tale of the head in the plant-pot. But the original song has a power and economy which neither of the copyists achieved. The (unnamed) sister, having found the body of her murdered lover, mourns it for three days, when she is forced by hunger to return home. She does not, of course, take the head, and she does not, of course, die of a broken heart. When her murderous brothers mock her, she is able only to reply bitterly:

★ The word "ballad" itself raises many problems of definition. We have qualified it as "ancient ballad" to differentiate the great, sung tales, some of them centuries old, from the many forms of song to which the term later became attached.

> Stand off, stand off, you bloody butchers,
> My love and I you have both slain.

It was what Brecht meant when he later insisted upon "reality" in his stories.

Another of the most widespread ballad tales, which even travelled from Europe and Britain to America, where it is part of the oral tradition of the Appalachians, is an even clearer archetype. It tells of a pair of young lovers, often soon to be married, who go for a walk, usually beside a river, but sometimes to a cave in a wood. Suddenly, and invariably for no given reason, the young man strangles, stabs, or beats the girl to death. In some versions he is hanged — without having denied or explained his action — in others the tale ends with the killing. A cursory glance into a collection of ancient ballads from almost any land will reveal any number of similarly stark and motiveless tales.

The influence of these ballads on Brecht the poet is simple to find. The first stanza of "Apfelböck, or The Lily of the Field"[9] reads:

> Mild was the light as Jakob Apfelböck
> Struck both his father and his mother down
> And shut their bodies in the linen press
> And hung about the house all on his own.

The ninth reads:

> And when they came to open the press door
> Jakob stood by, the light was mild and clear
> And when they asked him what he did it for
> Said Jakob Apfelböck: I've no idea.

The tenth, and final, stanza adds the air of mystery and ambiguity that is another archetypal element of the ancient ballad:

> A few days later the milk woman said
> She wondered what would happen by and by:
> Would Jakob Apfelböck, the child, perhaps
> Visit the grave where his poor parents lie?

Not only do we not learn why Jakob did it, but there seems a doubt that simple retribution will follow. The deeply moving ballad "On the

Infanticide Marie Farrar"[10] similarly tells, quite starkly, a simple tale of the utmost horror:

> Marie Farrar: month of birth, April
> An orphaned minor; rickets; birthmarks, none: previously
> Of good character, admits that she did kill
> Her child as follows here in summary.

In this poem Brecht employs another characteristic device — an exhortatory chorus:

> Therefore, I beg, make not your anger manifest
> For all that lives needs help from all the rest.

For the move from ballads between hard covers to ballads on stage we need look no further than the "Moritat" of Mack the Knife. Both the form and the assumption of the balladeers are there: the catalogue of Mackie's dreadful and apparently pointless crimes — they can hardly have done him any good — is sufficient in itself. He behaved how he behaved because that is how he was made.

Whether Brecht consciously chose to adopt this balladic form as the vehicle for his stage stories, or whether it is simply the way in which he naturally wrote, we can only guess at. But the one great model, coupled with his experiments with the form in poems, must have made it almost inevitable that his theatre writing would tend in that direction. The characteristic responses induced by a simply narrated story in which motive has been pared to the bone — emotional intensity and a pervasive ambiguity — were not at first clearly understood by Brecht. They were, as time went on, and especially after his "conversion" to the Marxist faith, effects which he was determined to keep under control. Later in his life Brecht came to realize the theatrical magic induced by the tension between inevitable empathy and his actors' attempts *not* to empathize. A similar tension, between the natural and ancient power of his way of story-telling and his determination not to let his audience be entirely carried away, is a large element of his greatest plays.

Although it is tempting neatly to separate the component parts of Brecht's technique for examination, it is, of course, impossible. As well as being a superb writer of stories, he had a gift for characterization which has rarely been equalled, but which is in some important ways inextricably mixed *with* and a product *of* his narrative technique. Even this element, however, owes an enormous amount to his ancient models, and to *Woyzeck*. Although in Büchner's play the protagonist's motive for the final act of violence is apparently a solid enough one — sexual jealousy — the delineation of thought processes and the decisive events in the tale are cut to such a bare minimum that the impression is of a human being suffering in the grip of shadowy elemental forces which lead inevitably to destruction. As in much of Brecht's writing, we have a clear *feeling* of character, but we are never allowed to make a trip inside Woyzeck's mind.* The resonances of the short scene between Woyzeck and a Jew are a good example. In a few dozen words of totally functional buying and selling dialogue, a whole world is created. Not a world of psychology, but a world that sums up centuries of hatred, persecution, prejudice and contempt. We learn — from the words and from the stage presence — about Woyzeck's state of mind, and we are given a portrait of a Jew as filtered through history and consciousness, in a few sentences which are apparently concerned with nothing but the price of a weapon. Brecht could conjure up fully-fledged, believable, even terrifying characters and insights in a similar way. Consider the Recruiting Officer and Sergeant who open *Mother Courage*; consider the policemen in *Baal*; consider the Corporal and the Ironshirt "Blockhead" in *Caucasian Chalk Circle*. No psychology, no *attempt* at insight, yet they all encapsulate soldiery, bestiality, violence and history.

It is not only minor characters who are created in this startling way. For despite Brecht's ability to bring his stage people to extraordinary life, his plays are not about the internal workings of the minds of even his most powerful protagonists. Most playwrights, as Brecht himself recognized, set out to show the private and personal responses of characters to disastrous situations which are, so to speak, "applied" to them by their creator: it is the desire to reveal the mind which leads the writer to invent his story, the character creates the situation. But Brecht, unlike the dramatists he despised but in exactly the manner of the ancient balladeer, was far more interested in the question *what* than the question *why*. He presents a situation, he presents characters: neither creates the other. His total lack of interest, as a story-teller, in causal psychology, coupled with his mischievous and/or misguided prognostications on individualism and society, especially after his

---

* Büchner's realization of the absurdity of even the attempt is stated in the first lines of *Danton's Death*: "Know one another? We would have to break open each other's skulls and squeeze the thoughts out of the brain tissue."

"conversion", have led to a great deal of confusion about his methods. The simple fact is that his plays abound with realized characters, dominant and otherwise. That he does not want microscopically to study their psyches is beside the point.

What Brecht *does* do, and what possibly makes him unique among modern writers, is to accept that people (real people) exist in their settings, and that the things which happen to them do so whatever their personalities, whatever their attitudes, whatever outsiders may imagine is going on in their heads. By giving us characters whose innermost souls we can only guess at, he takes a bold step towards achieving the "reality" he so deeply desired in art. As he matured, the method became increasingly relevant to his intentions. For in all but a very few of his works he used a "historicized" setting — real or imaginary — to make his points: and when one comes to examine history in reality, the most obviously lacking data is exactly the psychological information that other writers so often provide. One *has* no insight into the workings of the minds of the individual victims of history. Mother Courage is truly the portrait of an individual. She is rich, complex, fascinating. But what she thought about what was happening to her, what she felt about the life she was leading, what her awareness of existence was, is not only historically unfathomable, it is also irrelevant. She existed, if you like, as did Pete the Pipe, the Chaplain, Yvette: who needs to know, says Brecht, their innermost thoughts and agonies? We need to know that they were human, and that they suffered and died along with hundreds of thousands of other humans during a concrete historical event.

Unusual as this approach to characterization is, it becomes positively peculiar when one considers Brecht's beliefs. For although he saw it as a way to approach reality, and certainly not in conflict with his historical optimism, nobody — and least of all the communists — can see it as being politically positive in effect. His characters, who have souls, feelings, aspirations, the ability to "haggle away" the lives of their sons and then give silent screams of agony, are at the mercy of historical processes — which Brecht wishes (and possibly believes) will one day, through the application of a political system which will educate the human race to a pitch of reason as yet unknown, become impossible. If he were to do what other writers do, that is, make his protagonists *aware* of their historical situation, he would have to follow them in making his heroes react *against* it, attempt to *change* it. Mother Courage would not have been at the war — she had to travel 300 miles to get there — had she been aware; but had she been a Pelagea Vlassova, not an Anna

Fierling, what could she have done? Brecht is far too truthful an artist to tell politicians' lies: she could have starved to death or gone home again, nothing else. The communist critics who wanted her to have learned a lesson at the end wanted a different Mother Courage and a falsified historical situation. Brecht's Mother Courage may have learnt the full depths of human bitterness, but she had learnt nothing else, because there was nothing else to learn. She was a poor, benighted, tough and fascinating woman who needed a revolution in the world to save her, and everybody else, by preventing such a situation ever occurring. As Brecht put it after Helene Weigel's Berlin performance:

The tragedy of Mother Courage and her life, which the audience could feel deeply, lay in the fact that here was a terrible contradiction which destroyed a human being, a contradiction which could be resolved, but only by society itself in the course of long, terrible struggles. And the moral superiority of this way [Weigel's] of playing the part lay in the fact that the human being — even the most vital individual — was shown to be destructible. [11]

As so often, Brecht's honesty as a playwright was not matched by his honesty as a critic. The audience tended to feel a completely different tragedy: that this marvellous, villainous woman had undergone her sufferings because she was a victim of nothing more changeable than the human condition. Elsewhere Brecht wrote of the play:

Going through Mother Courage I note with some satisfaction how the war appears like an enormous field. . . every method of calculation. . . drawn from experiences of peace fails; boldness is no good, caution is no good, nor brutality, nor sympathy, everything brings destruction. [12]

That is much more as audiences tend to see it, and again they tend to see it as unavoidable. Brecht's view of it as a Marxist play, a play which would induce the recognition of the need to change the world, is not wrong. But it is optimistic.

Any idea Brecht had of *Galileo* as a play from which Marxist lessons of history could easily be drawn fails for similar reasons. It is the play in the *oeuvre* which comes closest to the traditional approach to historical subjects, in that its protagonist is an important historical figure rather than an unknown. But while Galileo may nowadays be seen as "a great man", that is because of retrospective admiration for his achievements rather than because (in Brecht's version of his life) he was allowed *at the time* to be great. In fact, the "great" men of the play are those with the power to dominate and regulate Galileo's life, even to the extent of forcing his recantation. Fascinatingly, Brecht's portrait of Galileo relies so little on causal psychology, portrays "what" rather than asking "why" so completely, that by a small number of minor alterations to the text, he was able, to his own satisfaction, to turn his creature from a man of whom he apparently approved to a man whom he claimed to have thought had altered the very course of history by a single act of betrayal. Stranger still, *both* versions remain in many respects self-portraits.

Galileo, unlike Mother Courage, did have a weapon, his genius, whereby he could perhaps have forced a change in the actions of the mighty. But in Brecht's portrayal he was as completely in the grip of history as Anna Fierling. The man we are shown is a man of contradictions. He is a glutton, a sensualist, a genius, a crook, a coward, possibly even a hero. In the first version he is seen as having achieved something fantastically important — the writing and dissemination of the *Discorsi* — by subterfuge coupled with the luck of Andrea's happening along to smuggle the manuscript out of the country. We are offered no explanation of his complex personality, but told, in effect: here is Galileo; believe in him; this is what he did; decide for yourself on the rights and wrongs of the matter. In the second, post-atomic-bomb version, Brecht claims (although it is not, as we have suggested, an entirely convincing claim) that Galileo could and should have altered history through the exercise of conscience and courage. It is utterly characteristic of Brecht that Galileo is shown throughout *not to possess* these requisite two qualities! All very well for him to tell Andrea: "Furthermore, I have come to the conclusion, Sarti, that I was never in any real danger" but what of the stage direction when he enters after his recantation "completely, almost unrecognizably, changed by his trial"? All very well for him to have claimed to have betrayed his profession, but what of the fact that he "risked the last miserable remains of my peace of mind by making a copy"? And if the actor introduces the required pause between "my" and "peace of mind", the true import of the speech is revealed: Galileo destroyed not only his peace of mind but what little eyesight remained to him by "using up the last ounce of light. . . for the last six months". The scene ends with the almost blind "traitor" asking his daughter, "How is the night?" Virginia replies, "Clear". It is a sad echo of an exchange in Scene 3, when Galileo's blackest times, unknown to him, are about to begin:

Virginia: How was the night, father?
Galileo: Clear.

Galileo's insistence that he believes in reason is similarly at variance with his final insistence that "the only purpose of science is to lighten the toil of human existence" — as heartrending, and at bottom as little to do with *reason*, as Einstein's statement that he would have been a locksmith had he realized what the discovery of the principle of the atom bomb would mean. Moreover, as a statement of Brecht's beliefs, Galileo's prognostications on reason should be seen in the context in which they are made. Consider the exchange in Scene 3:

Galileo: Look here, Sagredo! I believe in man and that means I believe in reason. Without that belief I wouldn't have the strength to get out of bed in the morning.
Sagredo: Then let me tell you this: I don't believe in reason. Forty years' experience has taught me that human beings are not accessible to reason.

Which man is right? Which is propounding Brecht's view? In Scene 14, Andrea says:

Even in ethics you were centuries ahead of us. . . Your hands are stained, we said. — You said: better stained than empty.

Galileo replies:

Better stained than empty. Sounds realistic. Sounds like me. A new science, a new ethics.

Not only does it sound like Galileo, but it sounds like Brecht, and it sounds like the "reason" that Sagredo despaired of in mankind. What is more, in Scene 4 Galileo had stated: "I submit that as scientists we have no business asking what the truth may lead to." Sad but true: one of Brecht's favourite slogans was, "Truth is concrete."

Complexity is piled on complexity by the mode of characterization in this play: the unexplored, unexplained relationship between the unhappy, human Virginia and her not unloving but totally dismissive father; the love relationship, too, between Andrea and Galileo, almost (perhaps we are meant to assume *in fact*) father and son, and the enormous emotional resonances that this blighted relationship gives to

Charles Laughton as Galileo, 1947. "He obstinately sought for the external: not for physics but the physicist's behaviour." (Willett, *Brecht on Theatre*, p. 166)

their final meeting. Again, as in *Mother Courage*, any hope Brecht may have had that this would be a play to instil revolutionary aspiration is lost in its very richness. Ostensibly Galileo feels for the lot of the common people (if not for his only daughter); ostensibly he sees science as being purely in the service of mankind. But whether he achieved something by subterfuge or betrayed the future by cowardice, he was a frail human being who despised people "whose brains were not capable of filling their bellies", and whom we both bless and pity for it.

Furthermore, because it is impossible not to see the protagonist as, in many ways, a self-portrait, the political ambiguities proliferate. Brecht believed in communism, as his Galileo believed in the Church, but both also believed in reason. Galileo's argument with the Church was *not* that new evidence required the abandonment of faith, but only that certain orthodoxies would have to be modified because of it: "Truth is the child of time, not of authority. Our ignorance is infinite, let's whittle away just one cubic millimeter."

When Brecht wrote the play, a critique of Stalinist communism was overdue, and it may not be too fanciful to equate Galileo's recantation "because I was afraid of physical pain" with Brecht's decision to settle in America and continue to write in a vacuum rather than risk liquidation or having, like Galileo, to toe the line of rigid orthodoxy.* Strangely too, the only exclusively political scene, Scene 10, in which a ballad singer demonstrates the popularization of Galileo's teachings as a way to social revolution, has the uncomfortable hallmarks of being inorganic, "grafted on". Even in Joseph Losey's magnificent film version of *Galileo* (unreleased for several years after it was made) the scene sticks out, embarrassingly, like a sore thumb. On stage it is usually worse. The political ambiguities of this dense play are further enriched by the Berliner Ensemble's decision to return to the original version for the production which went into their repertoire in 1977. East Berlin audiences — and highly placed members of the Ensemble — are perfectly prepared to admit that it is more relevant to life in East Germany than the later version *because* it can more easily be seen as a critique of the regime. Their sympathies have come full circle — back to Galileo as the foxy, ironic *survivor* who successfully uses a regime he cannot improve.

Brecht's hope for mankind, and the political "message" he wanted audiences to draw from his plays, was that human nature could, would and must change. Whether or not audiences do in fact receive this message, or whether they see the hope in *Mother Courage* and *Galileo*, for example, as being the hope that can be drawn from mankind's resilience and courage in the face of a destructive and unalterable world, will continue to be debated. But even before he became a Marxist, Brecht showed a marked reluctance to trust in the analytical intelligence of his audiences — a lack of trust which was one of the sources of his theatrical devices aimed at modifying their response.

* For an interesting sidelight on this, see *Understanding Brecht*, pp. 117–118, where Walter Benjamin records a conversation he had with Brecht about Brecht's poem, "The Peasant's Address to his Ox".

As we have seen, Brecht started writing plays partly because the theatre he was around him filled him with despair and disgust. The traditional way of telling a story in the theatre (which he came to call the "dramatic" way) was wrong for him because he neither believed in nor saw as desirable the "purification of the emotions" by catharsis (a dual response which became far stronger when he embraced Marxism). The "well-made play" infuriated him for its falsity, lack of seriousness and mediocrity, and the work of the Expressionists he considered more often masturbatory than revelatory. But as well as distrusting the writers, Brecht distrusted their audiences — who did, after all, not only tolerate the theatre of the day but actually support it. And the narrative technique which he chose (or which more probably came naturally to him) had a built-in disadvantage for a young cynic with a clear idea that he wanted to *alter* the "normal" response of audiences, wanted to destroy the "culinary" element: its ability to instil powerful emotions. Even worse, as he saw it: the more powerful the story *as a whole*, the more chance there was of its significant, serious elements being lost in an emotional rush.

Brecht is almost certainly wrong in this, but he can hardly be blamed for it. The effect of a story on the human being has never been explained or isolated, so he is entitled to his point of view. What is more, his distrust of his fellow humans' ability to extract "lessons" from history and literature grew rather than diminished. While even the communists saw his plays as anti-revolutionary, while it seems safe to say that anyone who read or saw his great plays without prior knowledge of the man would hardly identify them as Marxist, Brecht was quite confident that his was the only true method of galvanizing audiences to action. He seemed incapable of accepting that audiences could draw the "right" conclusions from other modes; even a play so blatantly critical of capitalist society as Hauptmann's *The Weavers* was for him merely a plea for piecemeal alleviation that was basically counter-productive.

Although even before he became a Marxist Brecht had concrete reasons, then, for thinking he needed devices to slow down a narrative, to erect a barrier to an overall emotional response, it should also be remembered that he was to some extent feeling his way as a playwright. Brilliant as *Baal* was, in many respects, it is clearly a 'prentice piece, and *Drums in the Night* almost certainly *needed* something to stop people "staring so romantically". Not, though, because it had anything particularly significant to say, but rather the opposite. It was, as he noted, a minor love story with off-stage drums; it was the story itself, the events narrated, that was wrong and would lead people to be carried away in a "romantic" way. Once he had started with these "epic" devices, there was clearly much to recommend them. His earliest stories, which probably would have achieved their social function without them, do not lose by being slowed down (they are pretty robust stories, after all), while some of his stories achieve their social aim *only* because of them.★ *The Threepenny Opera* is the best example of this. As we saw in Chapter 2, it is close to being a well-made play in its plotting, almost schematization. But the devices — particularly the songs *as epic devices* — give it a definite political thrust which transcends its limitations as a political story.

The more deeply involved Brecht became with Marxism, however, the more complicated grew his problems as a writer. It was in the late twenties and early thirties that his theoretical essays took on the didactic, hectoring tone that is such an unattractive feature of many of them, and that his desire to force an audience to draw the same conclusions as he did became at times almost hysterical. He claimed an enormous confidence in the ability of "the masses" to watch his plays rationally and be inspired to revolution by them, while at the same time revealing his continuing distrust of audiences by a proliferation of epic devices designed specifically to point up the parts which he feared they might miss. Brecht's confidence during this period in his abilities as a playwright is not hard to deduce from the essays of the era; nor is his total awareness that the complex, atavistic responses his stark and simple tales could induce needed staging devices to modify them. His frustrations sprang from the fact that, even with the devices, his audiences and critics — including the "friendly" ones — insisted on extracting not only different messages, but messages he could not conceive of as being there. Brecht's ambiguity, it is fairly safe to say, was far deeper than he even dreamed of.

Another facet of Brecht's difficulties at this time was his charac-

---

★ *Man Equals Man* is a good example of the former category; the first play to which he applied the term "epic", it actually achieves its social point about colonialism, ambiguous though that may be, through what it says rather than through the "epic" way in which it says it. It is interesting to note that in the late thirties Brecht described how a film version of Kipling's "Gunga Din", in which one of the Indians "betrayed his compatriots. . . sacrificed his life so that his fellow-countrymen should be defeated" amused and touched him despite its being an "utterly distorted account". No amount of epic presentation could have made it less distorted, but a different attitude to colonial history would make it perfectly possible to write an alternative: which *Man Equals Man* in some ways is.

teristic insistence that he was part of a new movement, or school, of play writing, which turned out, historically, to be none other than poor BB, out on a very lonely limb. His 1929 essay, "On Form and Subject Matter", is a sad affair, because its warblings about the need for a new subject matter are, in retrospect, a little pathetic:

Simply to comprehend the new areas. . . imposes a new dramatic and theatrical form. . . Petroleum resists the five act form. . . Even to dramatize a simple newspaper report one needs something much more than the dramatic technique of a Hebbel or an Ibsen. This is no boast but a sad statement of fact. [13]

We have already examined in detail in Chapter 4 where this sort of idea led him. *Saint Joan of the Stockyards* and *Round Heads and Pointed Heads* show his use of epic devices at its most militant. In other overtly communist plays, Brecht felt the need to *force* his audience not to be carried away by the overall story, but in these plays all the devices he can muster cannot rescue them from their irrevocable confusion. For once the master story-teller is not ambiguous but out of control; the devices that in his best plays make concrete and considered the individual elements of brilliantly told stories he feared might otherwise hypnotize, are desperate (and here unsuccessful) attempts to clarify the unclear.

Whether it was the personally tragic fact of his exile, or the cooling of his love affair with communism, or a combination of both, Brecht's direction as a playwright, as we have seen, changed during the 1930s. But while the emphasis on purely formal devices receded drastically, along with the barely digested political aspects, the basic elements which make his plays unique remained and were in many cases brought to the pitch of excellence that produced his greatest works. The narrative technique in particular became flexible, muscular and perfectly controlled. As a concomitant, the devices so vital in saving *The Threepenny Opera*, say, from "well-made play" falsity modified their function. The later, great plays had far less need of the theatrical trappings because they rely on a straightforward narrative method which, like that of the great ballads, has great power but no "cleverness". The power lies in the events that unfold and the people they unfold on and through.

Because the emotional power is inherent in the people and the events, not some artificial mix dreamed up by the writer, Brecht has of necessity to tell the story clearly and unemotionally. What has been so grossly misunderstood over the years (and it is partly his fault, a product of his inability to let his work speak for itself) is the simple fact that the emotion innate in the story (or the climactic parts of it) is not only *allowable*, but *necessary* to his avowed political aims. If a truly emotional event actually happens, we are bound to be moved by it — and moved, Brecht hoped, to say, "This character's suffering moves me because there is a way out for him." What is unallowable, in Brecht's view (and a function of the well-made play, to boot) is emotion instilled by the mode of telling, the arrangement of artificial plot elements in such a way that people are moved despite the fact that the elements, examined in isolation, are unreal and unimportant. In his latest as in his earliest writings on his own technique, Brecht insisted that the story *overall* should not make invisible the significance of its parts. In the "Short Organum", for instance, he wrote:

As we cannot invite the audience to fling itself into the story as if it were a river and let itself be carried vaguely hither and thither, the individual episodes have to be knotted together in such a way that the knots are easily noticed. . . The parts of the story have to be carefully set off against one another by giving each its own structure as a play within the play.[14]

The play within the play of Galileo's recantation is a real, awful event that is deeply moving. It is narrated in a way that makes it impossible not to wonder at the facts, at the historical setting, at the reactions of every character on the stage. To assume, as so much criticism does, that Brecht has somehow lost control of his story here is absurd. Without such "throat-grabbing" scenes this play in particular would be a dull and wordy affair indeed.

Where one can cross swords with Brecht's analysis is over the *type* of emotion his climactic scenes induce. For a man who made many highly tendentious statements, those on the emotions, ranging from the pseudo-psychological to the downright nutty ("The emotions always have a quite definite class basis"[15]) are among the hardest to come to terms with. His main bugbear, as is well known, was empathy, an essential element, as he saw it, of the old forms of theatre his plays were intended to replace. For, rightly or wrongly, Brecht was convinced that "dramatic theatre" induced a feeling that change in mankind is impossible, and therefore that his form of theatre *must* induce a determination to change. He wanted his plays to instil emotion at points in the narrative where one could not *simply* respond with pity, fear, horror and so on but where one would be forced further to seek a reason why, and, he hoped, seek to change the world because of it. This relatively simple *intention*, however, could only be achieved if emotions were as simply controlled (or even understood) as Brecht claimed. Galileo's recant-ation, in Losey's film of the play, brought several people at a private viewing to the point of bursting into tears — not merely of wanting to weep. The emotions induced, not surprisingly, were far from simple ones: complex forms of pity, for every character, oddly, not just for Galileo; and an awareness that a type of socially criminal act had been committed. Impossible, however, to be certain of the nature — or even the perpetrator — of the social crime, and impossible not to feel, as one tends to in Mother Courage's case, that the whole sad episode was a product of *human* weakness: it should not have happened, but it was inevitable. Also, though, an element of disgust was induced; an aware-ness that humans should be more honest, courageous, kind — presu-mably a socially useful feeling. As usual, Brecht is not necessarily *wrong*, merely too exclusive. He makes claims about specific emotional effects as though there were an actual way of measuring emotion, or of breaking it down into component parts in order to eliminate the parts he disapproves of. His refusal to trust audiences to draw the conclusions he wants them to is inextricably bound up with his refusal to accept that all his best dramatic writing is pregnant with many possibilities — over which he has little, or no, control.

The recantation scene is a useful example of another of the points of his own dramaturgy that Brecht either misunderstood or misrepre-sented — that of suspense. As early as 1931 in his notes to *The Three-penny Opera* and as late as 1949 in conversation with Friedrich Wolf he claims to look upon projected titles and other devices as ways of telling the story in advance, thus eliminating tension and the surprise element. This is, of course, nonsense. For a start, all that is revealed in advance is a little of what is to take place in the next short episode — and that in itself usually in a form that *sets up* a dramatic tension. For instance, Scene 3 of *Mother Courage* has a placard which reads:

Three years later Mother Courage and parts of a Finnish regiment are taken prisoner. She is able to save her daughter and her wagon, but her honest son dies.

and Scene 5's tells us among other things that:

Tilly's victory at Magdeburg costs Mother Courage four officers' shirts.

To suggest that these are devices which destroy suspense is equivalent to saying that the headlines in a popular tabloid newspaper make reading the stories unnecessary: in fact, they are there to whet the appetite. In *Galileo*, the element of suspense during the recantation scene is almost unbearable. We have been told, baldly, that he recants, and we are left to watch the varied hopes and agonies of the Little Monk, Federzoni, Andrea and the desperate, prayer-babbling Virginia. Our knowledge that the bell of St. Mark's is going to ring, when the characters on stage have decided Galileo has held out, produces an enormous dramatic tension, and the first stroke, coupled with Virginia's superbly logical and unexpected "He is not damned", delivers an intensely powerful emotional kick. We have known he will recant, the others have not; and the suspense lies in our desire to see how they will react, first to the waiting and then to the return of their fallen hero (or "saved" father). Brecht's "shift of emphasis" in his notes to *Mahagonny* may seem to cover the point, but it does not. [16] *Dramatic* theatre involved suspense as to the outcome, he wrote in those notes, and *epic* theatre suspense as to the process.* In this scene — as in many of his greatest — the placard, like a good headline, actually serves to increase our curiosity as to the outcome; the process of Galileo's recantation we are not shown. If the placards do serve a purpose — and the play within a play element noted above is an obvious one — it is not to destroy suspense, either in the piece overall or its individual parts. One suspects that Brecht knew this perfectly well.

Although in some ways Brecht's last great play, *The Caucasian Chalk Circle*, is uncharacteristic in tone — the effect of a good production is one of unalloyed joy — from the point of view of dramaturgy it is as complete an example as one may hope for. It has a story of classic simplicity that defies simple interpretation, it is bursting with characters who come across as solid, three-dimensional human beings while not revealing anything of their psyches, and it contains prose, poetry and song at once beautiful and functional. The other "epic" element which Brecht always insisted on — a social or revolutionary purpose — is there if you search hard enough for it. But, as we shall see, of all his major works this is the most difficult to accept as being political in the way he said he wanted; the meanings Brecht read into it, largely (as

---

* This translation may, anyway, make Brecht's meaning seem clearer than it actually is. Willett, not unreasonably, makes it a sporting metaphor — "Eyes on the finish" and "Eyes on the course". The German — *Spannung auf den Ausgang* and *Spannung auf den Gang* — as so often resists a definitive English rendering.

ever) from hindsight, are even for him less than convincing.

From the point of view of story, it is clear that *The Caucasian Chalk Circle* harks back to a different tradition from the one which was normally the wellspring of Brecht's technique. It is not a fearful ballad, not a tale that inspires horror, pity or awe, but rather in the mode of another ancient form, the fairy story. It has its fair share of villains — who, however, in keeping with the tradition, we cannot really fear or hate too much; it has its heroine who achieves her heart's desire in an almost magical fashion in the face of horrendous difficulties; and it has its kindly wizard or magician, who makes everything all come right in the end before disappearing without desiring or requiring that he be understood or thanked. Even the social element is similar to that of a folk tale: there is a harking back to princes and millers' daughters, to peasants who find penny purses, magic beans or golden geese. It is Brecht entirely off his guard, if you like, or at least a Brecht prepared for once to accept and celebrate the mystical joys of being alive. And if it is not his most serious play, it is arguably his most important in that it has a liberating life-enhancing quality that very few plays have ever matched.

The way Brecht chooses to tell his story is a splendid illustration of the differences between what he called the "dramatic theatre" and his own. Leaving aside the Induction for the present, it starts at the beginning — when Grusha Vachnadze, because of a military coup, finds herself in the position of having to look after a defenceless child — and moves straightforwardly and with the utmost concision to a point of apparently total disaster for the girl and her foundling. Then Brecht, in his most brilliant technical stroke ever, stops dead. When the second half of the play starts — and the effect is enhanced immeasurably by having a break here — Grusha and her child have been forgotten. We now begin at the beginning of what is apparently another story, a quite separate story, of how the villainous clerk Azdak becomes the Judge who saves the situation. This story, too, moves forward concisely and in a straight line, so that when Azdak and Grusha come together in the final scene, there is a shock of realization that has a genuinely magical effect: all that, one can only feel with wonder, to bring about this. It is a moment of absolute delight.

Arkadi Cheidze, the singer who is supposedly narrating the story, has told us at the end of Scene 1 (the Induction) that it is "actually two stories", and Willett and Manheim, taking him at his word, incredibly refer to "its awkward combination of two largely unrelated stories."[17] In fact, it is purely Brecht's decision to handle his narrative in this way which makes it appear to be two stories; he was as capable as the next dramatist of interweaving disparate elements to make up a homogeneous whole. That he had always viewed such a method with distrust hardly needs repeating. It is this element in *Galileo*, for example, that probably led him to call it "opportunistic", and in Chapter 7 we have noted that the Pete the Pipe and Yvette anecdote in *Mother Courage* is uncharacteristically "integrated" in a play whose narrative style is, as a whole, typically "epic". What is more, in *The Caucasian Chalk Circle* both strands are started at the same point, and take place in the same country during the same period of history. Many another dramatist would not only have interwoven the two, but interwoven also the lives of Azdak and Grusha. That Brecht chose not to is one of the reasons why the play is a masterpiece.

While Brecht ensured by this method of telling that the play could never be seen as "well-made", he was prepared to go much closer to more conventional forms of theatre in this play than in any other. As we saw above, the use of suspense is far more prevalent in his work than he recognized (or allowed), but in *The Caucasian Chalk Circle* he made use quite openly of suspense devices that can justifiably be described as cliff-hanging. The end of Scene 4, the point where we leave Grusha to meet Azdak, is a case in point. Simon Chachava, the kitchen-maid's fiancé, has returned from the wars at last to claim his bride. Grusha, through no fault of her own, has got married and acquired a child — although, totally in the fairy-tale tradition and against all the odds, she is still a virgin: that is "pure". For no convincing reason in the world, Grusha fails to tell Simon what's been going on:

Simon: Give me back the cross I gave you. Or better, throw it in the stream. (*He turns to go*)
Grusha: Simon Chachava, don't go away. It isn't mine, it isn't mine! (*She hears the children calling*) What is it, children?
Voices: Soldiers have come! — They are taking Michael away! (*Grusha stands aghast as two Ironshirts, with Michael between them, come towards her*)
Ironshirt: Are you Grusha? (*She nods*) Is that your child?
Grusha: Yes. (*Simon goes off*) Simon!

That is a deliberate tear-jerker, and a very effective one. Considering that we do not see Grusha again until the end of the play, a very effective one indeed. It is only one of several.

Brecht knew what to say and when to say it. His language, which can be conspicuous and flamboyant, can also be sparse and seemingly mundane. There is no point in trying to treat it adequately in a book intended primarily for people with little or no German. What we can say is that, even in translation, *The Caucasian Chalk Circle* exhibits the extraordinary range of his verbal orchestration. All the characters, many of the situations and most of the emotional effects are achieved through prose of scarcely-believable richness, and poetry that can achieve a limpid loveliness and the evocation of stark brutality. A few examples will suffice, as any reading of the piece will make the point more than adequately. On character alone, practically everything Azdak says reveals a complex humanity compounded of cunning, greed, generosity, venality, nobility and above all humour:

I'm an ignorant man. I haven't even a decent pair of trousers under my robe. See for yourself. With me, everything goes on food and drink. I was educated at a convent school. Come to think of it, I'll fine you ten piastres, too. For contempt of court.

Almost every character has a distinct mode of speech:

The Grand Duke: Am hunted. Ask for undivided attention. Make proposition.

For emotional effect, coupled with characterization, one need look no farther than the delightful wooing scene between Simon and Grusha — or the Soldier and the Young Lady, as they call each other. It is, startlingly, in the third person and is touching, funny and unique. The Singer evokes emotion while telling the story:

> As she was standing between courtyard and gate, she heard
> Or thought she heard, a low voice. The child
> Called to her, not whining but calling quite sensibly
> At least so it seemed to her: "Woman," it said, "Help me".

And he etches a dreadful, bloody time of civil war with savage economy:

> Great houses turn to ashes
> And blood runs down the street.
> Rats come out of the sewers
> And maggots out of the meat.
> The thug and the blasphemer
> Lounge by the altar-stone.

While the Grusha strand and the Azdak strand do not constitute two discrete stories, the Induction is often seen as being so inorganic as to be unplayable. It is more frequently omitted than played in British theatres, and in Russia said to be unacceptable because the picture it gives of Georgian peasants is completely unreal. This loss of Scene 1 is at once a pity (although not a tragedy) and a misreading. For although it appears to be grafted on expressly to provide a concrete political setting for a story that is otherwise a-political, it can be seen — and in good productions emerges — as a third element in the same folk tradition that actually enhances the magical effect as a whole. The Russian reaction is the key: the Georgian peasants are completely unreal. The point they *miss* is that the Georgian peasants are not *meant* to be real. The setting and the characters are idealized elements from a Golden Age as concrete and as unlikely as the Golden Age of Azdak's justice. A government expert talks poetically of why one loves one's own land — "the bread tastes better there, the sky is higher" — and the unwrapping and tasting of the cheese (performed with the required seriousness) produces an effect of touching tenderness. At the end of the scene the expert introduces a note of political reality by suggesting that the Singer shorten his tale because there are more important matters she must attend to. In fact, the Induction says, there is *nothing* more important. Cheidze replies simply: "No."

If one is going to insist on a socialist element in the play (and Brecht, as one would guess, does) this third strand of fairy tale multiplies the difficulties rather than diminishes them. At the end of the story of the chalk circle, we are told its meaning was this:

> That what there is shall belong to those who are good for it, thus
> The children to the maternal, that they thrive;
> The carriages to good drivers, that they are driven well;
> And the valley to the waterers, that it shall bear fruit.

Which is as neat a way as any of reminding us that we have been watching a play within a play about Georgian peasants. But the insult inherent in this to the members of the goat kolchoz (originally called Rosa Luxemburg, not Galinsk, and changed for reasons Willett and Manheim amusingly explain [18]) was recognized by Brecht in an updated optional epilogue:

Peasant Woman right: Arkadi Cheidze, you slyboots, friend of the valley thieves, how dare you compare us members of the Rosa Luxemburg collective with people like that Natella Abashvili of yours, just because we think twice about giving up our valley?[19]

It is not a negligible point. In any case, many people would question the morality of Azdak's judgment (although none could question his *lack* of morality!) and Brecht takes the sting out of it by having the Second Lawyer reveal that Natella only wants the child back because "The revenue of her estates. . . [is] tied to the heir" — a dramatic spilling of the beans that would ring ridiculously false if this were not a fairy tale, in which context it becomes delightful. The goat kolchoz not only loves the valley as Grusha loves Michael, but is also its natural mother. When Azdak asks Grusha if she does not want Michael to have the opportunity of being rich through going back to Natella, her answer is no. Michael is better off poor with Grusha. Why should not the same be true for the old goat kolchoz? It is worth noting, too, that Azdak (and therefore Grusha in the long run) is saved by only the second Mounted Messenger in Brecht's *oeuvre*. He did, after all, note in *The Threepenny Opera* that they arrive all too rarely in real life. Unlikely by the same token that the right kolchoz would get the valley? Finally, "the judge was always a rascal. Now the rascal shall be the judge"; the fruit-growers get the valley by virtue of the state, Grusha gets Michael by virtue of Azdak. With *Arturo Ui*, this play contains Brecht's finest and funniest court scenes. Like all the court scenes in all his plays, these show one thing and one thing only about justice: it is the tool of authority and therefore unattainable. Azdak is "almost" a good judge because he does not represent authority. As soon as he is appointed by a genuine authority, he knows he must disappear, because any Judge so appointed is a bad one. "Judgment must always be passed with complete solemnity — because it is such rot," he says. There is absolutely no suggestion, here as elsewhere, that things would be any different under any different form of authority.

There are hints in this play, as in *Galileo*, that Brecht, whether or not he regretted it afterwards, may have had Soviet communism somewhere in his mind when he wrote it. The part of Scene 5 in which Azdak, in a ferment of guilt at having saved the life of the Grand Duke, enters in chains dragging Shauva behind him, and demands "in the name of Justice. . . to be judged severely in a public trial!" sails extraordinarily close to being a satire of revolution. Azdak tells Shauva and three Ironshirts:

. . . A new age has come. . . Everything will be investigated, brought into the open. In future a man will prefer to give himself up. Why? Because he won't be able to escape the people. Tell them how I've been shouting all along Shoe-maker Street! . . . "Out of ignorance I let the Grand Swindler escape. Tear me to pieces, brothers!"

But Shauva reveals the response of the people:

They comforted him in Butcher Street, and laughed themselves sick in Shoe-maker Street. That's all.

Later in the scene, when the Fat Prince tries to have his nephew appointed Judge, the mock trial is introduced as "People of Grusinia versus Grand Duke". Azdak more realistically suggests that Grusinia "is not present in this court". While this part of the play is clearly a statement of the way the rich batten on the poor and a country is bled dry by its rulers, the overtones of the Stalinist show-trials are difficult to ignore. It may border on the fanciful, but the very name of the Governor who so richly deserved to lose his head has certain interesting echoes. He was Georgi Abashvili. Stalin was a Georgian, born Djugashvili.

We are not suggesting, of course, that Brecht wrote a right-wing play in *The Caucasian Chalk Circle*. In tone and in intention it is, like all his work, an illustration of the world's injustice and the necessity of change. The rich, in general, are seen as being nasty, the poor, in general, as not so bad. But while almost everything else he wrote is politically ambiguous, this play can perhaps more reasonably be seen as being only marginally concerned with things political. Brecht, sadly but not uncharacteristically, reacted to this "lack" with some hindsight notes which now and then border on idiocy. Azdak, for example, he describes as "utterly upright, a disappointed revolutionary posing as a human wreck,"[20] and many years later — after a reading, Willett and Manheim suggest, of Mao Tse-Tung's pamphlet *On Contradiction* — as "the disappointed man who is not going to cause disappointment in others".[21] Willett and Manheim also cite a Journal entry by Brecht indicating that while he was writing the play in 1944 he was "held up for a fortnight while he evolved social reasons for the judge's shabby eccentricities."[22]* Brecht also, in notes thought to date from 1954,

* The reason Brecht came up with, fascinatingly, was Azdak's "disappointment that the fall of the old rulers had not introduced a new era but merely an era of new ones". Again the link with Stalin's Russia is discernible, whether or not Brecht was aware that he was making it.

wrote: "The more Grusha does to save the child's life, the more she endangers her own; her productivity tends to her own destruction."[23] The use of a word like "productivity" in relation to a character so massively achieved as Grusha is little short of monstrous, but Brecht clearly believed that the character he had drawn had a genuine *choice* at the start of the play. In 1956 he is said to have claimed that "Inside the maid Grusha the child's interests and her own are at loggerheads with one another,"[24] and certainly he wrote in the "Short Organum":

Similarly in *The Caucasian Chalk Circle* the singer, by using a chilly and unemotional way of singing to describe the servant girl's rescue of the child as it is mimed on the stage, makes evident the terror of a period in which motherly instincts can become a suicidal weakness.[25]

This is perhaps the best single example of Brecht's misunderstanding the effect of his own writing. The beauty of the scene he is citing, the stunning emotional effect of the poetry, make the response he describes simply impossible. We know, everyone knows, that Grusha has no choice — saving the child is a matter of her simple humanity.* Likewise the famous and lovely line, "Terrible is the temptation to do good." When he first wrote the play, it read "Great is the temptation to do good." Not such a good line, indeed, but more in keeping with Brecht's personality: for the difficulty of being *evil* was one of his watchwords, and the subject of the fine poem "The Mask of Evil".[26] Brecht believed in good, and one of his main and key failings as a *political* writer is his love of his characters. Azdak, Mother Courage, Galileo, Grusha; all the way back to Macheath he portrays people who are not the functions but the creators of the anarchy that is society, that as a Marxist he is theoretically out to destroy. He is a despairing optimist who ought to hate his creations but loves them, who professes to believe in the necessity for, and the possibility of, a "better" sort of human being, but denies it with every major character he creates. *The Caucasian Chalk Circle* is a perfect embodiment of that dilemma.

If "epic theatre" (and its later modifications of nomenclature) were to stand up as a definition, it follows that other writers would be able to create plays identifiably *within* that definition. But although Brecht's influence has been enormous and incalculable, one can say with

---

* Brecht's astonishing advice to the actress of Grusha to look for a model in Brueghel's soulless and pinch-lipped scavenger "Dulle Griet" is a piece of transparent camouflage if ever there was one!

Pieter Brueghel the Elder, "Dulle Griet"

confidence that if a playwright set out today to write an "epic" play, he would not be able to: some might agree that he had achieved it, some would certainly deny it. For although Brecht saw it as a concrete entity — usually with the proviso that it was never totally realized — his view of his own method was flexible to the point of absurdity: it is not too far from the truth to say that, by "epic", he meant anything that he had written, unless he chose to call it otherwise.* Within his stated framework of telling a socially significant story in a "contradictory" manner, and pointing up elements that would lead to social progress by the use of technical devices that he claimed would induce in the audience specific responses, he produced an *oeuvre* whose richness and variety in subject matter and effect has been equalled possibly only by Shakespeare's.

Not so long ago, it was fashionable to use the word "epic" to describe the plays of other writers. In Britain John Arden, Peter Shaffer, Robert Bolt and others were mentioned, while in world drama plays by

---

* One sometimes wonders what Brecht would make of those bold and humourless experts who can usually be heard in the intervals of Brecht performances fulminating against the "un-epic", "un-gestic", "un-Brechtian" style of the production for all the world as if they knew what they were talking about.

Tennessee Williams, Max Frisch, Arthur Miller and even Pirandello were so called. More recently the cover-all term has been "Brechtian", which has been applied equally indiscriminately, usually to plays which have a loosely narrated — and almost invariably dull — story-line, and are full of undigested left-wing politics. It is a peculiar fact that the two legacies seen as being most definitely Brecht's are the "non-exciting" story and the naked political "message". Peculiar and sad: for Brecht was undoubtedly the greatest theatrical *story-teller* of this century, and the political aspect of his work is the one which, however serious he may have been in stressing it, he most signally failed at himself. He proclaimed communism, revolutionary clarity, direct appeal to the masses, and he wrote deeply ambiguous, politically "incorrect", and complex plays which could appeal only to people far more advanced educationally than the proletariat of any land is likely to be (allowed to be?) in the conceivable future.

The only play written in Britain in recent years that seems to come close to being *genuinely* in the mode of Brecht does so because it makes use of some of the mysterious and ancient elements of story-telling — as Brecht's plays do — rather than because it is an attempt to copy him. Edward Bond's *Saved* tells a stark and desperately simple story through the agency of characters into whose minds we have no hope of entering. It has a peculiarly distanced, primitive, Brueghel quality, despite being in a setting as far from Brecht as one could imagine — domestic, "naturalistic" and specifically in the present. Although emotionally crippled, the protagonists throb with life and live through a series of concrete events made historical, if at all, in that the characters are distanced from most audiences by being denizens of a world normally contacted only through the pages of the more lurid Sunday newspapers. The events are beyond their control and they have *nil* freedom to influence or alter anything. The language, while not poetic, is powerful, effective and intensely idiosyncratic, and the setting and costume have to be positively concrete in their excellence to make the story work. As in Brecht, the story is fulfilled only in the telling, in the physical statement of people in a setting that provides narrative elements the playwright usually lacks. As in Brecht, the immensely powerful emotional impact of the key scene — in this case, the stoning to death of a baby — is isolated and brought into harsh focus by its placing within the story. Strangely, Bond claims to see this utterly bleak piece as being in some way optimistic: an oddly Brecht-like stance.

Brecht, consciously or not, went backward in time for the essentials of his technique. By removing many of the artificial elements of theatre story-telling and replacing them with a starkly told series of events, he increased the reality, tension and emotional effect. He also, in many cases, increased the "magic" of the theatre story, while trying, if we are to believe some of his writings, to decrease or eliminate it. But while the bones of his dramaturgy can be isolated, the mix, and the magic, cannot. Let alone Hitler, let alone exile, much of Brecht's life, by most people's standards, was an emotional disaster. He believed in good, while knowing intimately the fact and the face of evil; he fought himself, and he fought everyone else. Yet his writing was almost invariably cool, detached, ironic and pared to the bone. His influence is mighty, and continuing; but all the theory in the world, his or anybody else's, will not turn out another Bertolt Brecht.

Notes

Chapter One: The Phenomenon of Brecht

1 *Observer*, 6 January 1955.
2 *Observer*, 26 June 1955.
3 *Observer*, 3 July 1955.
4 In John Willett, ed., *Brecht on Theatre*, London, 1964, p. 80.
5 Bertolt Brecht, *Collected Plays*, ed. John Willett and Ralph Manheim, London and New York, 1970 –, Vol. 7, London, 1976, p. xxv.
6 See *The Drama Review*, Vol. 12, No. 2, 1968, pp. 113–115.
7 Frisch's speech provides the starting point for Klaus Völker's article, "Brecht as a classic", in Ernst Wendt and others, *Bertolt Brecht*, Bad Godesberg, 1966, p. 27f.
8 Ronald Bryden, *The Unfinished Hero*, London, 1969, p. 40. To be fair, Bryden has a point about this particular play. We have come to the same conclusion in Chapter 8. The fault is the characteristic one of formulating general laws from a single example.
9 Cited by Ernst Wendt in *Bertolt Brecht*, p. 38.

Chapter Two: The Early Plays

1 Max Spalter, *Brecht's Tradition*, Baltimore, 1967, p. xii.
2 ibid., p. xi.
3 Bertolt Brecht, *Diaries 1920 – 1922*, trans. John Willett, London, 1979, p. 3.
4 ibid., p. 9.
5 *Collected Plays*, Vol. 1, London, 1970, p. 401.
6 *Diaries 1920 – 1922*, p. 127.
7 Cited in *Collected Plays*, Vol. 1, pp. viii – ix.
8 *Diaries 1920 – 1922*, p. 159.

Chapter Three: Brecht and Politics

1 *The Caucasian Chalk Circle*, Scene 5. Quoted from the translation by W. H. Auden in the version published by Methuen in 1963, p. 75. (Auden 'translated' the songs and James and Tania Stern translated the text.)

2 Cited in Klaus Völker, *Brecht: A Biography*, trans. John Nowell, London, 1979, p. 8.

3 This and the following quotation are cited in Völker, *Biography*, p. 110.

4 Brecht gave this interview shortly before his departure from Moscow, where he had witnessed the official opening of the Moscow Subway.

5 This and the previous quotation, also from Brecht's *Arbeitsjournal*, are widely noted and variously translated. See, for example, Völker, *Biography*, p. 274.

6 Quoted by Eric Bentley in "The Artist on Trial: Bertolt Brecht", *Encore*, Vol. XI, no. 5, September/October 1964, p. 18.

7 ibid., pp. 16–17.

8 Quoted in Klaus Völker, *Brecht Chronicle*, New York, 1975, p. 156.

9 ibid., p. 154.

10 Willy Haas, *Bert Brecht*, New York, 1970, p. 2.

11 Ronald Gray, *Brecht the Dramatist*, Cambridge, 1976, pp. 40–41.

12 ibid., p. 13.

13 Martin Esslin, *Brecht: A Choice of Evils*, London, 1959, p. xi.

14 Martin Esslin, *Brief Chronicles*, London, 1970, pp. 74–75.

15 See John Willett and Ralph Manheim, eds., *Poems 1913 – 1956*, London, 1976, p. 450, where the translation differs slightly from Esslin's.

16 Wendt, *Bertolt Brecht*, p. 8.

17 Völker, *Chronicle*, p. 85.

18 See Walter Benjamin, *Understanding Brecht*, trans. Anna Bostock, London, 1973, p. 119.

19 Völker, *Chronicle*, p. 88.

20 Ruth Fischer, *Stalin and German Communism*, Cambridge, Mass., 1948, p. 615.

21 See Wendt, *Bertolt Brecht*, p. 17.

22 The whole statement can be found in Gordon Kahn, *Hollywood on Trial*, New York, 1948.

23 Quoted by Eric Bentley in "The Artist on Trial: Hanns Eisler", *Encore*, Vol. XI, no. 5, September/October 1964, p. 36.

24 Völker, *Chronicle*, pp. 141–142.

25 See Völker, *Biography*, p. 331.

26 John Willett, *The Theatre of Bertolt Brecht*, London, 1959, p. 199.

27 Frederic Ewen, *Bertolt Brecht: His Life, His Art and His Times*, London, 1970, p. 452.

28 Many books on Brecht use the quotations cited here, see for example, Völker, *Biography*, pp. 354–358.

29 Völker, *Chronicle*, p. 141 (26 September 1951).

30 Esslin, *Choice of Evils*, p. 256.

31 Hubert Witt, ed., *Brecht as They Knew Him*, trans. John Peet, London, 1975, p. 93.

32 Haas, *Bert Brecht*, p. 77.

33 Esslin, *Choice of Evils*, p. 138.

34 Witt, *Brecht as They Knew Him*, p. 93.

35 Quoted in Esslin, *Choice of Evils*, p. 138.

36 Gray, *Brecht the Dramatist*, p. 53.

37 Esslin, *Choice of Evils*, pp. 138 and 140.

38 ibid., pp. 259 and 140.

39 See *The Mother*, trans. Lee Baxandall, New York, 1965, p. 154.

Chapter Four: In the Jungle of Intentions

1 *Poems 1913 – 1956*, p. 125.

2 Völker, *Biography*, p. 156.

Chapter Five: Hitler and the Power of Force

1 Willett, *Brecht on Theatre*, p. 100.

2 ibid., loc. cit.

3 *The Private Life of the Master Race*, English version by Eric Bentley, London, 1948, p. 7.

4 *Collected Plays*, Vol. 6, New York, 1976, p. 456.

5 *Poems 1913 – 1956*, p. 363.

Chapter Six: Brecht's Theory of Theatrical Performance

1 Willett, *Brecht on Theatre*, p. 233.

2 ibid., p. 110.

3 ibid., p. 185.

4 ibid., pp. 6 – 8.

5 Gray, *Brecht the Dramatist*, p. 72.

6 Cited in Christopher Innes, *Erwin Piscator's Political Theatre*, Cambridge, 1972, p. 77.

7 ibid., p. 58.

8 Willett, *Brecht on Theatre*, p. 22.

9 ibid., p. 71.

10 ibid., p. 246.

11 ibid., p. 104.

12 ibid., p. 88.

13 ibid., p. 198.

14 Constantin Stanislavsky, *An Actor Prepares*, Harmondsworth, 1967, p. 112.

15 Willett, *Brecht on Theatre*, p. 200.

16 ibid., p. 136.

17 ibid., pp. 104–105.

18 ibid., p. 36.

19 ibid., pp. 54–55.

20 *Poems 1913 – 1956*, p. 308.

21 Stanislavsky, *An Actor Prepares*, p. 81.

22 Cited in Innes, *Piscator's Theatre*, p. 118.

23 Willett, *Brecht on Theatre*, p. 142.

24 ibid., p. 109.

25 Benjamin, *Understanding Brecht*, p. 108.

26 *Poems 1913 – 1956*, p. 427.

27 Esslin, *Brief Chronicles*, p. 86.

28 Charles Marowitz and others, eds., *The Encore Reader*, London, 1965, p. 16.

29 *Poems 1913 – 1956*, p. 156.

30 Stanislavsky, *An Actor Prepares*, p. 163.

31 Willett, *Brecht on Theatre*, p. 23.

32 Bertolt Brecht, *The Messingkauf Dialogues*, trans. John Willett, London, 1965, p. 57.

33 Willett, *Brecht on Theatre*, p. 277.

34 *Poems 1913 – 1956*, p. 342.

35 Willet, *Brecht on Theatre*, p. 138.

36 ibid., p. 192.

37 *The Messingkauf Dialogues*, p. 48.

38 Willett, *Brecht on Theatre*, p. 277.

39 ibid., p. 157.

40 ibid., p. 129.

41 ibid., p. 121.

42 *Poems 1913 – 1956*, pp. 176–179.

43 Willett, *Brecht on Theatre*, pp. 193–194.

44 ibid., p. 194.

45 ibid., p. 82.

46 Bertolt Brecht and others, *Theaterarbeit*, Berlin, 1961, p. 387. There is a translation in Willett, *Brecht on Theatre*, p. 245.

47 *The Messingkauf Dialogues*, pp. 78–79.

48 Willett, *Brecht on Theatre*, p. 144.

49 ibid., p. 137.

50 ibid., p. 190.

51 ibid., p. 138.
52 Stanislavsky, *An Actor Prepares*, Chapter 9, esp. pp. 159–161.

Chapter Seven: Mother Courage: Brecht's Staging

1 Willett, *Brecht on Theatre*, p. 221.
2 Kenneth Tynan, *Tynan on Theatre*, Harmondsworth, 1964, p. 257.
3 Willett, *Brecht on Theatre*, p. 216.
4 This quotation is from the translation of the *Couragemodell* provided in *Collected Plays*, Vol. 5, New York, 1972, pp. 334–386. All subsequent unnoted quotations in this chapter are from the same source.
5 Cited in Keith Dickson, *Towards Utopia*, Oxford, 1978, p. 64.
6 Willett, *Brecht on Theatre*, p. 217.
7 ibid., p. 219.
8 ibid., p. 217.
9 ibid., p. 245.
10 Carl Zuckmayer, *A Part of Myself*, London, 1970, p. 267.
11 *Theaterarbeit*, p. 380.
12 See Willett, *Brecht on Theatre*, p. 129.
13 The final clause was an insertion by the actor, of which Brecht approved.
14 Roy Pascal, "Brecht's Misgivings", the 1977 Bithell Memorial Lecture, University of London Institute of Germanic Studies, pp. 4–8.
15 *Theaterarbeit*, p. 238.
16 Cited in Dickson, p. 108.
17 ibid., pp. 98–101.
18 ibid., p. 103.
19 Michael Morley, *A Student's Guide to Brecht*, London, 1977, p. 59.

Chapter Eight: In Search of a Theatre

1 *Poems 1913 – 1956*, p. 156.
2 See Völker, *Biography*, p. 222.
3 ibid., p. 226.
4 This is what Ernst Schumacher does in *Drama und Geschichte: Bertolt Brechts "Leben des Galilei" und andere Stücke*, Berlin, 1968.
5 Willett, *Brecht on Theatre*, p. 243.
6 *Poems 1913 – 1956*, p. 393.
7 Willett, *Brecht on Theatre*, p. 204.
8 Dickson, p. 92.
9 See Völker, *Biography*, p. 243.
10 Willett, *Brecht on Theatre*, pp. 91–99.

11 Gray, *Brecht the Dramatist*, p. 148.

12 Völker, *Biography*, p. 273.

13 *Collected Plays*, Vol. 6, p. 418.

14 ibid., p. 404.

15 ibid., p. 415.

16 ibid., p. 413.

17 ibid., p. 408.

18 For readers who wish to explore the play further, Keith Dickson's spirited defence of it, in historico-political rather than dramatic terms, is strongly recommended. See *Towards Utopia*, pp. 109–124.

Chapter Nine: Brecht's Dramaturgy

1   Willett, *Brecht on Theatre*, p. 15.

2   ibid., p. 23.

3   ibid., p. 25.

4   ibid., pp. 281–282.

5   ibid., p. 70.

6   ibid., p. 80.

7   ibid., pp. 279–280.

8   ibid., p. 251.

9   *Poems 1913 – 1956*, pp. 24–25.

10 *Poems 1913 – 1956*, pp. 89–92.

11 Cited in Morley, *A Student's Guide*, p. 59.

12 ibid., p. 57.

13 Willet, *Brecht on Theatre*, p. 30.

14 ibid., p. 201.

15 ibid., p. 145.

16 The reference here is to the famous comparative list, translated in Willett, *Brecht on Theatre*, p. 37.

17 *Collected Plays*, Vol. 7, p. xxv.

18 ibid., p. 316.

19 ibid., p. 324.

20 ibid., p. 302.

21 ibid., p. 305.

22 ibid., p. 314.

23 ibid., p. 305.

24 ibid., p. 307.

25 Willett, *Brecht on Theatre*, p. 203.

26 *Poems 1913 – 1956*, p. 383.

Chronology

1898   (10 February) Born in Augsburg.

1904–1908 Elementary School in Augsburg.

1908–1917 *Realgymnasium*, Augsburg. Joint editor of student periodical.

1917   Enrols at the University of Munich.

1918   First version of *Baal* finished by mid-June.
      Military service as medical orderly in an Augsburg V.D. ward.

1919   *Drums in the Night.* Reworking *Baal.*
      Sketches for Karl Valentin, the Munich-based comedian/clown.
      Son (named Frank after Wedekind) born to Paula Banholzer.

1921   *In the Jungle of Cities.*

1922   (29 September) First performance of *Drums in the Night.*
      Baal published in an edition of eight hundred copies only.
      (3 November) Marries Marianne Zoff.
      (13 November) Awarded Kleist Prize for *Drums in the Night.*

1923   (12 March) Daughter Hanne born.
      (9 May) first performance of *In the Jungle of Cities.*
      Meets Helene Weigel.
      (8 December) First performance of *Baal.*

1924   (19 March) First performance of *The Life of Edward II of England.*
      In September moves to Berlin to work for Max Reinhardt.
      (3 November) Son, Stefan, born to Helene Weigel.

1926   (26 September) First performance of *Man Equals Man*.
        During summer, begins a serious study of Marx and economics.

1927   (2 November) Divorced from Marianne Zoff.
        Beginning of collaboration with Kurt Weill.

1928   Collaborating with Elisabeth Hauptmann.
        (31 August) First performance of *The Threepenny Opera*.

1929   (10 April) Marries Helene Weigel.
        Baden-Baden Music Festival stages first performances of *The
        Flight of the Lindberghs* and *The Didactic Play of Baden-Baden on
        Consent*.

1930   (9 March) First performance of *The Rise and Fall of the City of
        Mahagonny*.
        Sues Nero Film Company over their version of *The Threepenny
        Opera*.
        (23 June) First performance of *He Who Says Yes*.
        (28 October) Daughter Barbara born to Helene Weigel.
        (10 December) First performance of *The Measures Taken*.

1931   In August completes (in collaboration with Dudow and others)
        filmscript of *Kuhle Wampe*.
        Finishes *Saint Joan of the Stockyards*.

1932   (17 January) First public performance of *The Mother*.
        (11 April) Radio version of *Saint Joan* broadcast.
        In May attends first showing of *Kuhle Wampe* in Moscow, prior to
        its being shown in Berlin on 30 May.
        Finishes *Round Heads and Pointed Heads*.

1933   (28 February) Escapes from Germany with Helene Weigel and
        Stefan. Barbara is smuggled out later. To Paris, via Prague,
        Vienna, Lugano.
        (7 June) *The Seven Deadly Sins* performed in Paris.
        Spends some of September in Paris with Margarete Steffin.
        Begins relationship with Ruth Berlau.
        Moves to Skovbostrand in Denmark in December.

1934   *The Threepenny Novel* published in Amsterdam.

1935   Visit to Moscow.

In April plans the series of sketches that were to form *Fear and Misery of the Third Reich*.

October to December visits New York to oversee production of *The Mother*. The visit is disastrous, though it gives him the chance to see several gangster films and to strengthen his collaborative relationship with Hanns Eisler.

1936   (4 November) First performance — in Danish in Copenhagen — of *Round Heads and Pointed Heads*.

1937   (17 October) First performance of *Senora Carrar's Rifles* in Paris.

1938   (21 May) First performance of eight of the scenes from *Fear and Misery* in Paris.

Completes in three weeks the first version of *Galileo*.

1939   In March begins work on *The Good Person of Setzuan*.

April to May moves into Sweden.

In November finishes *Mother Courage and Her Children* and *The Trial of Lucullus*.

1940   (17 April) Leaves for Finland with his family and Margarete Steffin.

In September completes *Mr. Puntila and His Man Matti*.

1941   In January works on the final version of *The Good Person*.

March to April writes *The Resistible Rise of Arturo Ui*, with some help from Margarete Steffin.

(19 April) First performance of *Mother Courage* in Zurich.

(15 May) Leaves Finland for America with his family, Margarete Steffin and Ruth Berlau. Steffin has to be left in Moscow, where she dies of tuberculosis. The rest continue via Vladivostok to California where friends have found Brecht a Santa Monica home.

1942   Among various film projects, co-writes a script for Fritz Lang's *Hangmen Also Die*. The film work is far from harmonious. Collaborating with Lion Feuchtwanger on a Saint Joan script.

1943   (4 February) First performance of *Good Person* in Zurich.

Finishes *The Visions of Simone Machard* and *Schweyk in the Second World War*.

(9 September) First performance of *Galileo* in Zurich.

(13 November) First son, Frank, killed fighting for the Germans in Russia.

1944   In September finishes *The Caucasian Chalk Circle*.
        Works with Charles Laughton on a new version of *Galileo*.

1945   (12 June) Performance of *The Private Life of the Master Race* in Bentley's English version in New York.
        In July completes his adaptation of *The Duchess of Malfi* for Elisabeth Bergner.
        In December completes English version of *Galileo*.

1947   (31 July) Laughton opens in *Galileo*.
        (30 October) Appears before House Un-American Activities Committee.
        (31 October) Flies to Paris.
        Completes work on version of *Antigone*.

1948   (15 February) First performance of *Antigone* in Chur in Switzerland.
        (5 June) First performance of *Puntila* in Zurich.
        In late October leaves for Berlin via Prague — because the American authorities refuse him a visa for the American zone.

1949   (11 January) Berlin opening of *Mother Courage*.
        Writes *The Days of the Commune*, while living in East Berlin.
        (8 November) Berliner Ensemble opens with *Puntila*.

1950   (15 April) First performance of adaptation of Lenz's *The Tutor*.
        Application for Austrian Citizenship approved. Settles in East Berlin.

1951   (17 March) First stage performance of *The Trial of Lucullus* by the Berliner Ensemble offends the authorities.
        (12 October) *Lucullus* re-opens with tactful modifications but no major rewriting.

1952   Publication of *Theaterarbeit*.

1953   (17 June) Uprising in East Germany. Brecht's reaction insufficiently heroic to please. He writes, but does not publish, a poem offering ironically "The Solution" to the East German government.

1954   (19 March) Berliner Ensemble moves into Theater am Schiff-
            bauerdamm, opening with adaptation of Molière's *Don Juan*.
            (7 October) First performance by Berliner Ensemble of *The
            Caucasian Chalk Circle*.
            (21 December) Receives Stalin Peace Prize in Moscow.

1955   In December begins rehearsing *Galileo*.

1956   In poor health after the Spring.
            (10 August) Attends rehearsal for the last time.
            (14 August) Dies.

Select Bibliography

a) *Brecht in Translation*

The series of volumes edited by John Willett and Ralph Manheim as *Collected Plays* (London and New York, 1970 and continuing) is the closest thing we have to a standard translation. Its limitations are referred to in the "Note on Texts and Titles" at the beginning of the book.

Poems 1913 – 1956, ed. John Willett and Ralph Manheim (London, 1976), is a valuable selection from Brecht's extensive poetic work. Among the many poems which illuminate the plays the following are particularly notable:

Morning Address to a Tree Named Green — a poem in praise of flexibility
From a Reader for Those who Live in Cities, No. 10
The Carpet Weavers of Kuyan-Bulak Honour Lenin — a parable that recalls the dispute over the valley in *The Caucasian Chalk Circle*
On Everyday Theatre — cf. the essay "The Street Scene"
The Chalk Cross — a twenty-five-line version of the story that provides one of the plays in *Fear and Misery of the Third Reich*
Speech to Danish Working-Class Actors on the Art of Observation
The Playwright's Song
Washing — recalls an occasion when Brecht taught the actress Carola Neher how one washes
Portrayal of Past and Present in One
On Judging
On the Critical Attitude
Theatre of Emotions
On Ease — a short poem that relates to Brecht's love of the ease that results from confidence in what one is doing
The Theatre, Home of Dreams
Showing Has to be Shown
On Speaking the Sentences
The Moment before Impact
The Play is Over
The Mask of Evil
The Democratic Judge — an American Judge who sounds like Azdak
Letter to Charles Laughton
Looking for the New and Old
The Curtains
The Lighting

The Songs
Weigel's Props
On Seriousness in Art

Brecht on Theatre, trans. and ed. John Willett (London, 1964) contains a selection from Brecht's writings on theatre, his *Schriften zum Theater*. The following essays are particularly useful:

Emphasis on Sport (pp. 6–9)
The Modern Theatre is the Epic Theatre (pp. 33–42)
The Question of Criteria for Judging Acting (pp. 53–56)
On the Use of Music in an Epic Theatre (pp. 84–90)
Alienation Effects in Chinese Acting (pp. 91–99)
On Gestic Music (pp. 104–105)
The Street Scene (pp. 121–129) — cf. the poem "On Everyday Theatre"
Short Description of a New Technique of Acting which Produces an Alienation Effect (pp. 136–147)
Alienation Effects in the Narrative Pictures of the Elder Brueghel (pp. 157–159)
A Short Organum for the Theatre (pp. 179–205) — essential reading
Stage Design for the Epic Theatre (pp. 230–233)
Theaterarbeit: an editorial note (pp. 239–246)
Notes on Erwin Strittmatter's Play 'Katzgraben' (pp. 247–251)
Appendices to the Short Organum (pp. 276–281)

The Messingkauf Dialogues, trans. John Willett (London, 1965), are published separately. Brecht never put these into final form, and they do not make easy reading, but at their best they display the flexibility of Brecht's thinking.

Theaterarbeit (Dresden, 1952 and Berlin, 1961) is an untranslated collection of essays, notes and documentation which sets out to show how the Berliner Ensemble works. For those who do not read German, there is still much to be gained from the photographic material assembled here. There are also selections from several *Modellbücher*. Some not very convincing discussion of these "model books" is included in *Brecht on Theatre* (pp. 211–225). There is, though, no doubt of their value as documentary evidence, nor of the fact that they provide a number of fascinating insights into ways of realizing the potential of a Brechtian text.

Diaries 1920 – 1922, trans. John Willett (London, 1979), is a selection, edited by Herta Ramthun, of early autobiographical and critical observations. We look forward to publication of translations from the later *Arbeitsjournal*, already available to German readers.

b) *Biographical Studies*
Frederic Ewen's *Bertolt Brecht: His Life, His Art and His Times* (London, 1970) is an earnest attempt to provide a context for Brecht's work. What is lacking is a sense of the man. Klaus Völker's *Brecht: A Biography* (trans. John Nowell, London, 1979) reveals more, and yet remains oddly unyielding. Most of the facts are in the same author's *Brecht Chronicle* (New York, 1975). The scattered

reminiscences in *Brecht as They Knew Him* (ed. Hubert Witt and trans. John Peet, London, New York and Berlin, 1974) make more attractive reading.

c)   *Critical Studies*
Martin Esslin, *Brecht: A Choice of Evils*, London, 1959. We hesitate to recommend this book for reasons we have tried to make clear in our own. What cannot be denied is that it is stimulatingly opinionated.

John Willett, *The Theatre of Bertolt Brecht*, London, 1959. This includes a lot of useful documentation of performances and publications. It is less interesting than it ought to be.

Walter Benjamin, *Understanding Brecht*, trans. Anna Bostock, London, 1973. This contains some brilliantly provocative writing, but is not as definitive as its adherents sometimes claim. We feel the need for a companion volume called *Understanding Benjamin*.

Keith Dickson, *Towards Utopia*, Oxford, 1978. A fascinating and important book, which argues for the consistency of Brecht's vision of a better world. Dickson is a polyglot, but readers should not be deterred by his erudition, He writes well, and with compassion.

Max Spalter, *Brecht's Tradition*, Baltimore, 1967. This provides Brecht with a lucidly presented background in German drama.

Peter Demetz, ed. *Brecht: A Collection of Critical Essays*, Englewood Cliffs, 1962.

Arnold Kettle, *Shaw and Brecht*, Milton Keynes, 1977. This Open Unversity Study Guide contains a great deal of good sense on Brecht.

Ernst Wendt and others, *Bertolt Brecht*, Bad Godesburg, 1966. The four essays in this book have been unfairly neglected.

Index of Brecht's Works

2   Unfinished plays, sketches, and adaptations

3   Film, novel, poems, and essays

General Index